INTRODUCING
LOGIC AND CRITICAL THINKING

INTRODUCING
LOGIC AND
CRITICAL
THINKING

The Skills of Reasoning *and* the Virtues of Inquiry

T. RYAN BYERLY

Baker Academic
a division of Baker Publishing Group
Grand Rapids, Michigan

Visit www.bakeracademic.com/professors
to access study aids
and instructor materials for this textbook.

Published by Baker Academic
a division of Baker Publishing Group
PO Box 6287, Grand Rapids, MI 49516-6287
www.bakeracademic.com

Printed in the United States of America

Library of Congress Cataloging-in-Publication Data
Names: Byerly, T. Ryan, author.
Title: Introducing logic and critical thinking : the skills of reasoning and the virtues of inquiry /
    T. Ryan Byerly.
Description: Grand Rapids : Baker Academic, 2017. | Includes bibliographical references and index.
Identifiers: LCCN 2017007503 | ISBN 9780801030819 (pbk. : alk. paper)
Subjects: LCSH: Logic—Textbooks. | Critical thinking—Textbooks.
Classification: LCC BC71 .B94 2017 | DDC 160—dc23
LC record available at https://lccn.loc.gov/2017007503

17 18 19 20 21 22 23   7 6 5 4 3 2 1

Contents

Preface for Instructors

It has become increasingly common for both Christian and non-Christian colleges and universities to offer and even require what we might call courses in "Logic *and*"—courses the formal titles of which typically begin with the words "Logic and" and end with something after the "and." Often what is included after the "and" is "Critical Thinking," though this is not universal. In any case, the expectation is that in courses of these kinds, students will learn about logic *and* they will learn about something else. What else they learn appears to vary widely from one institution to another and from one instructor to another.

When I have taught courses of this kind, I have thought that a very suitable subject to include for my students—in addition to logic—would be an introduction to intellectual virtues. The course would provide them both with the reasoning skills of formal logic and with an opportunity to reflect on, and even attempt to cultivate, virtues of inquiry. One problem I faced as an instructor, however, was that I could not find a single textbook that combined these subjects in the way I had in mind. That is why I've written *Introducing Logic and Critical Thinking*. My hope and expectation is that there are other instructors like me who would like to structure their courses in "Logic *and*" in this way and who would appreciate a single textbook that enables them to do so.

Some unique features of this textbook are designed to aid with instructional use. First, instructors should note that part 1 of the text, which significantly outstrips part 2 in length, intentionally includes a very substantial introduction to a wide range of techniques in deductive and inductive logic. It is my expectation that many instructors will use only sections of part 1. For some courses in "Logic *and*," a more thorough introduction to the methods of deductive and inductive logic is necessary, while for other courses a less thorough introduction is sufficient. I have attempted to write the text in such a way that instructors will not face significant difficulty in selecting sections from part 1 to cover at their discretion. For example, sections 2.4 and 2.5 might be considered too advanced for some introductory logic courses, as these sections introduce methods utilized in symbolic logic. Since these sections deal with relatively discrete methods, instructors can skip these sections and focus instead on the other methods discussed in chapter 2. At the same time, some instructors might welcome having a brief introduction to symbolic logic that could be used in a course with philosophy majors or honors students who seek a more thorough introduction to the discipline than many introductory logic texts provide.

Second, instead of having a separate section on informal fallacies, as is often the case with introductory textbooks, the approach I have taken is to discuss many of the most common informal fallacies in the context of the discussion of virtues of inquiry. For example, in the section on the virtue of trust in others, I discuss the *ad hominem* fallacy; in the section on the virtue of interpretive charity, I discuss the *straw man* fallacy; in the section on the virtue of introspective vigilance, I discuss the *post hoc* and *slippery slope* fallacies; and in the sections on the virtues of communicative clarity and audience sensitivity, I discuss the fallacies of *equivocation, amphibole,* and *begging the question.* Thus rather than discussing these informal fallacies in isolation, which can make them seem abstract, I have situated my discussion of these fallacies within the context of a broader discussion of intellectual virtues. Discussing them within the context of intellectual virtues allows the explanation for why these fallacies are problematic to be more strikingly illuminated.

A third feature worth highlighting about the textbook is that part 2, concerned with the virtues of inquiry, contains *practice exercises.* These consist of vignettes that briefly describe the way in which a character or group of characters conducts an inquiry. Students are asked to reflect on whether the character or characters do or do not display a particular virtue, and to defend their answers. In some cases, they are asked to offer recommendations about how the character could have conducted her inquiry more virtuously. For some examples included in these exercises, reasonable disagreement about how to evaluate the example is to be expected. From my vantage point, the primary purpose of the exercises is to serve as valuable conversation starters that can prompt more in-depth, thoughtful classroom discussion about the exercise of intellectual virtue and vice.

A final unique feature of the textbook is that it has been written intentionally with Christian students in mind. In several places, I briefly discuss how the Christian tradition might illuminate our understanding of a skill in reasoning or a virtue of inquiry. For example, the section on the virtue of intellectual generosity discusses a way in which a Christian conception of intellectual generosity may be more demanding than a secular conception. Similarly, I have intentionally selected practice exercises that in many cases will be of special interest to Christian students and instructors. In this way, the book should be especially attractive for courses in "Logic *and*" taught at Christian colleges and universities.

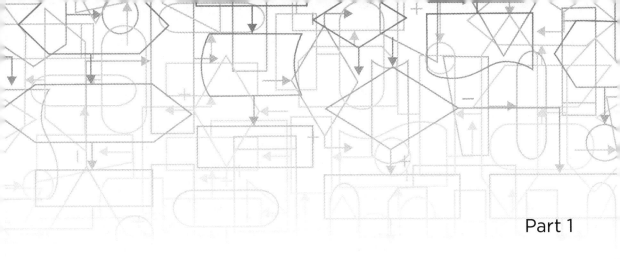

The Skills of Reasoning

The first part of this two-part book introduces some important skills that will help you to reason better. These are the skills taught in the discipline of logic as practiced within English-speaking institutions of higher education where this discipline focuses on identifying and evaluating arguments. Thus the chapters that compose the first part of this text explain certain widely used techniques that will assist you in identifying and evaluating arguments.

It is important that we do not confuse the skills of reasoning explained here with the virtues of inquiry that will be the focus of the second part of the text. There are various ways to distinguish between skills on the one hand and virtues on the other.[1] But perhaps the most important difference between the two is the following: a person is not deficient *as a person* for lacking any particular skills, but a person is deficient *as a person* for lacking virtues, including intellectual ones. By way of illustration, we would not say that a person was worse as a person for failing to have the basketball skills of LeBron James. Likewise, we would not say that LeBron James is better as a person for having the particular basketball skills he has. Of course, someone who doesn't have James's skills is worse *as a basketball player* than James. But the point here is that she is not worse *as a person* than James. However, a person who lacks virtues does lack something as a person. A person who is not courageous but is instead cowardly is worse off as a person than someone who is courageous. And the same goes for intellectual virtues and vices. A

1

person who is intellectually arrogant is worse off as a person than a person who is not intellectually arrogant.

The particular skills introduced in this first part of the book, then, are not necessary for making you better as a person. Learning to draw Venn diagrams and to construct formal proofs of arguments using the Proof Method does not make one a better human being. But this is not to say that acquiring these skills is not valuable at all. While having one particular skill does not make a person better as a person than other persons with different skills, it is nonetheless true that having *some* skill or other is of great value to us as persons. It would be bad for James if he had no skills at all—even bad for him as a person. To live excellent lives, we need some skills. And to lead intellectually excellent lives, we need some skills in reasoning. The skills in reasoning introduced here could be replaced by other skills—skills that don't require drawing overlapping circles to represent arguments or using arrows and wedges to symbolize premises in arguments. But without some skill set or other to aid one in reasoning, one does lack something as a person. It is important for our personal flourishing that we reason well, and having some skill set or other to help us with this makes a contribution to our flourishing.

While the particular skills of reasoning proposed here may be replaceable, they are nonetheless valuable for human flourishing. Moreover, they are skills that are widely (though not widely enough!) studied and acquired in English-speaking institutions of higher learning. By acquiring the skills of reasoning proposed in the first part of this text, you will have acquired a set of skills that makes a valuable contribution to living an excellent life as a person and that you can uniquely share with many other good reasoners educated in English-speaking institutions.

1

▶ ▶ ▶ ▶ ▶

Introduction to Arguments

Reflect for a moment on all the many things that you believe. Perhaps you believe some things about yourself: something about who you are, where you are, what you are up to, what constitutes your calling in life. Perhaps you believe some things about the community in which you find yourself: the community of your classmates, the community of your educational institution more widely, or your church, city, county, state, or national community. You might believe some things about the past: whether you ate a bagel for breakfast, whether your decision to pick up this book was a good idea, whether certain events recorded in the Bible are historical, or whether the American Revolution inspired the French Revolution. You might believe some things about the future: who will be the next president, what the housing market will be like next spring, what you will need in your life to make you truly happy, or whether you will one day have a glorified body in heaven.

You may very well believe some of these things in a kind of direct way based on your experiences. You believe that you are reading this book because of the visual and tactile experiences you are currently having, for example. Your belief that you are reading the book is not, perhaps, based on some other *beliefs* you have. Your belief that you are reading this book isn't based on your belief that this book says you are reading it, for instance. Rather, the experiences you are having are directly producing this belief in you. Maybe the same goes for some other beliefs you have. You believe you ate a bagel for breakfast because you seem to remember having eaten one. You hold this belief about the bagel not because of some other belief you hold. Some of your beliefs, then, may be held directly on the basis of your experiences and not on the basis of any other beliefs you hold.

Yet it remains the case that many of the beliefs you hold *are* held on the basis of other beliefs. You believe these things for certain *reasons*, we might say. Take, for instance, what you believe about who will be the next president. If you hold a belief about this matter, it will no doubt be one that is held on the basis of quite a number of reasons—reasons having to do with who you believe will be on the ballot, how you believe the country will fare between now and the next election, your views about what the American public believes about a wide range of important issues, and so on. You believe that so-and-so will be president *because of*, or *on the basis of*, these other beliefs you hold. And the same may go for many of the other beliefs you hold, such as your beliefs about what constitutes your calling in life, whose fault it was that your team lost, what the housing market will be like in the spring, and what will make for personal happiness.

An important feature of human life, then, is that many of the things we believe are things we believe on the basis of reasons.[1] Many Christian theologians have thought that our ability to hold beliefs on the basis of reasons—and to critically reflect on our reasons for belief—is an aspect of the image or likeness of God in us.[2] Certainly these rational capacities are part of what sets us apart from much of the rest of creation. Part of what it is to be a fully functioning human is to believe for reasons and to evaluate the reasons we have for belief.

An important additional observation about this key feature of human life—this fact that we believe many things on the basis of reasons—is that *reasons are often shareable*. If I believe something on the basis of a reason, and I am able to identify that reason, then I can share that reason with you. I can recommend it to you as a reason for you to believe what I believe. And you can do the same for me. You too can recommend that I believe some of the things you believe—for instance, what you believe about who will be the next president—by telling me your reasons for believing what you do about this. So the fact that humans believe many things on the basis of reasons—reasons that are often shareable—makes it possible for us to influence one another's beliefs by providing one another with reasons for belief.

How exactly do we do this? Our key mechanism is the presentation and defense of arguments. When we present an argument, we usually are interested in recommending that another person believe something on the basis of the claims made in that argument. We recommend that this person believe the conclusion of that argument on the basis of the premises of that argument. In section 1.1, we will more carefully define terminology like "argument," "premise," and "conclusion." For now, it is necessary only to understand that arguments are a key mechanism that we can use to influence the beliefs of others and that others can use to influence our beliefs. Indeed, in a certain way we can even use arguments in internal dialogues with ourselves. Strange as it might sound, most of us provide arguments to ourselves in an attempt to recommend to ourselves that we believe certain claims on the basis of others. Arguments, then, whether used privately or publicly, are absolutely central to the formation of many of the beliefs we hold.

This important role for arguments in the private and public processes of belief formation is evident in Scripture. The Hebrew prophets frequently employ arguments attempting to persuade the people of Israel to turn from their wicked ways. In many of the psalms, the writer seems to argue with himself about how to understand God's providence in his life. Jesus is fond of using arguments from analogy to defend key theological claims. And Paul's letters are densely packed with arguments. (Just consider how many times the word "for" appears in Paul's writings.) We see here clearly that arguments play a key role in the process of individual and social belief formation.

Because arguments play this central role in both the individual and social dimensions of belief formation, and because it matters what we believe and why we do so, it is important that we attend to what makes for *good* arguments versus what makes for *bad* arguments. Most of us take for granted that some arguments are better than others and indeed that some arguments are good while others are bad. We think that when someone recommends to us that we believe a claim on the basis of certain reasons, these reasons are sometimes good and sometimes not so good. We believe, then, that there are *evaluative* claims to be made about arguments. We can evaluate arguments for goodness and badness, for example. And we would prefer that those beliefs we hold on the basis of arguments be held on the basis of good arguments rather than bad ones.

This is where the discipline of logic makes a unique contribution to living a life of excellence as a human. As we have seen, humans are uniquely gifted in that we hold many beliefs on the basis of reasons that are shareable. We hold many beliefs on the basis of arguments for those beliefs. It is clear that we live more excellent lives when we hold the beliefs we do on the basis of good arguments rather than bad ones, and when the arguments we recommend to others for our beliefs are good arguments rather than bad ones as well. The discipline of logic is of immense value for helping us to accomplish these tasks because it is uniquely concerned with the evaluation of arguments. Indeed, **logic**, as we will define it, is *the study of the methods used to evaluate arguments*. Logic is all about arguments. The skills one acquires through studying logic enable one to do a better job of believing what one does on the basis of good arguments rather than bad ones. They aid one in recommending to others good arguments rather than bad ones in an attempt to influence others' beliefs. By studying logic, the student acquires skills that are important for flourishing as a human. By acquiring these logical skills in reasoning, we perhaps even display in fuller glory the image of God within us. We acquire skills that enable us to have a greater impact on our cultures for the kingdom of God, help us to navigate our own lives more wisely, and equip us for the pursuit of understanding. We neglect the discipline of logic at our peril.

1.1 Arguments vs. Nonarguments

We have said that logic is the study of the methods used to evaluate arguments and that arguments are often used for the purpose of convincing others (or ourselves) to hold certain beliefs on the basis of other beliefs. What we need now is a more precise definition of arguments that gets at their nature and not just one of their important functions. We need to explain what *makes* something an argument. By defining arguments and distinguishing them from important kinds of nonarguments, we will acquire our first important skill in logic.

For our purposes, we will define an **argument** as *a set of statements where one of those statements (the conclusion) is affirmed on the basis of the others (the premises)*. This way of defining the term "argument" obviously differs from our common understanding, where an argument might simply mean a shouting match. When Joe says, "Boo on you!" and Jim replies, "No, boo on your mom!" this is not an "argument" according to the above definition (though it may well count as an "argument" in the ordinary sense of that term). Our definition of "argument" focuses on the specific sense in which logicians use the term. Our definition tells us something about the component parts of arguments and the way these parts must be related if they are to constitute an argument. To use a construction analogy, both the building materials and how they are fastened together matter for whether we have constructed an argument. The component parts or building materials of an argument must be "statements," and for these to compose an argument they must be fastened together so that one of them is affirmed on the basis of the others. We will briefly examine both of these features of arguments—their components and their construction.

1.1.1 Statements: The Building Blocks of Arguments

The component parts or building materials of arguments are statements. For our purposes, a **statement** is *any sentence that is either true or false*. A sentence that is true (for example, "There are computers") is a statement. A sentence that is false (for example, "There aren't any computers anywhere in the world") is also a statement, albeit a false one. Even sentences that are not *known* to be true or false can be statements. It is not required that a statement be known to be either true or false but only that it be either true or false. So, for example, the sentence "There is life in other galaxies" is a statement. It is either true or false, even if it is not (yet) known to be either true or false.

Some sentences and strings of symbols do not compose statements. Any sentence that is neither true nor false is not a statement. Typically sentences that are questions or commands will not be statements. "Go home!" or "Would you like to excuse yourself?" are not typically statements, since they are not typically used as sentences that are either true or false. It is important to point out that sentences that have the form of commands or questions can sometimes be used to *make* statements. For example, the sentence "Believe me when I tell you I will lower taxes" might be used by a political candidate to make a statement—the statement that he or she will lower taxes—even though the sentence is expressed in the form of a command. Rhetorical questions like "Wouldn't you agree that logic is fun?" may likewise be used to make statements. When commands or questions are used in this way, we will treat them as statements, which can thus be used as components of arguments.

It should also be clear from the definition of "statement" above that strings of symbols that fail to compose sentences are also not statements. Thus "sdf ekp eoppld" is not a statement. We might imagine some language in which this string of symbols does compose a sentence, but it does not compose a sentence in English. And for our purposes we will be evaluating English arguments composed of English statements. "Sdf ekp eoppld" is not an English sentence and so cannot be an English statement or a component of any English argument.

One final remark about the nature of statements is in order. There are some sentences whose status as statements is disputable. According to some philosophers and theologians, sentences using moral or religious terminology are not statements. These philosophers and theologians believe that sentences using moral or religious terminology are neither true nor false. The purpose of these sentences is not to make any claims about the way the world is or to recommend belief to others, but instead to do something akin to expressing one's emotions.[3] Although this view of moral and religious discourse has some prominent advocates, it is certainly extreme. It sure seems that moral and religious discourse is offered for the purpose of recommending belief to others and making claims about the way the world is. Indeed, it is difficult if not impossible to affirm otherwise while taking moral and religious discourse seriously. We will not exclude religious and moral discourse from our purview here. For our purposes, the fact that a sentence uses moral or religious terminology will not disqualify that sentence from being a statement. Indeed, many of the examples we will examine in this book concern moral or religious claims, since some of the most hotly debated disagreements concern these claims. And we are interested here in aiding those who have a special interest in evaluating arguments about these matters.

1.1.2 The Construction of Arguments: Premise and Conclusion Indicators

We said above that arguments are composed of two or more statements, where a statement is a sentence that is either true or false. We must now say something about how these components or materials must be fastened together to form an argument. To have an argument, we need at least two statements, and we need one of them to be affirmed *on the basis of* or *because of* the others. The others need to be offered *as reasons for believing* the statement. In an argument, the statement that is affirmed on the basis of the others is called the "conclusion," and the statements on the basis of which the conclusion is affirmed are called the "premises."

With this understanding of the components and construction of arguments in view, consider the following examples of arguments:

1. Dr. Smith's grade distributions are exactly what the university is aiming for. So the complaints of Dr. Smith's students that Dr. Smith is not giving enough A's are wrong.
2. Planned Parenthood uses federal funds in a way that is not morally acceptable, for Planned Parenthood uses federal funds to perform abortions. And using federal funds to perform abortions is not morally acceptable.
3. You should vote for the Republican candidate for office because the Republican candidate will defend religious liberty.

In each example, we have an argument, because in each example we have a set of statements where one of these statements is affirmed on the basis of the other(s). In each of the examples, the hypothetical author of the passage attempts to supply a reason for believing one of the statements in the passage.

Some important features of these examples can help us to identify them as arguments. Each example includes either a premise indicator or a conclusion indicator. **Premise indicators** are *words or phrases indicating that what comes immediately after them is a premise on the basis of which a conclusion is affirmed*. Examples of premise indicators are "because" and "for." A fuller list of these indicators is included in figure 1.1. **Conclusion indicators** are *words or phrases indicating that what comes immediately after them is a conclusion affirmed on the basis of premises supplied elsewhere in the argument*. Examples of conclusion indicators are "therefore" and "so." A fuller list of conclusion indicators is included in figure 1.2.

Figure 1.1
Premise Indicators

Because	Owing to
For	As
Inasmuch as	Since
After all	

Figure 1.2
Conclusion Indicators

Therefore	Accordingly
Consequently	It follows that
So	Hence
Thus	Whence
For this reason	

See if you can spot the premise and conclusion indicators in examples 1–3 above. In example 1, we have the conclusion indicator "So." This word indicates that what comes after it is a conclusion affirmed on the basis of what came before it. This conclusion indicator helps us to identify example 1 as an argument because it shows us that it is composed of statements where one (the second) is affirmed on the basis of the other (the first).

Example 2 uses the premise indicator "for." This premise indicator tells us that what comes after it is a premise on the basis of which the claim preceding the word "for" is affirmed. In this passage, we have an argument that begins with a conclusion and then supplies reasons for affirming that conclusion.

The conclusion also comes first in example 3, which uses the premise indicator "because." Here the claim that follows the word "because" is a premise on the basis of which the claim that precedes the word "because" is affirmed.

Notice that example 3 offers us an argument using only one sentence. We might ask how it composes an argument, since our definition of an argument requires at least two statements. The answer is that, strictly speaking, a statement need not be a sentence but can be a clause that *could* function on its own as a sentence that is either true or false. In example 3 we get two such clauses, one before the word "because" and one after it. So even though we don't get two sentences in example 3, we do get an argument because we get at least two clauses that can function alone as sentences that are either true or false, and one of them is affirmed on the basis of the other. Here the linking word "because" functions to indicate this very fact about their relationship.

While very many arguments employ premise or conclusion indicators like those used in 1–3, not all arguments do. Some arguments are presented without premise or conclusion indicators. For example, consider the following passage:

4. We should go to Busch Gardens this weekend. It's one of the last times it will be open this year, all of our friends are going, and it's a lot of fun.

In this argument, there is no word or phrase that indicates to the reader that the first sentence is the conclusion of the argument. The reader has to figure this out herself using her knowledge of the author of the passage and of the context in which it is offered. Sometimes the absence of premise and conclusion indicators can lead to interpretive confusions. It can be difficult to tell whether the author intended to provide an argument or not.

1.1.3 Arguments vs. Nonarguments

We have said quite a bit now about the nature of arguments, their components, and some tips for identifying them. We will conclude this section by identifying some types of passages that, though not arguments, are often confused with arguments. These types of passages are composed of sets of statements, but the statements are not related to one another in the right way to form arguments, because none of the statements is affirmed on the basis of the others. Some of these types of passages are more difficult to distinguish from arguments than others.

One common type of passage that does not form an argument is a report. A **report** is *a set of statements where none of the statements is affirmed on the basis of the others and where the statements are offered for the purpose of simply providing the reader with information*. The primary purpose of reports, then, is informational; no conclusion is drawn in a report. The following passage is an example of a report:

5. The study revealed that building the new stadium would cost around five billion dollars. To make a profit, the average ticket price per event would need to be around forty dollars. The city would also need to extend the light rail from the suburbs to the downtown area. It is estimated that 45 percent of the population would attend an event at the stadium at least once during its first year.

While example 5 is composed of many statements, these statements are not related to one another in the right way to form an argument. None of them is affirmed on the basis of any of the others. The primary purpose for which a passage like example 5 would be offered is simply to provide the reader with information.

Of course, it might be that by providing the reader with this information, the author hopes the reader will draw a particular conclusion—perhaps, for example, that the building project is feasible. And it is clear that the information in a report may be highly relevant for the purpose of drawing such conclusions. This is indeed part of why reports can be confused with arguments. We can mistakenly think that a person is advocating a position when she makes a report because of the relevance that the report has for that position. But if no conclusion is affirmed in a passage, that passage does not compose an argument—no matter how relevant the information of the report is to one conclusion or another.

A second type of passage that is commonly mistaken for an argument is a mere conditional statement. A **mere conditional statement** is *an "if . . . then" statement that is not used to either affirm or deny either of its component clauses.* All "if . . . then" statements are conditional statements; they have two component clauses that could function as independent sentences but that are related in a conditional manner. So, for example, the sentence "If the star pitcher doesn't play, then the team will lose" is a conditional statement. It relates two clauses using an "if . . . then" construction. But what makes a conditional statement a *mere* conditional statement is that it is not used to affirm or deny either of the clauses that compose it. The conditional statement in the example just mentioned doesn't clearly affirm or deny either that the star pitcher won't play or that the team will lose. It states only that there is an "if . . . then" relationship between these claims and can thus be assumed to be a mere conditional statement.

Of course, in some conversational contexts, if someone were to make this conditional statement, we would reasonably interpret him as affirming or denying one of its components. For instance, imagine that you and I are sitting in the stands, and it is clear to us that the star pitcher is not playing. I ask you, "Will the team win?" and you respond by making the conditional statement above: "If the star pitcher doesn't play, then the team will lose." Here it seems that your assertion does function to affirm one of the component parts of the conditional statement—namely, that the team is going to lose. And the statement supplies a reason for this assertion as well—namely, that the star pitcher isn't playing. So in this conversational context, we should treat your utterance of this conditional statement as constituting an argument.

The foregoing highlights a certain complication in identifying whether a particular passage composes an argument. As interpreters of the passage, if we are to determine whether the passage composes an argument, we must know something about the context in which it is offered. Here is a rule of thumb: *If the context does not clearly indicate that a conditional claim is used in order to affirm or deny one of its component clauses, then treat the conditional statement as a mere conditional statement; if it is clear that the conditional statement does function to affirm or deny one of its component clauses, then treat the conditional statement as composing an argument.*

A third type of passage that is commonly and mistakenly thought to compose an argument is an illustration. An **illustration** is *a set of statements where none of the statements is affirmed on the basis of the others, and where one of the statements is explained or clarified through the use of an example.* The primary purpose of the illustration is not to argue in favor of the statement or statements it illustrates but to clarify the statement or statements. Here is an example of an illustration:

> 6. Some claims are true simply because of the meaning of the words that compose them. So, for instance, the claim "All bachelors are males" is true because of the meaning of "bachelor" and "male."

The passage above provides us an example of an illustration. The first statement made in example 6 is illustrated by the second statement. The second statement provides one example of the phenomenon that is stated to exist in the first statement. The purpose of the illustration is not to defend the first statement or argue that it is true but simply to provide an example of it.

Illustrations can be easily confused with arguments for two reasons. First, as in example 6, they sometimes employ words or phrases that are often used as conclusion indicators. While example 6 uses the word "So," this word does not function as a conclusion indicator in this passage. It instead indicates that what comes after it is an illustration. The word "thus" is also sometimes used in this way. A second reason illustrations are commonly mistaken for arguments is that the illustrations could often be used to provide arguments for those claims they illustrate if this were deemed desirable. This is so in example 6. If the author deemed it desirable to *argue* for the first claim in her passage, she might do so by pointing to the second claim in her passage. In doing so she would appeal to the sentence "All bachelors are males" not as an illustration of her claim that some sentences are true simply because of the meaning of the words that compose them, but as a reason for affirming this claim. The word "So" would still not be functioning as a premise indicator in this instance, but the illustration indicated by the "So" would be employed to provide evidence of the claim that preceded it.

How can one distinguish between arguments and illustrations, if that which can be used for an illustration can also sometimes be used to provide a premise in an argument? Distinguishing between arguments and illustrations can require some interpretive sensitivity on the part of the reader. When we encounter a passage that includes an example that could be used to compose either an illustration or an argument, we must consider whether the statement the example is about is controversial in the conversational context. If the statement is not controversial, then the example is likely offered merely as an illustration. This seems to be the case with example 6 above. If the statement is controversial, however, then the example may indeed be offered as a premise in defense of the statement. A rule of thumb here is this: *Assume that examples are used to provide illustrations of statements rather than arguments for them unless those statements the examples are about are controversial in the conversational context; if the statements the examples are about are controversial, then treat the passage as an argument.*

The final type of passage that is sometimes confused with an argument is an explanation. An **explanation** is *a set of statements where none of the statements is affirmed on the basis of the others and where some of the statements tell the reader why one of the other statements is true.* The primary purpose of explanations is not to defend or argue in favor of a statement but to provide the reader with an understanding of why the statement is true. Here is an example of an explanation:

7. The sidewalk is wet because the sprinklers have been on.

In example 7, the author is likely offering an explanation for why the sidewalk is wet. The explanation—namely, that the sprinklers have been on—provides the reader with an understanding of why the sidewalk is wet. Its purpose is not to convince the reader that the sidewalk is wet but to explain to the reader why this is so.

Explanations can be confused with arguments because they often employ words or phrases that can be used as premise indicators. Example 7 uses the premise indicator "because," for instance, but here the word "because" does not function as a premise indicator. Rather, the word "because" indicates that what comes after it will explain why what comes before it is true.

What we saw with illustrations is also the case with explanations: that which can be used to provide a good explanation can also often be used to provide a good argument. If, for instance, we needed to find an argument for thinking that the sidewalk is wet, then example 7 might serve that purpose. Why think the sidewalk is wet? Well, the sprinklers have been on. Whether a passage like example 7 composes an argument or an explanation depends once again on the conversational context. A first rule of thumb for discerning whether a passage composes an argument or an explanation is much like our rule for sorting out arguments and illustrations. *If the statement that is either explained or argued for is controversial in the conversational context, then treat the passage as an argument; if it is not controversial, treat the passage as an explanation.*

A second rule of thumb for distinguishing arguments and explanations can also be useful. When attempting to discern whether a passage is an argument or an explanation, we should also ask whether that which is offered as either an explanation or an argument is the sort of thing that would make sense of the claim for which it either explains or argues. If not, then the passage is probably an argument. Consider this example:

8. Jesus did many miracles other than those recorded in the Gospels, because the Gospel of John says he did.

That the Gospel of John says Jesus performed many miracles other than those recorded in the Gospels doesn't *make sense of why* Jesus performed many miracles not recorded in the Gospels. That John tells us this happened is not the sort of thing to explain why it happened. So example 8 is best understood as an argument rather than an explanation. Here, then, is a second rule of thumb: *If the potential premise or explanation is not the sort of thing to make sense of the statement that is either argued for or explained, then the passage is probably an argument; if the potential premise or explanation would indeed make sense of the statement that is either argued for or explained, then the passage is likely an explanation.*

1.1.4 Summary

In this section, we defined some key terms (argument, statement, premise indicator, and conclusion indicator) and offered some tips for identifying whether a passage composes an argument or some other type of statement that is not an argument (a report, a mere conditionals statement, an illustration, or an explanation). It should be clear from our discussion that determining whether a passage composes an argument requires some sensitivity to the interests of the author of the passage one is considering and to the context in which that passage is offered. The first step in acquiring the skills necessary for doing a good job evaluating arguments is to learn to identify them.

Exercise 1.1

A. Statement or Not a Statement? Identify whether each of the following composes a statement or does not compose a statement. If it does not compose a statement, explain why it doesn't.

1. Martin Luther King Jr. lived during the Revolutionary War.
2. It is good to honor one's father and mother.

Key Ideas for Review

Logic is the study of the methods used to evaluate arguments.

An **argument** is a set of statements where one of those statements (the conclusion) is affirmed on the basis of the others (the premises).

A **statement** is any sentence that is either true or false.

Premise indicators are words or phrases indicating that what comes immediately after them is a premise on the basis of which a conclusion is affirmed.

Conclusion indicators are words or phrases indicating that what comes immediately after them is a conclusion affirmed on the basis of premises supplied elsewhere in the argument.

A **report** is a set of statements where none of the statements is affirmed on the basis of the others and where the statements are offered for the purpose of simply providing the reader with information.

A **mere conditional statement** is an "if . . . then" statement that is not used to either affirm or deny either of its component clauses.

An **illustration** is a set of statements where none of the statements is affirmed on the basis of the others, and where one of the statements is explained or clarified through the use of an example.

An **explanation** is a set of statements where none of the statements is affirmed on the basis of the others and where some of the statements tell the reader why one of the other statements is true.

---

3. Table sit three hike hike balloon.

4. Bring it on!

5. The philosophers keep asking, "Why?"

6. I don't like hot pillows.

7. There is something in nature that can cure cancer.

8. Sally was so upset about missing the shot.

9. Science aims to discover truth.

10. So that we can be happy.

B. Argument or Nonargument? Identify whether each of the following quoted passages composes an argument. If a quoted passage does not compose an argument, identify whether it composes a report, a mere conditional statement, an illustration, or an explanation.

1. A furniture website states, "The table is made of a dark kind of wood. It stands well on its own and does not hobble. It is accompanied by four sturdy chairs made of the same material. The entire set can fit in the average dining room space quite easily."

2. One child says to another, "Go with me! There will be clowns and elephants and people swinging from the trapeze. It's going to be awesome."

3. A preacher says, "Sometimes a good person will allow someone he loves to suffer. Thus good fathers will permit their children to suffer so that their children will learn important life lessons."

4. A concerned consumer says, "That car company really should work on their product, shouldn't they? Customers almost never buy from them more than once."

5. A mother tells her daughter, "If you are going to get your license, you have to go through the driver's education course."

6. A wife tells her husband, "Going to the mailbox will only waste your time. After all, it's Sunday."

7. A political candidate says, "The leaders of that country are evil people, and we will not negotiate with evil people. So we will have no talks with them."

8. A student admits to his professor, "I didn't get a good grade because I didn't do enough practice exercises."

9. A book says, "We can be confident that the New Testament documents are a reliable source of historical information, since if they weren't, then no other ancient documents would be either."

10. A historian claims, "The framers of the Constitution were heavily influenced by European political philosophers. So, for instance, Thomas Jefferson was influenced by John Locke."

1.2 Evaluating Arguments

In section 1.1 we introduced key concepts that enable us to better identify arguments. The next step is to learn to evaluate the arguments we identify. After all, we hope that the arguments on the basis of which we believe things and the arguments that we employ to influence the beliefs of others are *good* arguments rather than *bad* arguments. Fulfilling this hope requires skills in evaluating arguments—skills that enable us to better ascertain what value an argument has.

In this section, our aim is to acquire some additional key concepts that will help us with this work of evaluating arguments. In particular, our concern will be to learn several distinct evaluative properties or features that arguments can have. Each evaluative feature we will learn is either a way an argument can be good or way an argument can fail to be good. Once we learn what these evaluative features are, our concern in the remainder of part 1 will be to learn methods we can use to identify when arguments possess these features.

1.2.1 Evaluating Arguments in Two Steps

The process involved in evaluating arguments can be conceived of as a two-step process. The first step is concerned with determining whether the premises of the argument are true. If one or more of the premises of an argument isn't true, then it would be a mistake to believe the conclusion of the argument on the basis of these premises. For example, consider the following argument:

1. All animals are omnivores. And all omnivores eat. So all animals eat.

Even if the conclusion of this argument is true, it would be a mistake to believe it on the basis of the argument's premises. This is because at least one of the premises—namely, the premise that all animals are omnivores—is false.

A second step in evaluating arguments involves identifying the relationship between the premises of the argument and its conclusion. In particular, it is important to identify in what way, if at all, the truth of the premises of an argument would support its conclusion. If an argument has only true premises, but the truth of its premises doesn't support its conclusion, then it is still a mistake to believe the conclusion on the basis of those premises, despite their truth. For example, consider the following argument:

2. Some animals are herbivores. And no herbivores eat meat. So no animals eat meat.

The premises of this argument are true. However, it would be a mistake to believe the conclusion on the basis of these premises. The reason for this is that the premises are not related in the right kind of way to the conclusion. Even though the premises of example 2 are true, they don't support its conclusion adequately for us to believe that conclusion on the basis of them.

The full process of evaluating an argument involves evaluating both the truth or falsity of its premises *and* the relationship between its premises and its conclusion. If we overlook either of these steps, we have not completed the process of evaluating an argument. In principle it doesn't matter in what order we complete these two steps. However, it can often be helpful to begin with the second step, since it is likely to be much easier to achieve agreement with others regarding this second step than it is to achieve agreement regarding the first step. Consider, for example, the following argument:

3. Either Jesus never really died or he did in fact rise from the dead. But Jesus really did die. So Jesus did in fact rise from the dead.

Arguments like the one presented in example 3 are hotly debated today, as they have been for centuries. But even those who strongly disagree about the truth of the premises of this argument can fairly easily reach agreement about the relationship between these premises and the conclusion of the argument. Both those who affirm that the premises of the argument are true and those who do not can fairly easily agree that *if* the premises of the argument are true, they would confirm its conclusion. *If* we assume that Jesus either didn't die or did rise, and *if* we assume that Jesus did die, then it has to be true that Jesus did rise. The only remaining question regards the truth of these assumptions.

Example 3 illustrates how agreement can often be reached concerning the relationship between the premises of an argument and its conclusion, even if agreement can't be reached so easily regarding the truthfulness of the argument's premises. The example also illustrates how we can often make progress in a conversation with others with whom we disagree by focusing first on evaluating the relationship between the premises of an argument and its conclusion. Specifically, we make progress by identifying more clearly where our disagreement originates. Those who disagree about the conclusion of the argument presented in example 3 are unlikely to disagree about whether the premises of example 3, if true, would support its conclusion. This means that their disagreement is likely instead to be concerned with the truth of one or both of the premises. And this is where their future discussion should focus.

In this way, beginning with the second step of our two-step evaluative process can be quite helpful. And as it turns out, the skills of reasoning we will discuss in the next two chapters are concerned precisely with this step of the process of evaluating arguments. These skills will enable us to methodically identify whether the premises of arguments adequately support their conclusions, and by doing so they will help us to make progress in dialogue with others by directing our attention to the origins of our disagreements.

1.2.2 Key Evaluative Features: Validity, Invalidity, Soundness, Unsoundness

The skills we will learn in the next two chapters will help us to discern the relationship between the premises of arguments and their conclusions, and will thereby help us to determine which key evaluative features arguments possess. It is now time that we introduce the key features that we will identify with these skills.

The first key evaluative feature is validity. A **valid** argument is *an argument in which the truth of the premises absolutely guarantees the truth of the conclusion—an argument in which it is impossible for the premises to be true and the conclusion false.* An argument is valid if and only if the truth of its premises would guarantee the truth of its conclusion. If the premises are true, the conclusion has to be true also. If there were a scale that measured the extent to which the premises of an argument can confirm the conclusion of an argument, validity would lie at the very peak of this scale.

We've seen some examples of valid arguments already. Example 3 above, for instance, is a valid argument: *if* it is true that either Jesus never really died or he did in fact rise from the dead, and *if* it is true that Jesus really did die, then it has to be true that Jesus rose from the dead.

Example 1 is also a valid argument: *if* all animals are omnivores, and *if* all omnivores are things that eat, then this would guarantee that all animals are things that eat. It is impossible for it to be the case that all animals are omnivores, and that all omnivores eat, but *not* that all animals eat.

Notably, example 1 is valid even though one of its premises is clearly false. This illustrates an important fact: the validity of an argument does not directly relate to the truth or falsity of its premises. Nor does the validity of an argument have direct implications for the truth or falsity of its conclusion. Rather, the validity of an argument is concerned with the *relationship* between the truth of the argument's premises and the truth of its conclusion. The argument is valid if and only if the following relationship obtains: the truth of the argument's premises (whether they are true or not) would guarantee the truth of its conclusion (whether it is true or not). Accordingly, there can be valid arguments with true premises and a true conclusion, false premises and a false conclusion, or false premises and a true conclusion. The only kind of argument that cannot be valid is an argument that has all true premises and yet a false conclusion.

Look back now at example 2. The argument in example 2 is not valid but is rather what we will call invalid. An **invalid** argument is *an argument in which the truth of the premises does not absolutely guarantee the truth of the conclusion—an argument in which it is possible for the premises to be true and the conclusion false.* We can tell that the argument in example 2 is invalid because the premises are true while the conclusion is false. Thus the truth of its premises do not guarantee the truth of its conclusion. Given our definition of what it is for an argument to be valid, example 2 is not a valid argument. Any argument that is not valid is invalid. So example 2 is an invalid argument. It is an argument in which the truth of the premises does not guarantee the truth of the conclusion, an argument in which it *is* possible for the premises to be true and the conclusion false.

Being valid is one way an argument can be good, while being invalid is one way an argument can fail to be good. However, the fact that an argument is valid doesn't imply that it is good in every respect. Nor does the fact that an argument is invalid imply that it is bad in every respect. This is because there are additional ways arguments can be good or fail to be good other than by being valid or invalid.

As we saw earlier in this section, a different way for an argument to be good is to have only true premises. When an argument has only true premises *and* is valid, we call it a sound argument. A **sound argument** is *a valid argument with only true premises*. An argument is sound if and only if it has both features—it is both valid and has only true premises. An interesting fact necessarily follows—namely, that every sound argument has a true conclusion. This is guaranteed by the two features of sound arguments. Given that an argument is valid (the first feature of sound arguments), the truth of its premises would guarantee the truth of its conclusion. And the second feature of sound arguments is that their premises *are* true. So it follows that the conclusion of any sound argument is true as well.

By contrast, an **unsound argument** is *an argument that is not sound*. There are two ways for an argument to be unsound. An argument can be unsound by failing to be valid or by failing to have only true premises. Of course, some arguments fail in both respects: they are both invalid and have at least one false premise. These arguments, we might say, are doubly unsound.

In chapter 2 we will study deductive logic. **Deductive logic** is *the study of the methods used to evaluate arguments for validity or invalidity*. Whereas logic in general is the study of the methods used to evaluate arguments, deductive logic is a particular branch of logic that studies the methods used to evaluate arguments for the specific evaluative properties of validity or invalidity. But before turning to deductive logic, we must introduce some further key evaluative features.

1.2.3 Key Evaluative Features: Strength, Weakness, Cogency, Uncogency

In discussing validity in the previous subsection, we imagined a scale that measures the extent to which the premises of an argument confirm its conclusion. Validity sits at the very peak of this scale. In valid arguments, the truth of the premises absolutely guarantees the truth of the conclusion. It's impossible for the premises to be true and the conclusion false.

There are cases, however, in which the truth of an argument's premises would support the truth of its conclusion without supporting it to *this* extent. In these cases, it's *possible* for the premises to be true and the conclusion false, but this is *unlikely*. The premises don't guarantee the truth of the conclusion, but they make it more likely than not. We will call arguments with this feature strong arguments. A **strong** argument is *an argument in which the truth of the premises makes the conclusion more likely than not without absolutely guaranteeing the conclusion*. Here's an example of a strong argument:

4. Most students who took the logic quiz scored below 95 percent. So Sam, who took the quiz, scored below 95 percent.

In example 4, the truth of the premise doesn't guarantee the truth of the conclusion. It's *possible* for the premise to be true and the conclusion false. After all, Sam might be an especially strong student—the exception rather than the rule. Nonetheless, the truth of the premise does make it more likely than not that the conclusion is true. If all you had to go on concerning Sam's score was that most students scored below 95 percent, and you didn't know anything about Sam's relative standing in the class, the safe bet to make (if you had to) would be that he scored lower than 95 percent. In this way, the argument is one in which the premises make the conclusion likely to be true without guaranteeing it.

We have defined strong arguments using the language of likelihood. It is also possible to define strong arguments using the language of probability. Using probabilistic language, a strong argument is one in which the probability of the conclusion given the premises is greater than 50 percent and less than 100 percent. Saying that the probability is greater than 50 percent is a different way to say that the conclusion is more likely than not given the premises, while saying that the probability is less than 100 percent is a different way to say that the conclusion is not guaranteed by the premises.

In contrast to strong arguments, there are weak arguments. A **weak** argument is *an argument in which the truth of the premises does not make the truth of the conclusion more likely than not*. To use probabilistic language, they are arguments in which the probability of the conclusion given the premises is 50 percent or less.

Imagine that we tweak the conclusion of example 4 to get the following:

5. Most students who took the logic quiz scored below 95 percent. So Sam, who took the quiz, scored above 95 percent.

In example 5, the conclusion is more likely to be false than true, given the premise. So example 5 is a weak argument.

The final two key evaluative concepts we need to introduce are those of cogency and uncogency. A **cogent** argument is *a strong argument with only true premises*. Like a sound argument, a cogent argument has two and only two required features. To be cogent, an argument must be strong, and it must have only true premises. If we supposed that the premise in example 4 were indeed true, then example 4 would be a cogent argument. Any argument that is both strong and has only true premises is cogent.

By contrast with cogent arguments, there are uncogent arguments. An **uncogent** argument is *an argument that is not cogent*. It is either a weak argument or an argument that is strong but has at least one false premise. Of course, some arguments are both weak and have at least one false premise. Such arguments, we might say, are doubly uncogent. If the premise in example 5 were false, for instance, it would be a doubly uncogent argument.

Whereas deductive logic is the branch of logic concerned with evaluating arguments for validity or invalidity, **inductive logic** is *the study of the methods used to evaluate arguments for strength or weakness.* In chapter 3 we will study inductive logic, looking at several methods used to test whether arguments are strong or weak.

1.2.4 Relationships between Key Evaluative Features

Putting the information from the two previous subsections together, we can draw some interesting conclusions about the relationships between these key evaluative features of arguments. For example, we can determine that some invalid arguments are strong arguments. This is because for an argument to be invalid, all that is required is that the truth of its premises doesn't guarantee the truth of its conclusion. But strong arguments have this feature. The truth of their premises makes the truth of their conclusion more likely than not but doesn't guarantee its truth.

Many relationships of this kind can be discerned. As an aid to discerning them, take a look at the Argument Evaluation Tree in figure 1.3. In this figure, the lower-level categories represent what we call "mutually exclusive" and "jointly exhaustive" subcategories of the upper-level categories. For example, within the category of the arguments, there are the subcategories of valid arguments and invalid arguments. No arguments are both valid and invalid (that is, validity and invalidity are mutually exclusive), and all arguments belong to either the valid category or the invalid category (that is, these categories are jointly exhaustive). With this background, try to use figure 1.3 to answer the following question: Can cogent arguments be valid?

It turns out the answer is no. This is because all cogent arguments must be strong, but all strong arguments are invalid. No invalid arguments are valid, of course, so no cogent arguments are valid arguments.

This conclusion—and others that can be drawn using figure 1.3—may initially seem strange, since in our everyday speech we use some of our key vocabulary from this section in ways that differ from how that vocabulary has been defined here. For example, in ordinary English it is often the case that calling an argument "strong" does not imply that the truth of the argument's premises do not guarantee its conclusion. Recall that we saw something similar to be true of the key term "argument": it too has uses in ordinary English that differ from the technical meaning it is given in the discipline of logic.

Figure 1.3
Argument Evaluation Tree

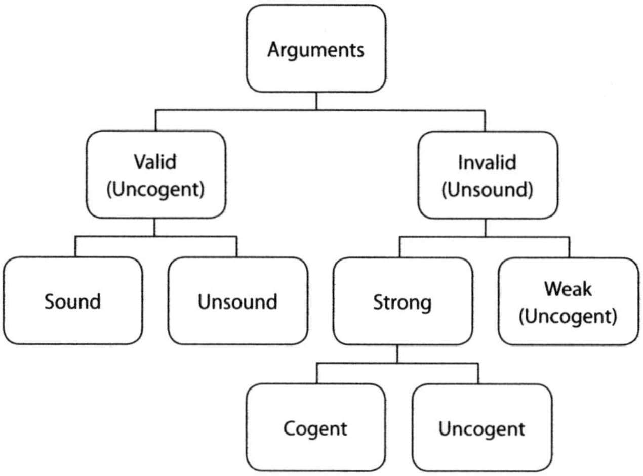

Because we often employ this chapter's key terminology in ways that depart from how that terminology is defined here, it is important that we acquire a working understanding of these terms and their definitions and continue to use them consistently for class purposes. If the vocabulary isn't acquired and used consistently as we have defined it, our study of logic will not help us to inculcate skills of reasoning. It will only confuse us. With this in mind, the section exercises below are designed to further strengthen your acquisition of this key vocabulary.

1.2.5 *Summary*

This section has introduced several evaluative properties of arguments that will help enable us to determine the value that arguments have. The key evaluative properties of validity, invalidity, soundness, unsoundness, strength, weakness, cogency, and uncogency have been defined, and their relationships have been illustrated. The subdisciplines of deductive and inductive logic, which will be studied in more detail in the next two chapters, have also been introduced.

Exercise 1.2

A. True or False? Using your knowledge of the key vocabulary introduced in this section, determine whether the following statements are true or false.

1. A valid argument can have a false conclusion.

2. A strong argument can be uncogent.

Key Ideas for Review

A **valid** argument is an argument in which the truth of the premises absolutely guarantees the truth of the conclusion—an argument in which it is impossible for the premises to be true and the conclusion false.

An **invalid** argument is an argument in which the truth of the premises does not absolutely guarantee the truth of the conclusion—an argument in which it is possible for the premises to be true and the conclusion false.

A **sound** argument is a valid argument with only true premises.

An **unsound** argument is an argument that is not sound.

Deductive logic is the study of the methods used to evaluate arguments for validity or invalidity.

A **strong** argument is an argument in which the truth of the premises makes the conclusion more likely than not without absolutely guaranteeing the conclusion.

A **weak** argument is an argument in which the truth of the premises does not make the truth of the conclusion more likely than not.

A **cogent** argument is a strong argument with only true premises.

An **uncogent** argument is an argument that is not cogent.

Inductive logic is the study of the methods used to evaluate arguments for strength or weakness.

3. If a strong argument has only true premises, it is valid.

4. If a valid argument has a false premise, it is unsound.

5. Any argument with a false premise is invalid.

6. An argument with only true premises and a true conclusion can be uncogent.

7. Deductive logic is the study of the methods used to evaluate arguments for strength or weakness.

8. Some valid arguments are weak.

9. All sound arguments are uncogent.

10. If a valid argument has a false conclusion, it must have at least one false premise.

B. Practice with Arguments. Using your knowledge of key vocabulary introduced in this section, attempt to construct arguments with the features listed below.

1. A valid argument with a false conclusion.

2. A weak argument with only true premises.

3. A sound argument.

4. A cogent argument.

5. A strong argument with a true conclusion but at least one false premise.

2
▶ ▶ ▶ ▶ ▶

Deductive Logic

In chapter 1 we briefly introduced the fields of deductive and inductive logic. Deductive logic, we said, is the study of the methods used to evaluate arguments for validity or invalidity. In this chapter, our focus is on deductive logic understood in this way. We will discuss five methods commonly employed to determine whether arguments are valid or invalid. Using these methods can contribute to completing the two-step process for evaluating arguments that we introduced in chapter 1.

Each of the five sections in this chapter is concerned with either a method used to test whether arguments are valid or a method used to test whether arguments are invalid. As we will see, each method is limited in some way. None of the methods by itself will enable you to discern whether every single argument is valid or invalid. For each method, there will be some valid arguments that the method does not enable you to conclude are valid and some invalid arguments that the method does not enable you to conclude are invalid. Nonetheless, the methods we will discuss do have widespread applicability. Many of the arguments you encounter on a daily basis can be determined to be valid or invalid by using one or more of these methods. Moreover, by learning these methods, you will also acquire skills that will enable you to better *construct* valid arguments of your own.

The five methods for evaluating arguments covered in this chapter are not exhaustive. Other methods are used to evaluate whether arguments are valid or invalid besides these. However, the five covered here are perhaps the most commonly used due to their widespread applicability. Acquiring these skills will put you in a much better position to evaluate arguments for validity or invalidity than you would be in without comparable skills and will allow you to share in the skills of deductive logic learned by many other people educated in colleges and universities in the English-speaking world.

2.1 Famous Forms Method

The first method, which is called the **Famous Forms Method**, is *a method used to determine whether an argument is valid by determining whether the argument's form conforms to a famous valid argument form*. This method takes three steps. First, you identify the form of the argument you are evaluating. Second, you check to see if the form of this argument conforms to one of the **famous valid argument forms** we will discuss below. Third, you conclude that the argument is valid if its form conforms to one of these famous argument forms.

2.1.1 Identifying Argument Forms

To employ the Famous Forms Method, we need to first learn how to identify an argument's form, or pattern of reasoning. We'll illustrate how to do this with the following example.

1. If Sam ate chili, then Sam will be happy. Sam ate chili. So Sam will be happy.

For purposes of using the Famous Forms Method, we identify an argument's form by replacing any repeated statements in the argument with capital letters, such as P or Q. It is important when doing this replacement that we consistently replace the same repeated statement with the same letter. For example, we might replace the repeated statement "Sam ate chili" in example 1 with the letter C in both premises. It is also important to replace different repeated statements with different letters. For example, since we're using the letter C for "Sam ate chili," we might use the letter H for "Sam will be happy." The result of performing this replacement is:

2. If C, then H. C. So H.

Example 2 gives us the form of the argument in example 1.

In some cases, identifying an argument's form requires us to do slightly more than simply replace its repeated statements with capital letters. Often we must perform the additional step of making the argument's logical connectives more explicit in a conventional manner. An argument's **logical connectives** are *those words or phrases that an argument uses in order to make larger state-ments out of smaller ones.*[1] For instance, in example 2 the first premise uses the "if . . . then" logical connective. It uses this connective to build the larger statement "If C, then H" out of the smaller, repeated statements C and H. Sometimes in English we express the "if . . . then" connective without explicitly stating the word "then." For example, we might have written example 1 as:

3. If Sam ate chili, Sam will be happy. Sam ate chili. So Sam will be happy.

Here the word "then" is left out, though we clearly have the same argument we did in example 1. When we identify the form of an argument like example 3, we will adopt the convention of supplying the word "then," making the logical connective used in the argument more explicit. The result is the argu-ment form indicated in example 2.

In addition to using "if . . ." rather than "if . . . then," there are other ways to express the "if . . . then" logical connective in English. For example, instead of "If Sam ate chili, Sam will be happy," we often use statements like "Given that Sam ate chili, Sam will be happy," or "Assuming that Sam ate chili, Sam will be happy," or "Sam will be happy if Sam ate chili," or "Sam ate chili only if Sam will be happy." In all of these cases, our convention will be to write the "if . . . then" connective as "if . . . then" when we attempt to identify the form of the argument.

In addition to the "if . . . then" logical connective, there is also the "either . . . or" connective and the "not" connective. Consider the following example that uses both.

4. Either Sam ate chili or Sam ate pizza. Sam did not eat pizza. So Sam ate chili.

Here let's replace "Sam at chili" with C as before and "Sam ate pizza" with P. The first premise will now be:

5. Either C or P.

The same would have been true if the "either" had been left out of the first premise in example 4. As with our "if . . . then" connection above, so too our convention, when we give the form of statements that use "or" or "either . . . or," will be to write "either . . . or" in the way we have in example 5.

What about the second premise in example 4? It doesn't quite repeat "Sam ate pizza" verbatim. Rather, it denies "Sam ate pizza" by saying "Sam did not eat pizza." There are other ways of saying the same thing—of denying that Sam ate pizza. For example, we could say, "It is not the case that Sam ate pizza" or "Sam didn't eat pizza." In any of these cases, for purposes of identifying the form of the argument, our convention will be to write the second premise as follows:

6. Not-P.

Thus the form of the argument in example 4 is:

7. Either C or P. Not-P. So C.

Along with replacing repeated statements with capital letters and making statements' logical connectives explicit in a conventional manner, there are two further ways in which we can adjust an argument to help identify its form.

First, notice that in each of our examples we have indicated the conclusion with the conclusion indicator "So." This will be our convention, whether or not the word "so" appears in an argument whose form we are attempting to identify. Imagine that in place of example 4 we had:

8. Sam ate chili, for either Sam ate chili or Sam ate pizza, and Sam didn't eat pizza.

Example 8 doesn't use a conclusion indicator. Instead, it uses a premise indicator. Nonetheless, when we state the form of arguments like example 8, our convention will still be to use the conclusion indicator "so" to mark the conclusion rather than using a premise indicator.

Notice something else about example 8. While it gives us the same argument as example 4, the order of the premises and conclusion has changed. But when using the Famous Forms Method, we will always state premises prior to conclusions when giving an argument's form.

Finally, notice again something interesting about example 8. The second premise—the last statement—begins with the word "and." For the purposes of using the Famous Forms Method, we will never write the word "and" when determining an argument's form. In cases like the present one, we will simply overlook the word "and" and write only "Not-P" for the second premise. The same goes for other conjunctions like "but" or "however." Thus, employing our conventions for identifying argument forms, the form of argument 8 will be:

9. Either C or P. Not-P. So C.

We have now identified six conventions we will employ when identifying an argument's form as part of the Famous Forms Method. All of these conventions are summarized in figure 2.1. Replacing an argument's repeated statements with capital letters and following these conventions is all that is necessary for completing the first step of the Famous Forms Method: identifying the argument's form.

Figure 2.1
Conventions for Identifying an Argument's Form

- Write "if . . . then" for "if . . . ," "if . . . then," ". . . only if . . . ," "given that . . . ," and other stylistic variants of "if . . . then."
- Write "either . . . or" for "or" or "either . . . or."
- Write "Not-P" for any sentence that denies a statement you have represented by P.
- Use the conclusion indicator "so" and no premise indicators.
- Write premises before conclusions.
- Eliminate conjunctions such as "and" or "but."

2.1.2 Famous Valid Argument Forms

Once you have identified an argument's form, the next step of the Famous Forms Method asks you to check whether this argument form conforms to one of the famous valid argument forms. An argument form **conforms** to a famous valid argument form *if it exactly matches it, or if it matches it except that it uses different letters or puts its premises in a different order*. In this subsection, we will identify these famous valid argument forms and explain what it is for an argument form to conform to one of them.

There are five famous valid argument forms. The argument forms are called "famous" because they are so widely used. They are valid argument forms because any argument with a form that conforms to one of them is a valid argument. Thus when we complete step two of the Famous Forms Method and find out that an argument has a form that conforms to one of the famous valid argument forms, we can conclude that it is a valid argument.

The first famous valid argument form is called *modus ponens*, which is Latin for "the way of affirming." This argument form is:

If P, then Q.
P.
So Q.

An example of an argument that has a form that conforms to *modus ponens* is:

10. If Ellie pays her rent, the landlord will keep quiet. Ellie pays her rent. So the landlord will keep quiet.

If we replaced "Ellie pays her rent" with P and "the landlord will keep quiet" with Q throughout example 10, the resulting argument form would exactly conform to *modus ponens*. Example 10, then, is a valid argument.

The second famous valid argument form is called **modus tollens**, which is Latin for "the way of denying." This argument form is:

If P, then Q.
Not-Q.
So not-P.

An example of an argument that has a form that conforms to *modus tollens* is:

11. If Ellie paid her rent, then Ellie's bank account is now low. Ellie's bank account isn't now low. So Ellie didn't pay her rent.

If we replaced "Ellie paid her rent" with P and "Ellie's bank account is now low" with Q throughout example 11, the resulting argument form would exactly conform to *modus tollens*. Example 11, then, is a valid argument.

The third famous valid argument form is called the **disjunctive syllogism**, due in part to its prominent use of a disjunction—an "either . . . or" statement. Two ways to state the form of disjunctive syllogism are:

Option 1	Option 2
Either P or Q.	Either P or Q.
Not-Q.	Not-P.
So P.	So Q.

In each case, one of the two options presented in the first premise (here, P or Q) is denied in the second premise, and it is therefore concluded that the other option must be correct.

An example of an argument that has a form that conforms to disjunctive syllogism is:

12. Either Ellie paid her rent or Ellie bought a new television. Ellie didn't buy a new television. So Ellie paid her rent.

If we replaced "Ellie paid her rent" with P and "Ellie bought a new television" with Q throughout example 12, the resulting argument form would exactly conform to the first option for a disjunctive syllogism. Example 12, then, is a valid argument. If the second premise in 12 had instead been "Ellie didn't pay her rent" and the conclusion had been "So Ellie bought a new television," then the argument's form would have exactly conformed to the second option for a disjunctive syllogism.

The fourth famous valid argument form is called the **constructive dilemma**. Like the disjunctive syllogism, it begins with a disjunctive, "either . . . or" claim. However, rather than denying one of the two options presented by the disjunction, in a constructive dilemma claims are made about what is the case if each one of these disjuncts is correct, and a disjunctive conclusion is drawn on this basis. Two options for representing the form of constructive dilemma are:

Option 1	Option 2
Either P or Q.	Either P or Q.
If P, then R.	If P, then R.
If Q, then S.	If Q, then S.
So either R or S.	So either S or R.

An example of an argument that has a form that conforms to constructive dilemma is:

13. Either Ellie paid her rent or Ellie bought a new television. If Ellie paid her rent, then her landlord will keep quiet. If Ellie bought a new television, then her roommates will be upset. So either Ellie's landlord will keep quiet or her roommates will be upset.

If we replaced "Ellie paid her rent" with P, "Ellie bought a new television" with Q, "Ellie's landlord will keep quiet" with R, and "Ellie's roommates will be upset" with S throughout example 13, the resulting argument form would exactly conform to the first option for constructive dilemma. Example 13, then, is a valid argument.

The final famous valid argument form is the **hypothetical syllogism**. Like *modus ponens* and *modus tollens*, it begins with a conditional, "if . . . then" statement. But unlike these other argument forms, its second premise and its conclusion are also conditional statements. Hypothetical syllogisms look like this:

If P, then Q.
If Q, then R.
So if P, then R.

An example of an argument that has a form that conforms to a hypothetical syllogism is:

14. If Ellie paid her rent, then Ellie's bank account is now low. If Ellie's bank account is now low, then Ellie cannot now buy a new television. So if Ellie paid her rent, then Ellie cannot now buy a new television.

If we replaced "Ellie paid her rent" with P, "Ellie's bank account is now low" with Q, and "Ellie cannot now buy a new television" with R throughout example 14, the resulting argument form would exactly conform to the hypothetical syllogism. Example 14, then, is a valid argument.

Now that we have introduced the five famous valid argument forms, what remains is for us to learn how to discern when an argument's form conforms to one of these famous forms. Sometimes this is perfectly straightforward. For example, if we identify the forms of any of the arguments in examples 10 through 14 in exactly the manner specified above, then the resulting forms would exactly match one of the famous valid argument forms. Whenever we have a case of an exact match like this, we can conclude that the argument's form conforms to the relevant famous valid argument form and is therefore valid.

An argument's form can conform in two ways to a famous valid argument form even without exactly matching this form. The first way is if the argument's form is exactly like one of the famous argument forms except that it uses different letters from the famous argument form. For instance, return to example 1 from earlier in this section:

1. If Sam ate chili, then Sam will be happy. Sam ate chili. So Sam will be happy.

We identified the form of example 1 as:

2. If C, then H. C. So H.

The form identified in example 2 is exactly like *modus ponens*, except that it uses C in place of P and H in place of Q. Anytime an argument's form is exactly like one of the famous valid argument forms, except that it has different capital letters in place of the capital letters used in the famous form, we can conclude that the argument form conforms to the famous valid argument form and is thus valid.

When attempting to discern whether an argument form you have identified conforms to a famous valid form, it is helpful to see if you could *consistently* replace the letters in the form you have identified with letters used in the famous form and get as a result a form that exactly matches the famous form. For instance, in example 2, if we replace C consistently with P and replace

H consistently with Q, we get an exact match with *modus ponens*. We can therefore conclude that the form identified in example 2 conforms to *modus ponens*.

There is a second way in which an argument form can conform to one of the famous forms without exactly matching it. This is if its premises are in a different order from the order they appear in the famous form. For instance, imagine that instead of example 1 we had:

15. Sam ate chili. If Sam ate chili, then Sam is happy. So Sam is happy.

When we attempt to identify the form of example 15 using the same capital letters we used previously, we get:

16. C. If C, then H. So H.

The argument form identified in example 16 doesn't exactly match *modus ponens*. However, it does conform to *modus ponens*. The reason is this: if we consistently replace the capital letters used in example 16 with the capital letters used in *modus ponens*, we get an argument form that is exactly like *modus ponens*, except that the premises are in reverse order. To see this, simply replace C with P and replace H with Q. You get:

17. P. If P, then Q. So Q.

The argument form identified in example 17 is exactly like *modus ponens* except that its premises are in a different order from the order of the premises in *modus ponens*. When an argument's form is related to any of the famous valid argument forms in this way, the argument form conforms to the relevant famous form and is therefore valid.

With these remarks in mind, you are now ready to start applying the Famous Forms Method. To apply the method, first attempt to discern an argument's form. Then attempt to discern whether that form conforms to a famous valid argument form in one of the ways we have just identified, either by exactly matching it or by matching it with the exception of the capital letters it uses, the order of its premises, or both. If the argument form does conform to a famous valid argument form, then the argument is valid.

2.1.3 Using the Famous Forms Method Effectively

The Famous Forms Method has great utility. To use it most effectively, keep two observations in mind. First, arguments can have more than one form, but if any of their forms conforms to a famous valid argument form, then they are valid. This is the case even if some of their forms do not conform to a famous valid argument form.

Consider the following example:

18. If Ellie either paid her rent or bought a new television, then Ellie's bank account is now low. Ellie either paid her rent or bought a new television. So Ellie's bank account is now low.

One way to identify the form of argument 18 is to replace "Ellie paid her rent" with P, "Ellie bought a new television" with Q, and "Ellie's bank account is now low" with R. If we do this, then the argument form we end up with is:

19. If either P or Q, then R. P or Q. So R.

The argument form in example 19 doesn't conform to one of the famous valid argument forms, as it doesn't exactly match any of them or match one except that it employs different letters or has premises in a different order.

Nonetheless, example 18 is a valid argument and can be shown to be valid by using the Famous Forms Method. Rather than replacing "Ellie paid her rent" with P and "Ellie bought a new television" with Q, we can replace "either Ellie paid her rent or Ellie bought a new television" with P. And rather than replace "Ellie's bank account is now low" with R, we can replace it with Q. If we do, the result is:

20. If P, then Q. P. So Q.

And example 20 exactly matches *modus ponens*.

Something that is nicely illustrated by examples 19 and 20 is the notion of a main logical connective. The **main logical connective** of a statement is *the logical connective that operates on the entire statement as opposed to simply a subpart of the statement*. In the first statement of example 19, the main logical connective is the "if . . . then" connective. Whereas this connective operates on the entire statement, the "either . . . or" connective operates only on the first part of the "if . . . then" statement. Another way to say this is that the statement, taken as a whole, is an "if . . . then" statement rather than an "either . . . or" statement. By definition, a **conditional statement** is *a statement in which the main logical connective is the "if . . . then" connective*. It is this fact that enables us to identify the argument's form as conforming to *modus ponens*. Using the notion of a main logical connective, we can similarly define a disjunction and a negation. A **disjunction** is *a statement in which the main logical connective is the "either . . .*

or" connective, and a **negation** is *a statement in which the main logical connective is the "not" connective.*

Many arguments involving statements that deny other statements can also be evaluated more effectively using the Famous Forms Method if we keep in mind that they have multiple forms. For example, consider:

21. If Sam ate chili, then Sam didn't eat pizza. But Sam did eat pizza. So Sam didn't eat chili.

Here, instead of replacing "Sam ate pizza" with a capital letter, we will use the Famous Forms Method most effectively if we replace "Sam didn't eat pizza" with a capital letter. If we replace "Sam ate chili" with P and "Sam didn't eat pizza" with Q, then the resulting argument form will exactly match *modus tollens*. However, if we instead replace "Sam ate pizza" with a capital letter, then the resulting argument form will not conform to a famous valid argument form.

The moral of this first observation is that employing the Famous Forms Method effectively can sometimes take some creative work. There are often multiple ways to represent an argument's form. When employing the Famous Forms Method, we need to check whether any of these ways of representing the argument yields a form that is consistent with a famous valid argument form. If any of them does, then the argument is valid.

The second observation concerns an important limitation of the Famous Forms Method—namely, that the method can be used only to determine that an argument is valid. It cannot be used to determine that an argument is invalid. Even if you have checked all the forms an argument can have and have found that none of them matches one of the famous valid argument forms, this does not allow you to conclude that the argument is invalid. Indeed, we will see some examples in later sections of arguments that are valid even though none of their forms conforms to a famous valid argument form. To use the Famous Forms Method effectively, then, we must be careful not to use it to draw the conclusion that any argument is invalid but only that arguments with a form conforming to a famous valid argument form are valid.

2.1.4 Summary

This section has introduced the Famous Forms Method, used to determine if an argument is valid. The method involves identifying an argument's form and then checking to see whether it conforms to a famous valid argument form. We have explained how to identify an argument's form and provided a list of conventions to be followed in this book. We have identified the five famous valid argument forms: *modus ponens*, *modus tollens*, the disjunctive

Key Ideas for Review

The **Famous Forms Method** is a method used to determine whether an argument is valid by determining whether the argument's form conforms to that of a famous valid argument form.

The **famous valid argument forms** are the five commonly employed argument forms given below. Any argument with a form that conforms to one of these argument forms is a valid argument.

Modus Ponens	Modus Tollens	Disjunctive Syllogism (options 1 and 2)	
If P, then Q.	If P, then Q.	Either P or Q.	Either P or Q.
P.	Not-Q.	Not-Q.	Not-P.
So Q.	So not-P.	So P.	So Q.

Constructive Dilemma (options 1 and 2)		Hypothetical Syllogism
Either P or Q.	Either P or Q.	If P, then Q.
If P, then R.	If P, then R.	If Q, then R.
If Q, then S.	If Q, then S.	So if P, then R.
So either R or S.	So either S or R.	

Logical connectives are those words or phrases that an argument uses in order to make larger statements out of smaller ones.

An argument form **conforms** to a famous valid argument form if it exactly matches it, or if it matches it except that it uses different letters or puts its premises in a different order.

A **main logical connective** of a statement is the logical connective that operates on the entire statement as opposed to simply a subpart of the statement.

A **conditional statement** is a statement in which the main logical connective is the "if . . . then" connective.

A **disjunction** is a statement in which the main logical connective is the "either . . . or" connective.

A **negation** is a statement in which the main logical connective is the "not" connective.

syllogism, the constructive dilemma, and the hypothetical syllogism. And, finally, we have discussed how to determine when an argument's form conforms to one of these famous forms.

Exercise 2.1

A. Using the Famous Forms Method. Write the forms of the following arguments. Then use the Famous Forms Method to determine if the arguments are valid. If the validity of an argument cannot be determined in this way, say that it cannot be determined.

1. If Jesus did not rise from the dead, your faith is in vain. But your faith is not in vain. So Jesus did rise from the dead.

2. Either you are with me or you are against me. You are with me. So you're not against me.

3. If we confess our sins, we should forgive others. For if we confess our sins, God forgives our sins. And if God forgives our sins, we should forgive others.

4. Either you study or you go to the party. If you study, you will regret not going to the party. If you go to the party, you will regret not studying. So either you will regret not going to the party or you will regret not studying.

5. We should go on vacation, for, assuming that we don't want to upset the children, we should go on vacation. And we don't want to upset the children.

6. Either we'll see the Eiffel Tower or we'll see the Louvre. We won't see the Louvre. So we'll see the Eiffel Tower.

7. If you study hard, you'll make a good grade. You didn't study hard. So you won't make a good grade.

8. The rats will be back tonight, for it's going to rain. And if it's going to rain, the rats will be back tonight.

9. Either the elephants are playing a trick on us or they prefer water to soda. So they prefer water to soda, for they are not playing a trick on us.

10. We will help with the discipleship if you will preach a revival for us. We won't help with the discipleship. So you won't preach a revival for us.

B. Using the Famous Forms Method (Advanced). Follow the same instructions as for exercise A.

1. We forgot to pray only if we were distracted. We weren't distracted. So we didn't forget to pray.

2. Either our child-rearing manuals need revision or it is good for children to play outside and it is good for children to sing songs inside. It is not good for children to play outside or for children to sing songs inside. So our child-rearing manuals need revision.

3. If the star player wasn't injured, we didn't lose. We lost. So the star player was injured.

4. If you either brush your teeth or comb your hair, you'll get to bed later than you planned. If you get to bed later than you planned, you'll need more coffee in the morning or you'll be groggy at the office. So if you

either brush your teeth or comb your hair, you'll need more coffee in the morning or you'll be groggy at the office.

5. We should be humble, for we shouldn't fail to imitate Jesus. And we should be humble given that we shouldn't fail to imitate Jesus.

6. If Paul were psychologically disturbed, he couldn't have been as effective as he was. But Paul either encountered Jesus or Paul was psychologically disturbed. And if Paul encountered Jesus, then we should listen to him. So either Paul couldn't have been as effective as he was or we should listen to him.

7. The arena will become empty, for if the season ticket holders stop attending, the arena will become empty. But given that the arena will become empty if the season ticket holders stop attending, the arena will become empty.

8. Either Sally paid the higher fee or she parked farther away. But if Sally either paid the higher fee or parked farther away, then she's going to be upset. So Sally's going to be upset.

9. The Bears can't win the division, for the Bears can win the division only if the Tigers lose. And the Tigers won't lose.

10. If the Gospel writers were poorly informed, then they weren't in a good position to write truthful narratives if they wanted to. The Gospel writers were in a good position to write truthful narratives if they wanted to. So they were not poorly informed.

2.2 Counterexample Method

This section introduces a second method used in deductive logic, the **Counterexample Method**, which is *a method that provides provisional evidence of the invalidity of an argument by constructing a good counterexample to the form of that argument that makes all of its key logical vocabulary explicit.* Unlike the Famous Forms Method of the previous section that can be used only to determine that an argument is *valid*, the Counterexample Method can be used only to provide evidence that an argument is *invalid*. Further, unlike the Famous Forms Method, the Counterexample Method can provide only provisional evidence. When we apply the Counterexample Method to an argument successfully, what we learn is that there is good reason to think that the argument is invalid. It will always be possible, however, that this good reason can be overcome by *better* reason for thinking that the argument is valid. So when we successfully apply the Counterexample Method to an argument, what we learn is that *in the absence* of better reason for thinking the argument is valid, we should conclude that the argument is invalid.

This kind of provisional evidence concerning the invalidity of an argument can be quite valuable. Imagine that I give you the following argument for thinking that God doesn't take up time:

1. If God takes up space, God takes up time. God doesn't take up space. So God doesn't take up time.

And imagine I insist that the argument is valid and has true premises, but you think the argument is invalid. If you could successfully provide provisional evidence that the argument is invalid, then this would help us to make progress in our discussion of the argument, for by providing provisional evidence that the argument is invalid, you would put pressure on me to somehow provide better evidence that the argument is valid. If I'm unable to do this, then we should provisionally conclude together that our evidence better supports the conclusion that the argument is invalid. Until someone is able to provide better evidence than we currently have for thinking that the argument is valid, our evidence should lead us to conclude that the argument is invalid.

Can the Counterexample Method be employed to provide provisional evidence for the invalidity of the argument in example 1? It turns out that it can. To see how, we need to explain the key features of the method. The Counterexample Method involves three steps. For the first step, we identify the form of the argument. The procedure for doing this is very similar to the procedure we used to identify the form of arguments when applying the Famous Forms Method, with two important caveats we will identify in just a moment. For the second step, we attempt to construct a good counterexample to the argument's form. We'll explain what a good counterexample is below. For the third step, we conclude that there is provisional evidence that the argument is invalid if we have been able to construct a good counterexample to the argument's form.

2.2.1 Identifying Argument Forms

Recall that an argument's form is the pattern of reasoning the argument employs. As we said in section 2.1, all arguments have multiple forms. For example, example 1 has the form:

2. P. Q. So R.

We get this form for example 1 if we replace the entirety of the first premise with P, the second premise with Q, and the conclusion with R. But, example 1 also has the form:

3. If P, then Q. Not-P. So not-Q.

We get this form for example 1 if we replace "God takes up space" with P and "God takes up time" with Q.

Given that almost all arguments have multiple forms, how do we select which form to use when employing a method of deductive logic that requires that we identify the argument's form? The form we select is guided by the aims of the method in question. When we used the Famous Forms Method, the aim of the method was to discern whether arguments have a form matching one of the famous valid argument forms. When we identified the forms of arguments for purposes of using this method, we selected the argument form that was most likely to match one of the famous valid forms. This led us to adopt some conventions for identifying argument forms that we will now alter when using the Counterexample Method. In the Counterexample Method, our aim is no longer to discern whether an argument has a form matching one of the famous valid argument forms. Our aim instead is to identify whether there are good counterexamples to the form of the argument that have as good a chance as any of the argument's forms of being valid. When identifying an argument's form for the sake of employing the Counterexample Method, we will identify a form of the argument that has as good a chance of being valid as any form the argument has.

In order to identify a form of an argument that has as good a chance as any of the argument's forms of being valid, we will select a form that makes all the argument's key logical vocabulary explicit. The **key logical vocabulary** of an argument is *the argument's logical connectives, quantifiers, and copulas.* We will discuss each of the three components of the key logical vocabulary in turn.

As we said in the previous section, logical connectives include the "if . . . then" connective, the "either . . . or" connective, and the "not" connective. Here they also include the "and" connective, which is employed in any sentence in which "and" is used in between two statements. These statements are called "conjunctions," and we can define them in a way similar to how we earlier defined other kinds of statements. A **conjunction** is *a statement in which the main logical connective is the "and" connective.* For purposes of using the Counterexample Method, we will write an "and" when representing sentences that use any stylistic variant of "and" in this way. Stylistic variants of "and" include "however," "moreover," and "but." Thus, for example, using P to stand for "It is raining" and Q to stand for "It is cloudy," we would represent the statement "It is raining and it is cloudy" as "P and Q." Representing conjunctions in this way marks one important difference from our procedure in the Famous Forms Method.[2]

The second and third sets of key logical vocabulary that we will always render explicit when identifying an argument's form for the sake of employing the Counterexample Method, will be used only when we are assessing arguments that employ categorical statements. **Categorical statements** are *statements that assert that a relationship obtains between classes or categories of things.* For example, consider the following argument:

4. All fish are animals. Some animals are living things. So some fish are living things.

This argument uses categorical statements exclusively. It has two premises that are categorical statements and a conclusion that is a categorical statement as well.

The second set of key logical vocabulary, then, is the quantifier. The **quantifier** is *the word in a categorical statement that signals how much of the subject class the statement is concerned with.* Each categorical statement has four elements: a quantifier, a subject term, a copula, and a predicate term. In the first premise of example 4, the quantifier is "all," while in the second premise and conclusion, the quantifier is "some." While the first premise is concerned with all the fish, the second premise is concerned with some of the animals. When assessing arguments that use categorical statements, we must be clear about the meaning of the quantifier "some." When used in categorical statements, "some" means *at least one.* "Some" does *not* mean *not all.* Thus, for example, the claim "Some animals are living things" means that at least one animal is a living thing, but it does not mean that not all animals are living things. In addition to the quantifiers "all" and "some," other categorical statements use the quantifier "no"—as, for example, in the statement "No fish are birds." In sum, whenever we are assessing an argument that employs categorical statements, we will use the quantifiers "all," "some," or "no" as we identify the argument's form.

The copula is the third set of logical vocabulary we will always render explicit when identifying the form of an argument for the sake of using the Counterexample Method. The **copula** is *the form of the verb "to be" that is employed in the categorical statement.* In example 4 the only copula used is "are." In some categorical statements, the copula "are not" is instead used. For example, "Some fish are not birds" uses the copula "are not."

In addition to the quantifier and copula, categorical statements also include a subject term and a predicate term. The **subject term** is *the first class or category named in the categorical statement.* For example, in the first premise of example 4, the subject term is "fish." The **predicate term** is *the second class or category named in the categorical statement.* So, for example, in the second premise of example 4, the predicate term is "living things." When we identify the form of an argument that employs categorical statements, we will use capital letters to stand for the terms in the argument. Each time the same term appears in the argument, whether it appears as the subject term or the predicate term, we will replace it with the same capital letter.

Let's apply our procedure for identifying argument forms to example 4. If we keep the quantifiers and copulas explicit and replace "fish" with F, "animals" with A, and "living things" with L, we get the following argument form:

5. All F are A. Some A are L. So some F are L.

The form identified by example 5 is ready to be used in the second step of the Counterexample Method.

Let's apply our procedures for identifying argument forms for the sake of the Counterexample Method to three more examples before we move on to the second step of constructing good counterexamples. Consider the following arguments:

6. If Sally is a follower of Jesus, Sally's life bears fruit. Sally's life bears fruit. So Sally is a follower of Jesus.
7. Either our income tax will be raised or our homeowner's insurance will increase. Our income tax will be raised. So our homeowner's insurance won't increase.
8. No Christians are Muslims. Some Muslims are taxpayers. So some Christians are not taxpayers.

See if you can identify the form of each of these arguments that makes all of its key logical vocabulary—its logical connectives, quantifiers, and copulas—explicit.

In example 6, if we replace "Sally is a follower of Jesus" with P and "Sally's life bears fruit" with Q, we get the following form:

9. If P, then Q. Q. So P.

In example 7, if we replace "Our income tax will be raised" with P and "Our homeowner's insurance will increase" with Q, we get the following form:

10. Either P or Q. P. So not-Q.

In example 8, if we replace "Christians" with C, "Muslims" with M, and "taxpayers" with T, we get the following form:

11. No C are M. Some M are T. So some C are not-T.

Examples 9–11 can now be employed for the second step of the Counter-example Method: attempting to construct good counterexamples. As it turns out, the second step of the Counterexample Method can be employed to provide provisional evidence that examples 6–8 as well as examples 1 and 4 from earlier are all invalid.

2.2.2 Providing Good Counterexamples

Once we have identified the form of the argument we are assessing that makes all of its key logical vocabulary explicit, the next step of the Counter-example Method is to attempt to construct a good counterexample to that argument form. A **good counterexample** to an argument form is *an argument that uses this argument form where the premises are well-known truths and the conclusion is a well-known falsehood*. Given that the premises are known to be true and the conclusion is known to be false, we can conclude that the argument is invalid. This in turn allows us to conclude that the argument form that the original argument used is an invalid argument form. An **invalid argument form** is *an argument form in which some arguments that employ the form are invalid*. This allows us to conclude that there is provisional evidence that the original argument is itself invalid. In the absence of better reason to think that the original argument is valid, our current evidence indicates that the argument is invalid.

Let's try to construct some good counterexamples to the argument forms employed by examples 1, 4, 6, 7, and 8. These will be arguments that use the forms of 1, 4, 6, 7, and 8 but have premises that are well-known truths and a conclusion that is a well-known falsehood. To construct such arguments, we need to replace the capital letters of the forms of examples 1, 4, 6, 7, and 8 with either new statements or, if the forms employ categorical statements, new categories. In attempting to construct good counterexamples, it is often helpful to start with the conclusion, making sure that it is an obvious false-hood, and then to work backward.

Start with example 1. Recall that its form was:

3. If P, then Q. Not-P. So not-Q.

Since this argument form doesn't use categorical statements, we need to replace the capital letters P and Q with statements. And we need to pick a statement for Q that will make the conclusion, not-Q, a well-known falsehood. It's well known that "All fish are animals"; let's use this for Q. This yields:

12. If P, then all fish are animals. Not-P. So it is not the case that all fish are animals.

We now need to pick a statement for P that will make the premises well-known truths. The statement needs to be something that is itself false (so that premise two is true) but nonetheless something that *if* true would imply that all fish are animals. "All fish are dogs" would do the trick. It's known to be false that all fish are dogs, but if all fish *were* dogs, this would imply that all fish were animals. If we replace P with "All fish are dogs" we get:

13. If all fish are dogs, then all fish are animals. It's not the case that all fish are dogs. So it's not the case that all fish are animals.

Example 13 gives us a good counterexample to the argument form employed by the argument of example 1. This shows that the argument form employed by example 1 is an invalid argument form: some arguments that use this form are invalid. The argument form used by example 1—the argument form identified by example 2—is known by logicians as the fallacy of **denying the antecedent**. This argument form looks very much like *modus tollens*, a famous valid argument form. In *modus tollens* the second premise denies the consequent of the conditional "if . . . then" claim employed in the first premise. The **consequent** is *the part of a conditional statement that immediately follows the word "then."* In the argument form of example 2, however, the second premise instead denies the antecedent of the conditional employed in the first claim. The **antecedent** is *the part of a conditional statement that immediately follows the word "if."*

A similar fallacy occurs in example 6. Recall that the argument form of example 6 was:

9. If P, then Q. Q. So P.

The argument form of example 9 looks a lot like *modus ponens*, a famous valid argument form. But whereas in *modus ponens* the second premise affirms the antecedent of the "if . . . then" claim, in the argument form of example 9 the second premise affirms the consequent. Logicians call the argument form of example 9 the fallacy of **affirming the consequent**. This argument form can be shown to be invalid by replacing P and Q with the same statements we used to provide a good counterexample to the previous example. Using these same statements for P and Q, we get:

14. If all fish are dogs, then all fish are animals. All fish are animals. So all fish are dogs.

As example 14 indicates, the argument form of example 9 is an invalid argument form. And this provides provisional evidence for thinking that the argument of example 6, which uses the argument form of example 9, is also invalid.

Skip now to example 7. Its form was:

10. Either P or Q. P. So not-Q.

The argument form of example 10 looks a lot like disjunctive syllogism, a famous valid argument form. However, whereas in disjunctive syllogism the second premise *denies* a **disjunct**—*one of the statements in an "either . . . or" claim on either side of the "or"*—in the argument form in example 10 the second premise *affirms* one of the disjuncts. Accordingly, logicians call the argument form of example 10 the fallacy of **affirming a disjunct**.

To construct a good counterexample to the argument form of example 10, we should begin by picking a statement for Q that will make the conclusion, not-Q, a well-known falsehood. Let's use the statement "All fish are animals." That gives us:

15. Either P or all fish are animals. P. So it's not the case that all fish are animals.

We now need to select a statement for P that will make the premises well-known truths. As it turns out, this is pretty easy. All we need to do is select a statement for P that is a well-known truth, and then the second premise will be a well-known truth. The first premise is a well-known truth regardless of what we pick for P because the statement "All fish are animals" is already a well-known truth. If either disjunct of an "either . . . or" claim is true, that claim is true by definition. Similarly, if either disjunct is a well-known truth, the "either . . . or" claim as a whole is a well-known truth. So let's replace P with "All fish are living things." This gives us:

16. Either all fish are living things or all fish are animals. All fish are living things. So it's not the case that all fish are animals.

Example 16 is a good counterexample to the argument form of example 10. While the first premise may strike you as odd, this is only because you are thinking of the meaning of "either . . . or" claims in a way that differs from the way that we are treating them here. We often hear "either . . . or" claims and assume they mean that either the first option is true or the second option is true *but not both*. However, when we use the "either . . . or" logical connective, it is instead intended to be understood as meaning that either the first option is true or the second option is true *or both are true*. This is known as an inclusive "or." Because the "or" in examples 10 and 16 is inclusive, the first premise of example 16 is a well-known truth. Since the second premise is a well-known truth also, and the conclusion is a well-known falsehood, example 16 provides a good counterexample to the argument form of example 10 and so provides provisional evidence that the argument of example 7 is invalid.

Our final two examples—4 and 8—use categorical statements. Thus we will replace the capital letters in their argument forms with classes or categories rather than with statements. Start with the argument of example 4. Its form was:

5. All F are A. Some A are L. So some F are L.

To produce a good counterexample to this argument form, it will be helpful to start with the conclusion. We need to pick categories for F and L that will make the conclusion a well-known falsehood. Let's use "fish" for F and "dogs" for L. That will give us:

17. All fish are A. Some A are dogs. So some fish are dogs.

We now need to pick a category for A that will make the premises well-known truths. It needs to be a category to which all fish belong and to which at least some dogs belong. Let's use the category of "animals." This yields:

18. All fish are animals. Some animals are dogs. So some fish are dogs.

Example 18 is a good counterexample to the argument form in example 5, and so it provides provisional evidence that the argument of example 4 is invalid.

Finally, take the argument of example 8. Its form was:

11. No C are M. Some M are T. So some C are not-T.

Again, let's begin our construction of a good counterexample by starting with the conclusion. We need to pick categories for C and T that will make the conclusion a well-known falsehood. Let's use "fish" for C and "animals" for T. This yields:

19. No fish are M. Some M are animals. So some fish are not animals.

We now need to pick a category for M that will make the premises well-known truths. M needs to be a category to which no fish belong but to which at least some animals belong. Let's use "dogs." If we do, we get:

20. No fish are dogs. Some dogs are animals. So some fish are not animals.

Example 20 is a good counterexample to the argument form of example 11. Recall that "some dogs are animals" means only that at least one dog is an animal; it does not mean that it is not the case that all dogs are animals. Because example 20 provides a good counterexample to example 11, it provides provisional evidence that the argument of example 8 is invalid.

2.2.3 *Using the Counterexample Method Effectively*

We'll conclude with two tips for using the Counterexample Method effectively. First, as you may have noticed in the previous subsection, it can be very helpful when using the Counterexample Method to pick statements or terms that refer to very well-known things. This is because we need to create premises that are well-known truths and conclusions that are well-known falsehoods. In the previous subsection, we used statements or terms that referred to animals. Other possibilities are statements or terms that refer to colors, numbers, or even celebrities.

Second, it is important to observe an additional limitation of the Counterexample Method. We've already seen that the Counterexample Method is limited in that it can provide evidence only of an argument's invalidity, not its validity, and it can provide only provisional evidence at that. The Counterexample Method is also limited in that its successful application depends to some extent on our creativity. Its successful application depends on our being able to think of statements or categories that will enable us to produce good counterexamples. With some examples this can be easy, but other examples may be more difficult. You won't always be able to find a good counterexample to an argument form (some argument forms are valid, after all!), but sometimes you will find a counterexample only after a fair amount of hard work.

2.2.4 *Summary*

This section introduced the Counterexample Method—a method whereby we identify provisional evidence of the invalidity of an argument by constructing a good counterexample to the argument's form. We learned the proper procedure for identifying argument forms for the purpose of employing the Counterexample Method and observed ways in which this procedure differs from the procedure employed for identifying argument forms for the purpose of using the Famous Forms Method. We then identified techniques for constructing good counterexamples and reviewed limitations of the Counterexample Method.

Key Ideas for Review

The **Counterexample Method** is a method that provides provisional evidence of the invalidity of an argument by constructing a good counterexample to the form of that argument that makes all of its key logical vocabulary explicit.

The **key logical vocabulary** of an argument is the argument's logical connectives, quantifiers, and copulas.

A **conjunction** is a statement in which the main logical connective is the "and" connective.

Categorical statements are statements that assert that a relationship obtains between classes or categories of things.

The **quantifier** is the word in a categorical statement that signals how much of the subject class the statement is concerned with.

The **copula** is the form of the verb "to be" that is employed in the categorical statement.

The **subject term** is the first class or category named in the categorical statement.

The **predicate term** is the second class or category named in the categorical statement.

A **good counterexample** to an argument form is an argument that uses this argument form where the premises are well-known truths and the conclusion is a well-known falsehood.

An **invalid argument form** is an argument form in which some arguments that employ the form are invalid.

Denying the Antecedent	Affirming the Consequent	Affirming a Disjunct (options 1 and 2)	
If P, then Q.	If P, then Q.	Either P or Q.	Either P or Q.
Not P.	Q.	P.	Q.
So not-Q.	So P.	So not-Q.	So not-P.

The **consequent** is the part of a conditional statement that immediately follows the word "then."

The **antecedent** is the part of a conditional statement that immediately follows the word "if."

A **disjunct** is one of the statements in an "either . . . or" claim on either side of the "or."

Exercise 2.2

A. Identifying Argument Forms. Identify the form of each of the following arguments that is most relevant for employing the Counterexample Method.

1. Either you will vote or I will vote. I will vote. So you won't vote.

2. Some good stewards are rich people. No rich people are people who receive government entitlements. So no people who receive government entitlements are good stewards.

3. If we go to the opera, then we will have to end work early and get dressed up fancy. So if we will have to end work early, we will have to get dressed up fancy.

4. Either we pay for swimming lessons or our son will continue to dog paddle. If our son continues to dog paddle, we will be embarrassed. So if we pay for swimming lessons, we will not be embarrassed.

5. Some foreigners are people who talk with unusual accents. Some people who talk with unusual accents are not trustworthy people. So some foreigners are not trustworthy people.

6. We owed a lot in taxes in 2015. If we owed a lot in taxes in 2015 and 2016 is not relevantly different from 2015, then we will owe a lot of taxes in 2016. So if we owe a lot in taxes in 2016, then 2016 is not relevantly different from 2015.

7. No environmentally friendly vehicles are fast vehicles. But all fast vehicles are fun vehicles. So no environmentally friendly vehicles are fun vehicles.

8. If God knows what you will do before you do it, then either you can't do otherwise than what you do or what you do explains why God holds the beliefs he does. You can do otherwise than what you do. So if what you do explains why God holds the beliefs he does, then God doesn't know what you will do before you do it.

9. No grocery deliveries are exciting events. But some exciting events are dangerous events. So no grocery deliveries are dangerous events.

10. All questions are welcome occurrences in the classroom. Some welcome occurrences in the classroom are occasions for laughter. So some questions are not occasions for laughter.

B. Counterexamples. Construct a good counterexample to each of the following argument forms.

1. If P, then Q. Not-P. So not-Q.
2. Some A are B. No A are C. So no B are C.
3. Either P or Q. So if Q, then not-P.
4. If P and Q, then R. P. So either Q or R.
5. No A are B. No B are C. So no A are C.
6. Some A are B. All B are C. So some A are not C.
7. If either P or Q, then R. Not-R. So not-P and not-Q.
8. Some A are not B. No A are C. So some B are C.
9. P. Either Q and R, or P. So not-Q and not-R.
10. All A are B. Some B are not C. So some A are not C.

C. Forms and Counterexamples. Provide a good counterexample to each of the argument forms you identified for the examples in exercise A.

2.3 Venn Diagram Method

In the previous section, we introduced categorical statements—statements that affirm that a relationship obtains between classes or categories of things. We also saw that categorical statements are sometimes employed to form arguments. The arguments we saw in the previous section that employed categorical statements were all a special kind of argument called a **categorical syllogism**, which is *an argument with three categorical statements: two premises and one conclusion. These three statements employ three different terms, and each term is used twice in the argument.* (Look back at exercise 2.2 A.10 or 2.2 B.10 for examples.)

In the previous section we employed the Counterexample Method to evaluate categorical syllogisms. This method can provide us with provisional evidence concerning the invalidity of a categorical syllogism. In this section we will introduce an additional method to evaluate categorical syllogisms: Venn diagrams, named after the logician John Venn. A **Venn diagram** is *a diagram of three overlapping circles, one labeled S, one labeled P, and one labeled M, corresponding to the subject and predicate terms of the conclusion of a categorical syllogism and the middle term of that syllogism.* By using Venn diagrams, we can represent the premises of categorical syllogisms with three overlapping circles and then use this representation to determine if the categorical syllogism is valid. We will call this the Venn Diagram Method. The **Venn Diagram Method** is *a method used to determine an argument's validity that involves representing the premises of a categorical syllogism on a Venn diagram and then concluding that the syllogism is valid if this diagram also unambiguously represents that the conclusion of the syllogism is true.* This method can allow us to determine conclusively that a categorical syllogism is valid. It can also provide provisional evidence that a categorical syllogism is invalid. Moreover, as we will see below, Venn diagrams can be applied to arguments that are not originally stated as categorical syllogisms. This can be done by converting these arguments into categorical syllogisms and then applying Venn diagrams.

2.3.1 Evaluating Categorical Syllogisms with Venn Diagrams

In this subsection, we'll learn how to evaluate categorical syllogisms using Venn diagrams. Let's start with an example:

1. All Christians are sinners. No sinners are people who can judge others. So no Christians are people who can judge others.

The argument in example 1 is a categorical syllogism. It uses three categorical statements: two premises and one conclusion. And these statements employ three different terms, repeating each twice. The three terms are "Christians," "sinners," and "people who can judge others." We'll illustrate how to use Venn diagrams by using one to evaluate this argument.

The first step for applying a Venn diagram to a categorical syllogism is to draw three overlapping circles in the way illustrated below (figure 2.2). Each circle represents one of the three terms of the argument being evaluated. We will label these three terms S, P, and M. We use the label S for the subject term of the conclusion, P for the predicate term of the conclusion, and M for what we call the middle term. The **middle term** of a categorical syllogism is *the term that appears in both of its premises.* In example 1, S stands for "Christians," P for "people who can judge others," and M for "sinners."

Figure 2.2

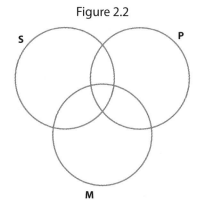

Once we have drawn three overlapping circles in this way, our next step is to represent the information provided by the argument's premises. To complete this step properly we must always represent information provided by universal premises first. A **universal statement** is *a categorical statement that is concerned with all members of its subject class and that uses the quantifier "All" or "No," as in statements of the form "All S are P" and "No S are P."* By contrast, a **particular statement** is *a categorical statement that is concerned with only some members of its subject class and that uses the quantifier "Some," as in statements of the form "Some S are P" and "Some S are not P."* As it turns out, the argument in example 1 contains two universal premises. Because it does, the order in which we represent the information provided by these premises does not matter. The order matters only when we have one universal premise and one particular premise.

Let's start by representing the information provided by the first premise. It claims that all Christians are sinners. Thus, using our letters to represent these terms, it claims that all S are M. In order to represent this information in our diagram, we shade in all the S circle that doesn't overlap with the M circle. Doing so indicates that there is nothing in the S circle that is not in the M circle. In other words, if there is anything at all in the S circle, then it is also in the M circle. All S (Christians), if there are any, are M (sinners). Completing this shading will make our diagram look like this (figure 2.3):

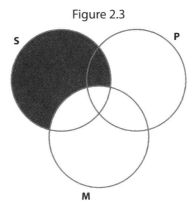

Figure 2.3

Notice that when we complete this shading, we shade in an area of overlap between the S circle and the P circle—the area that does *not* also overlap with the M circle. What this indicates is that if there is anything that is *both* an S and a P, it is *also* an M. This is correct, of course, since we already know that if anything is an S, it is an M. Thus if anything is an S *and* a P, it is also an M.

More generally, whenever we represent the information of a universal affirmative premise, like premise 1 of example 1, we will represent that information in the way we just have. An **affirmative statement** is *a categorical statement that affirms that some or all members of the subject class are members of the predicate class, as in statements of the form "All S are P" or "Some S are P."* Whereas "All S are P" is a universal affirmative premise, "Some S are P" is a particular affirmative premise. If we wanted to represent the universal affirmative premise "All P are M" or "All M are S," we would follow the same procedure above in shading in all the circle representing the subject class of each of these except for that part that overlaps with the circle representing the predicate class. To see what this would look like, consult figures 2.4 and 2.5, respectively.

Returning to our task of representing the argument of example 1 on our Venn diagram, our next step is to represent the information provided by the second premise. This premise claims that no sinners are people who can judge others. Or, using our capital letters, it claims that no M are P. In order to represent this on our diagram, we will shade in all the area of overlap between

Figure 2.4   Figure 2.5

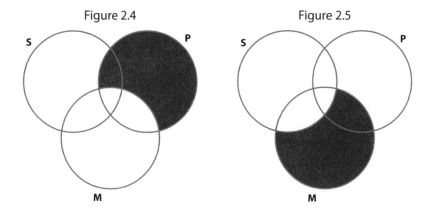

the M circle and the P circle. This indicates that nothing is both an M (sinner) and a P (a person who can judge others). Combining the information from our first premise with the information from our second premise, we get the following (figure 2.6):

Figure 2.6

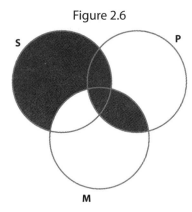

Notice that when we shaded in the area of overlap between the M and P circles, this also involved shading in the small, pizza-slice-like area of overlap between the S, M, *and* P circles. This indicates that there is nothing that is an S, an M, *and* a P, which makes sense since we have already granted that there is nothing that is an S and an M.

Just like with our representation of the information from our first premise, anytime we represent the information of a universal negative premise, like our second premise, we will represent it in the way we have here. A **negative statement** is *a categorical statement that denies that some or all members of the subject class are members of the predicate class, as in statements of the form "No S are P" or "Some S are not P."* The former are universal negative premises, while the latter are particular negative premises. When representing all universal negative premises we will always shade in the area of overlap between the two circles representing the subject and predicate classes of these premises. Thus, for example, if we wanted to represent "No S are P" or "No M are S" we would do so as follows (figures 2.7 and 2.8, respectively):

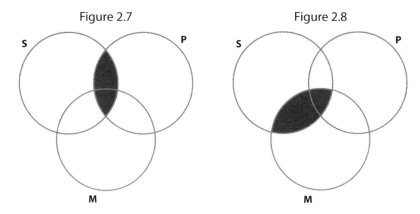

Figure 2.7   Figure 2.8

It is worth observing briefly something interesting about the way we have represented both universal affirmative premises and universal negative premises. The way we are representing these premises does not include any information about whether there are any members of the subject or predicate classes of these terms. For example, the way we represented universal affirmative premises indicates that *if* there are any members of the subject class, then they are also members of the predicate class; but it doesn't indicate that there actually *are* any members of the subject or predicate classes. Similarly here, the way we are representing universal negative statements indicates that *if* there are any members of the subject class, they are *not* members of the predicate class; but it does not indicate that there *are* any members of the subject or predicate classes.[3]

Returning to our evaluation of the argument of example 1, we are now in a position to use the Venn diagram in figure 2.6 to determine whether the argument of example 1 is valid. When we use a Venn diagram to determine whether an argument is valid, our procedure is to check whether the Venn diagram contains a representation of the conclusion of the categorical syllogism. We check for this only after having represented the premises of the syllogisms as in figure 2.6. In example 1, the conclusion is "No Christians are people who can judge others." Using our capital letters, this says "No S are P." We saw in figure 2.7 what it looks like to represent the universal negative claim "No S are P." It involves shading in the area of overlap between the S and P circles. So we need to check to see whether this area in figure 2.6 is shaded. It turns out that it is. This is because when we represented premise 1, it included shading in the area of overlap between S and P but *not* M, and when we represented premise 2, it included shading in the area of overlap between M, P, and S. Because figure 2.6 contains a representation of the conclusion of the argument in example 1, we can conclude that the argument is valid.

Following the procedures we have introduced thus far will enable you to use Venn diagrams to evaluate categorical syllogisms that use only universal premises. But what about categorical syllogisms that use particular premises as well? This is our next topic. Let's try an example that uses both a particular affirmative premise and a particular negative premise:

2. Some nonbelievers are atheists. Some atheists are not happy people. So some nonbelievers are not happy people.

Again, we'll use S to represent "nonbelievers," since this is the subject term of the conclusion; P to represent "happy people," since this is the predicate term of the conclusion; and M to represent "atheists," since this is the middle term. Since we have only particular premises, the order in which we represent the information of our premises does not matter.

Let's start with the first premise. Using our letters, this premise claims that some S are M, meaning that there is *at least one* S that is an M. To represent this, we will use the symbol x to indicate that there is at least one S that is an M. We'll put this x in the area of overlap between the S and M circles (figure 2.9):

Figure 2.9

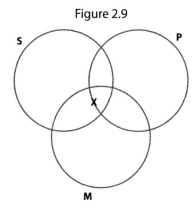

Notice that we put the x on the line that runs through the area of overlap between the S and M circles. While we know that there is at least one S that is an M, we do not know whether this S is *also* a P, or whether it is *not* a P. Thus we deliberately put the x on this line to indicate that we do not know whether there is something that is an S, a P, and an M, or only something that is an S and a P but not an M. In some cases when we are representing particular affirmative statements of the form "Some S are P," we *will* know that there aren't any S that are both P *and* M. We'll look at an example of this kind momentarily.

Our next step for evaluating the argument of example 2 is to represent the second premise. This premise claims that some atheists are *not* happy people. Or, using our letters, it claims that some M are *not* P. In order to represent this, we will use an X to indicate that there is at least one M that is not a P. We will need to put this X in the area of the M circle that does not overlap with the P circle. Again, since we do not know whether this M that is not a P is an S or is not an S, we will put this X on the line that runs through the area of the M circle that doesn't overlap with the P circle. The Venn diagram in figure 2.10 contains this representation, along with the representation of the first premise.

Figure 2.10

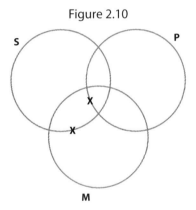

We are now in a position to use our Venn diagram to determine whether the argument of example 2 is valid. In order to be able to conclude that it is valid, it needs to be the case that figure 2.10 contains a representation of the conclusion of the argument in example 2. That conclusion said that some atheists are not happy people. Or, using our letters, it said that some S are not P. In order for our diagram to represent this conclusion, the diagram must include an X in the area of the S circle that does not overlap with the P circle. Does it?

It turns out that it does not. Or, to be precise, we simply cannot determine that it does. This is because for each X on our diagram, we do not know that it belongs in the area of the S circle that does not overlap with the P circle. One X is on the line of the P circle in the area of overlap between the S circle and the M circle. But we put this X on this line precisely to indicate that we do not know whether it belongs inside or outside the P circle. Similarly, we put our other x on the line of the S circle in the area of the M circle that is outside the P circle. This is to indicate that we do not know whether this x belongs in the S circle or outside it. Our diagram, then, represents that we do not know that there is an x in the S circle that is not in the P circle. Because of this, our diagram does not enable us to draw the conclusion that the argument of example 2 is valid. In order to enable us to draw the conclusion that an argument is valid, our Venn diagram of its premises needs to represent that its conclusion is unambiguously true.

We have thus far used Venn diagrams to represent an argument with only universal premises and an argument with only particular premises. We will conclude with an example that uses one particular premise and one universal premise:

3. Some deities are not people who have flaws. All saints are people who have flaws. So some deities are not saints.

For our Venn diagram, we'll use S for "deities," P for "saints," and M for "people who have flaws." Because we have one universal premise and one particular premise in this argument, we must begin filling in our Venn diagram by representing the information from the universal premise. This is so even though our universal premise comes second. Using our letters, this premise states that all P are M. Thus we need to shade in all the area of our P circle that does not overlap with the M circle (figure 2.11).

Figure 2.11

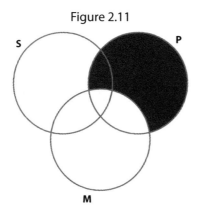

Next, we need to represent our first premise. Using our letters, it says that some S are not M. Thus we need to put an x in the area of the S circle outside the M circle. However, unlike in the Venn diagrams in figures 2.9 and 2.10, this time we *do* know exactly where this x must go. Since the area of the S circle that is outside the M circle but overlaps with the P circle is shaded, we know that no x can go in this area. Thus if there is to be an x in the area of the S circle outside the M circle, it must go in the area of the S circle that is outside *both* the M circle *and* the P circle. We represent this as follows (figure 2.12):

Figure 2.12

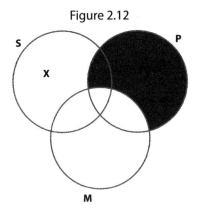

The Venn diagram in figure 2.12 represents that there is something in the S circle that is outside both the M circle and the P circle. This will now allow us to conclude that the argument of example 3 is valid, for in order to conclude that the argument is valid, we simply need figure 2.12 to represent that the conclusion of example 3 is true. This conclusion says that some S are not P. And, indeed, figure 2.12 does represent this. It represents that there is an S that is neither a P nor an M. And, of course, this is sufficient for us to know that there is an S that is not a P.

2.3.2 *Transforming Arguments into Categorical Syllogisms*

Thus far we have learned how to use Venn diagrams to determine if categorical syllogisms are valid. If we learn how to transform arguments that are not stated as categorical syllogisms into categorical syllogisms, we can expand the range of arguments that we can use Venn diagrams to evaluate. This subsection identifies three kinds of arguments that we can transform into categorical syllogisms using some simple techniques.

First, some arguments are very nearly categorical syllogisms except that instead of using predicate terms in the way that categorical statements do, one or more of the statements that compose these arguments use predicate adjectives or verbs other than a copula. Consider the following argument:

4. Some people with anger problems have hypertension. All people who have hypertension need medical attention. So some people with anger problems need medical attention.

Example 4 is not a categorical syllogism because it does not have three *terms*, each used twice. As we've seen, terms are words or phrases that represent classes or categories of things. But the words or phrases in the predicate position of the statements in example 4 are not words or phrases that represent classes or categories. There is no category of "have hypertension" or "need medical attention." Moreover, the statements in example 4 do not employ copulas, which are essential elements of categorical statements.

Nonetheless, while example 4 is not a categorical syllogism, it is *nearly* one. By making some very simple alterations to example 4 we can transform it into a categorical syllogism without harming its original meaning. All that is needed to transform example 4 into a categorical syllogism is to replace its verbs with copulas and to nominalize its predicates—that is, to turn them into nouns. In order to turn the predicates of the statements in example 4 into nouns, we can simply introduce phrases like "things that . . ." or "people who . . ." preceding the verb phrases used in these statements. Applying these procedures we get:

5. Some people with anger problems are people who have hypertension. All people who have hypertension are people who need medical attention. So some people with anger problems are people who need medical attention.

This simple transformation yields a categorical syllogism with three terms, each used twice. We are now in a position to apply the Venn diagram method to this argument.

A second kind of argument that can be transformed into a categorical syllogism is one that is concerned with single individuals rather than with classes or categories. Consider this example:

6. The president is a powerful person. All powerful people are people who carry great responsibility. So the president carries great responsibility.

This argument is not a categorical syllogism in part because it is concerned with "the president," which is not a class or category of things. Nonetheless, arguments of this kind can be transformed, if somewhat awkwardly, into categorical syllogisms. This can be achieved by introducing a phrase like "people who are identical to . . ." or "things that are . . ." and then replacing singular predicate nouns with plural ones. Thus we can transform example 6 into:

7. All people who are identical to the president are powerful people. All powerful people are people who carry great responsibility. So all people who are identical to the president are people who carry great responsibility.

While admittedly somewhat awkward, example 7 does give us a categorical syllogism that is faithful in meaning to example 6 and that can now be evaluated using a Venn diagram.

A third kind of argument that can be transformed into a categorical syllogism is one that departs from categorical syllogisms by employing stylistic variants of categorical statements. For example, statements of the form "At least one S is a P" are stylistic variants of the categorical statement "Some S are P." Statements of the form "If anything is an S, it is a P" are stylistic variants of the categorical statement "All S are P." Statements of the form "Nothing that is an S is also a P" are stylistic variants of the categorical statement "No S are P." And statements of the form "Not all S are P" are stylistic variants of the categorical statement "Some S are not P." When we encounter arguments that employ stylistic variants of categorical statements like these, we can sensibly transform them into categorical syllogisms. Consider the following example.

8. No one who is an idolater is a follower of Jesus. At least one follower of Jesus is a Bible reader. So not all Bible readers are idolaters.

We can sensibly transform example 8 into:

9. No idolaters are followers of Jesus. Some followers of Jesus are Bible readers. So some Bible readers are not idolaters.

Since example 9 is a categorical syllogism, we can now evaluate it using a Venn diagram.

2.3.3 Summary

This section introduced the Venn Diagram Method, used to determine if categorical syllogisms are valid. The method involves representing the premises of a categorical syllogism on a Venn diagram and then determining if the argument is valid by determining whether the diagram unambiguously represents that the conclusion of the argument is true. The section also illustrated how we can transform arguments that are not presented as categorical syllogisms into categorical syllogisms for purposes of evaluating them using the Venn Diagram Method.

Exercise 2.3

A. Venn Diagrams. Use Venn diagrams to evaluate the following categorical syllogisms. If the Venn diagram allows you to conclude that the syllogism

Key Ideas for Review

A **categorical syllogism** is an argument with three categorical statements: two premises and one conclusion. These three statements employ three different terms, and each term is used twice in the argument.

A **Venn diagram** is a diagram of three overlapping circles, one labeled S, one labeled P, and one labeled M, corresponding to the subject and predicate terms of the conclusion of a categorical syllogism and the middle term of that syllogism.

The **Venn Diagram Method** is a method used to determine an argument's validity that involves representing the premises of a categorical syllogism on a Venn diagram and then concluding that the syllogism is valid if this diagram also unambiguously represents that the conclusion of the syllogism is true.

The **middle term** of a categorical syllogism is the term that appears in both of its premises.

A **universal statement** is a categorical statement that is concerned with all members of its subject class and that uses the quantifier "All" or "No," as in statements of the form "All S are P" and "No S are P."

A **particular statement** is a categorical statement that is concerned with only some members of its subject class and that uses the quantifier "Some," as in statements of the form "Some S are P" and "Some S are not P."

An **affirmative statement** is a categorical statement that affirms that some or all members of the subject class are members of the predicate class, as in statements of the form "All S are P" or "Some S are P."

A **negative statement** is a categorical statement that denies that some or all members of the subject class are members of the predicate class, as in statements of the form "No S are P" or "Some S are not P."

is valid, indicate that it is valid. If the diagram does not, indicate that it does not.

1. Some medicines are liquids that should not be taken with alcohol. All liquids that should not be taken with alcohol are liquids that should not be taken with bourbon. So some medicines are liquids that should not be taken with bourbon.

2. No reasons for belief are reasons for religious agnosticism. Some reasons are reasons for religious agnosticism. So some reasons are not reasons for belief.

3. All people who are centered on others are people who are quick to forgive. Some people who are quick to forgive are not people who are slow to apologize. So some people who are slow to apologize are not people who are centered on others.

4. Some biblical scholars are people who deny the resurrection. No people who deny the resurrection are faithful Christians. So some biblical scholars are not faithful Christians.

5. Some good decisions are tough decisions. All tough decisions are decisions that require weighing the good and the bad. So some good decisions are decisions that require weighing the good and the bad.

6. All things that begin are things that are caused. Some things that exist are not things that are caused. So some things that exist are not things that begin.

7. No religious views are views about which there is complete agreement among experts. Some views that improve one morally are not views about which there is complete agreement among experts. So some views that improve one morally are religious views.

8. Some actions that improve people's lives are actions that are unfair. No actions that are unfair are actions that you are required to perform. So some actions that improve people's lives are not actions that you are required to perform.

9. Some expensive purchases are not fun purchases. All fun purchases are purchases people look forward to making. So some expensive purchases are not purchases people look forward to making.

10. No events that occurred in the past are events we can now change. Some events that occurred in the past are events we would like to change. So some events we would like to change are not events we can now change.

B. Transforming Arguments. Transform each of the following arguments into a categorical syllogism. Then use a Venn diagram to evaluate it. If the diagram allows you to conclude that the argument is valid, indicate that the argument is valid. If it does not, indicate that it does not.

1. Some university presidents make a lot of money. All people who make a lot of money face many temptations. So some university presidents face many temptations.

2. Some prayers are answered neither "yes" nor "no." If any prayer is answered neither "yes" nor "no," it is answered "wait." So some prayers are answered "wait."

3. God is all powerful. Nothing that is all powerful is also divisible. So God is not divisible.

4. No vegetarians eat meat. Some vegetarians are not healthy. So some people who are healthy are not people who eat meat.

5. No politicians should receive money from donors that would influence their decisions if elected. All businesses are donors that would influence the decisions of politicians if elected. So no politicians should receive money from businesses.

6. If any job is taken by an immigrant, it is not also taken by a national. Some jobs taken by nationals are jobs that should be taken by nationals. So some jobs taken by immigrants are jobs that should be taken by nationals.

7. Stephen Curry is a great three-point shooter. Some great three-point shooters had fathers who were great three-point shooters. So Stephen Curry had a father who was a great three-point shooter.

8. At least one president has been shot. No one who has been shot has been protected perfectly. So at least one president has not been protected perfectly.

9. Nothing that is destructive of the well-being of children is a character trait a parent should possess. Neglect is destructive of the well-being of children. So neglect is not a character trait a parent should possess.

10. Some terrorist acts are committed by religious people. Not all acts committed by religious people are committed for religious reasons. So not all terrorist acts are acts committed for religious reasons.

2.4 Proof Method

This section introduces the Proof Method. The **Proof Method** is *a method used to determine that an argument is valid by constructing a proof of the argument's conclusion where each step of the proof is justified by an implication rule, an equivalence rule, or an indirect proof rule.* The Proof Method offers a significant advantage over the Famous Forms Method and the Venn Diagram Method—the other two methods we have surveyed that can be employed to determine that an argument is valid. Namely, it can be used to determine that more complex arguments are valid. The Famous Forms method can be employed only to determine that arguments with a few specified forms are valid. The Venn Diagram Method can be employed only to determine that categorical syllogisms are valid. The Proof Method, by contrast, can be employed to determine that a very wide range of arguments with quite different forms are valid.

To explain how to use the Proof Method, we will begin by introducing its unique symbols. We will then introduce the notion of a proof and the rules of implication, equivalence, and indirect proof that are employed by the Proof Method.

2.4.1 The Symbols of the Proof Method

Like the Famous Forms Method and the Counterexample Method, the Proof Method involves representing arguments in such a way that their logical connectives are made explicit. Indeed, like the Counterexample Method, it requires representing arguments in such a way that *all* of their logical connectives are made explicit. However, it is common when using the Proof Method to use special symbols to represent these logical connectives rather than representing them as we have in previous sections with English words or phrases.

For purposes of employing the Proof Method, we will symbolize the logical connective "if . . . then" with the arrow symbol: →. Any statement that employs an "if . . . then" claim or one of the stylistic variants of the claim will be symbolized using the arrow. We will symbolize the "either . . . or" connective using the wedge: ∨. We will symbolize the "and" connective using the dot: ·. And, we will symbolize the "not" connective using the tilde: ~.

Here are some illustrative examples. Using P for the first statement in each example, Q for the second statement (if there is more than one statement), and our new symbols for the connectives, see if you can symbolize each of them:

1. Fred ate chocolate and Fred ate a banana.
2. Fred ate chocolate if Fred ate a banana.
3. Either Fred ate chocolate or Fred ate a banana.
4. Fred did not eat chocolate.

Using our new symbols, and employing P and Q to stand for the statements employed in these arguments, we get:

5. P · Q
6. Q → P
7. P ∨ Q
8. ~P

There is one final symbol to introduce—the parentheses: (and). These parentheses are used to disambiguate otherwise ambiguous symbolizations of statements. For example, consider the following complex statements:

9. If Fred ate chocolate or Fred ate a banana, Fred ate something.
10. Fred ate chocolate and Fred ate a banana, or Fred didn't eat anything.
11. If Fred didn't eat anything, then Fred neither ate chocolate nor ate a banana.

If we attempt to symbolize examples 9–11 without using parentheses or some other kind of disambiguation device, we will get symbolizations that are ambiguous between multiple readings. For example, if we tried to symbolize example 9 with only the dot, arrow, wedge, and tilde—letting P, Q, and R stand for its first, second, and third statements—we would get:

12. P ∨ Q → R

Look at what falls on either side of the arrow in example 12. It is unclear whether the antecedent of the "if . . . then" statement represented by the arrow is P ∨ Q or just Q. If it is just Q, then this means that the second disjunct isn't just Q, but Q → R. Using our parentheses, the difference is between the following:

13. (P ∨ Q) → R
14. P ∨ (Q → R)

Example 12 by itself is ambiguous between examples 13 and 14, which are significantly different statements. Because it is ambiguous in this way, example 12 fails to offer an adequate representation of example 9 and cannot be employed in the Proof Method. To be employable in the Proof Method, a statement needs to have all ambiguity removed. Given the placement of the comma, the "if," and the "either" in example 9, it is best to symbolize it as example 13.

Return to examples 10 and 11. Using P, Q, and R for the first, second, and third statements in each and remembering to make all logical connectives explicit, see if you can symbolize them. If you symbolized them correctly, you got:

15. (P · Q) ∨ ~R
16. ~P → ~(P ∨ Q)

For example 10, the placement of the comma makes it clear where the parentheses should be placed. We use the tilde in the second disjunct because we are aiming to make all logical connectives explicit. Thus R should be understood here to be representing "Fred ate something" rather than "Fred didn't eat anything." Similarly, in example 11, P stands for "Fred ate something." Again, the placement of the comma along with the placement of the "if" and the "either" indicates that the parentheses for example 11 need to fall on the right-hand side of the arrow, as they do in example 16. Finally, in example 16 we symbolize the consequent of example 11—"Fred *neither* ate chocolate *nor* ate a banana"—as the negation of a disjunction. In general, we symbolize statements that use "neither" as claiming that "not either" of the relevant disjuncts is true.

More than one pair of parentheses may be used in symbolizing a very complex statement. For example, consider:

17. Either Fred ate chocolate and Fred ate a banana, or Fred neither ate chocolate nor ate a banana.
18. If Fred either ate chocolate or ate a banana, and Fred didn't eat chocolate, then Fred ate a banana.

In symbolizing example 17, we'll use P for "Fred ate chocolate" each time it occurs and Q for "Fred ate a banana" each time it occurs. Noting the placement of the comma, we should symbolize example 17 as:

19. $(P \cdot Q) \vee \sim(P \vee Q)$

Notice that there are two sets of parentheses here. The first set clarifies that the entire conjunction $P \cdot Q$ and not just Q is the first disjunct of the first disjunction in example 19. The second set clarifies that what is negated is not just P, but $P \vee Q$.

Try symbolizing example 18. Notice that the "then" comes only after "and Fred didn't eat chocolate." Thus when symbolizing we should place the arrow after our symbolization of this statement. Let's use P for "Fred ate chocolate" and Q for "Fred ate a banana" each time these occur. Making sure to symbolize all logical connectives, we get the following:

20. $((P \vee Q) \cdot \sim P) \rightarrow Q$

Notice that we get two open parentheses, or left-hand parentheses, in a row. The second one is closed, or countered with a right-hand parenthesis, after the first Q, whereas the first is closed after the second P. The outer pair of parentheses clarifies for us that the entire conjunction $(P \vee Q) \cdot \sim P$ is the antecedent of the conditional. The inner pair of parentheses clarifies that the entirety of $P \vee Q$ is the first **conjunct**, or *the statement on one side of "and" in a conjunction.*

With these new symbols (and one additional one we will introduce in the section below on equivalence rules), we will be able to symbolize arguments for the purpose of employing the Proof Method. The next step is to learn how to construct proofs using rules of implication, equivalence, and indirect proof.

2.4.2 Constructing Proofs

When using the Proof Method, our aim is to construct a proof of an argument's conclusion. A **proof** of an argument is *a set of symbolic statements that begins with symbolized representations of the argument's premise(s) and ends with a symbolized representation of its conclusion, where each other statement in the set is justified by a rule of implication, equivalence,* *or indirect proof.* To see what proofs look like, we need to introduce some of these rules. We'll start with the **rules of implication**, since many of them are already familiar from the Famous Forms Method.

The inference rule **MP**, for *"modus ponens,"* allows us to conclude from statements of the form P → Q, and P, that Q. Suppose we had the following argument:

> 21. If Fred ate chocolate, then Fred ate something. Fred ate chocolate. So Fred ate something.

Using P for "Fred ate chocolate" and Q for "Fred ate something," we could symbolize this argument as follows:

> 22.
>
> P → Q
>
> P
>
> So Q

To construct a proof of example 22, we need to write down a series of statements, beginning with its premises and ending with its conclusion, where each step following the statement of the premises is justified by a rule of implication, equivalence, or indirect proof. As it turns out, the inference rule MP allows us to do this in just one step. The conclusion, Q, is justified by the first and second premises, given the rule MP. To indicate this by constructing a formal proof, we will write the following:

> 23.
>
> 1. P → Q [premise]
> 2. P   [premise]
> 3. So Q   from 1,2 by MP

Notice here that we numbered each premise of the argument, labeled each premise as a premise, and then wrote down a justification for any steps following these premises. The justification—here "from 1,2 by MP"—will always cite one or more of the previous claims in the argument, together with a rule of implication, equivalence, or indirect proof. For our purposes here, the order in which the premises are listed will not be important. So, for example, we could just as well have written "from 2,1 by MP."

Let's introduce some additional implication rules. From claims of the form P → Q, and ~Q, the rule **MT**, for *"modus tollens,"* allows us to infer ~P. From claims of the form P v Q and ~Q, the rule **DS** for "disjunctive syllogism" allows us to infer P. Likewise, DS allows us to infer from P v Q and ~P that Q. The rule **HS**, for "hypothetical syllogism," allows us to infer from claims of the form P → Q and Q → R that P → R. And, the rule **CD**, for "constructive dilemma," allows us to infer from claims of the form P v Q, P → R, and Q → S, either R v S or S v R.

Thus far our implication rules have included only those rules already introduced when we discussed the Famous Forms Method. To this list, we'll add three more. The rule of **Simp**, for "simplification," allows us to infer from claims of the form P · Q either P or Q. If we have P · Q, Simp allows us to infer P, and Simp allows us to infer Q. The reason for this is that we know that conjunctions are true only if both of their conjuncts are true.

The rule **Conj**, for "conjunction," allows us to infer from claims of the form P and Q, that P · Q. The reasoning here is very similar to that employed to defend Simp. We know that a conjunction is true if each of its conjuncts is true, so the rule Conj allows us to infer a conjunction from the truth of each of its conjuncts.

Finally, the rule **Add**, for "addition," allows us to infer from P either P v Q or Q v P. In other words, Add allows us to add disjuncts. The justification for this is that we know a disjunction is true if either of its disjuncts (or both) is true. Thus if we know that P is true, we know that any disjunction of which P is a disjunct is true.

Table 2.4.1 lists the rules of implication we've just introduced.

TABLE 2.4.1

Rules of Implication

MP	MT	DS (options 1 and 2)		HS	CD (options 1 and 2)	
P → Q	P → Q	P v Q	P v Q	P → Q	P v Q	P v Q
P	~Q	~Q	~P	Q → R	P → R	P → R
So Q	So ~P	So P	So Q	P → R	Q → S	Q → S
					R v S	S v R

Simp (options 1 and 2)		Conj	Add (options 1 and 2)	
P · Q	P · Q	P	P	P
So P	So Q	Q	So P v Q	So Q v P
		So P · Q		

Before moving on to introduce the rules of equivalence and rules of indirect proof, let's get some practice constructing proofs with these rules of implication. Below are three examples that are already symbolized:

24.

    $P \rightarrow Q$

    ~R

    $\sim R \rightarrow P$

    So Q

25.

    $P \cdot \sim Q$

    Q v R

    So R

26.

    $(P \lor Q) \rightarrow R$

    Q

    So R

Start with example 24. Unlike with example 22, there's no rule of implication that allows us to move directly from the premises to the conclusion here. We're going to have to get to the conclusion through multiple steps.

When doing more complex proofs like example 24, it can often be helpful to work backward from the conclusion. This procedure involves looking for the conclusion in the premises and then thinking about what it would take to prove the conclusion from these premises. In example 24, the conclusion is Q. Looking for Q in the premises, we find that it appears as the consequent of the conditional in the first premise. We have $P \rightarrow Q$ there. Thinking about our rules, what else would we need in addition to $P \rightarrow Q$ to prove Q? If we had P in addition to $P \rightarrow Q$, then we could prove Q by MP. So we need, or would like to be able, to prove, P. Again, let's look for P in the premises to see if there's a way to prove it. Notice that P shows up as the consequent of the third premise. That premise gives us $\sim R \rightarrow P$. If we had ~R, we could use this premise to prove P by MP. It turns out that ~R is our second premise. So here's our plan: use MP, ~R, and $\sim R \rightarrow P$ to prove P. Then use the P we've proved, along with $P \rightarrow Q$ and MP, to prove Q. Writing this down formally with all the premises numbered and labeled, and each step after the premises justified, we get the following proof:

27.

    1. $P \rightarrow Q$ [premise]

    2. ~R   [premise]

    3. $\sim R \rightarrow P$ [premise]

    4. P   from 2,3 by MP

    5. Q   from 1,4 by MP

Providing a proof for example 24 used only one rule of implication, but we had to apply it twice.

Give example 25 a try. Again, try starting with the conclusion, looking for it in the premises, and thinking about how to prove it using the premises and rules of implication. Here, when we look for the conclusion, R, in the premises, we see it in premise 2 as one of two disjuncts. We know that we can prove a disjunct using DS if we can show that the other disjunct is false. Here that disjunct is Q. Can we prove that Q is false? It turns out that we can because we have ~Q as one conjunct in a conjunction in premise 1. So by Simp and 1, we can conclude that ~Q. Here's how we can use these steps to construct a formal proof of 25:

28.

    1. P · ~Q [premise]
    2. Q v R [premise]
    3. ~Q   from 1 by Simp
    4. R   from 2,3 by DS

Here we used two implication rules to reach our conclusion.

Finally, try example 26. Here we see that the conclusion is the consequent of a conditional. Thus if we could prove the antecedent of the conditional, we could prove the conclusion by MP. The antecedent is itself a disjunction. One way to prove a disjunction is to find one of its disjuncts. If we do, we can use Add to add the other disjunct. It turns out here that the second premise gives us one of the disjuncts. So we can use this strategy:

29.

    1. (P v Q) → R [premise]
    2. Q   [premise]
    3. P v Q   from 2, by Add
    4. R   from 3,1 MP

Using the strategy we've suggested—finding the conclusion in the premises and then thinking about how to prove it given those premises and the rules— can be difficult and demand creativity. It takes some practice. The practice exercises at the end of this chapter will help with this process.

Let's now introduce the equivalence rules. Unlike the implication rules, the equivalence rules allow us to move in two directions. With implication rules, we could move only from the implying claims to the implied claim. With the equivalence rules, we can move from either equivalent claim to the other equivalent claim. Indeed, this is precisely what it is to say that the claims are equivalent—*logically* equivalent. They play exactly the same role from a logical point of view. Here in particular they make exactly the same contribution to constructing proofs.

We'll use ten **rules of equivalence**. The first is **DN**, for "double negation." It allows us to move back and forth from claims of the form P to claims of the form ~~P (*not* not-P). From P, by DN, we can conclude ~~P; from ~~P and DN we can conclude P.

Second is **Comm**, for "commutation." It allows us to move back and forth from claims of the form P v Q to claims of the form Q v P and from claims of the form P · Q to claims of the form Q · P. In other words, it allows us to switch the places of conjuncts or disjuncts.

Third is **Re**, for "redundancy." It allows us to introduce or eliminate redundant statements. In particular, it allows us to move back and forth from claims of the form P to claims of the form P · P or claims of the form P v P.

Fourth is **Cont**, for "contraposition." It allows us to move back and forth from claims of the form P → Q to claims of the form ~Q → ~P. This rule should be intuitive from what we already know from the implication rule MT—namely, that from P → Q and ~Q we can infer ~P. Equivalently, from P → Q we can infer ~Q → ~P. Moving the other direction, from ~Q → ~P to P → Q, uses the same reasoning but with different statements in the positions of antecedent and consequent in the conditionals. From ~Q → ~P, MT tells us that ~~P (or P by DN) will imply ~~Q (or Q by DN).

The fifth rule, **As**, for "association," allows us to move parentheses. It allows us to move back and forth from (P v Q) v R to P v (Q v R) and back and forth from (P · Q) · R to P · (Q · R). These rules should be intuitive from what we already know about the meanings of disjunctions and conjunctions. We already know that disjunctions are true if any of their disjuncts are true. Thus (P v Q) v R is true if either P v Q is true or R is true. But in turn, P v Q is true if P is true or R is true. Thus (P v Q) v R is true if P, Q, or R is true. The same can be said of P v (Q v R). Each statement is true if and only if one or more of P, Q, or R is true. They are logically equivalent. Likewise, we already know that a conjunction is true if and only if both of its conjuncts are true. Thus we know for both (P · Q) · R and P · (Q · R) that it is true if and only if P, Q, and R are all true. The statements, again, are logically equivalent.

The five remaining rules are more complicated, though you can find a convenient summary of all the equivalence rules in table 2.4.2 and justifications of each rule in relevant endnotes. Let's start with **Ex**, for "exportation." Exportation allows us to move back and forth from claims of the form (P · Q) → R to claims of the form P → (Q → R).[4]

Rule seven is **MI**, for "material implication." MI tells us that we can move back and forth from statements of the form P → Q to statements of the form ~P v Q.[5]

The next two rules allow us to exchange or shift around wedges and dots. First is **Dist**, for "distribution." This rule allows us to move back and forth from P · (Q ∨ R) to (P · Q) ∨ (P · R) and back and forth from P ∨ (Q · R) to (P ∨ R) · (P ∨ R). Notice that the pattern is the same in each case. Moving from left to right, we put the first item on the left-hand side as the first item in each pair of parentheses on the right; the first logical connective on the left becomes the logical connective inside the parentheses on the right, and the second logical connective on the left becomes the logical connective linking the pairs of parentheses on the right.[6]

Rule nine is **DeM**, for "De Morgan's," named after nineteenth-century logician Augustus De Morgan. It allows us to move back and forth from ~(P · Q) to ~P ∨ ~Q and back and forth from ~(P ∨ Q) to ~P · ~Q.[7]

The final equivalence rule is **ME**, for "material equivalence." In order to state this rule, we need to introduce one additional symbol, the double arrow: ↔. The double arrow represents the logical connective "if and only if." You may have noticed this expression being used several times already throughout this book. But until now we have not had a special way to represent it in arguments. For purposes of using the Proof Method, we will use the double arrow to represent the "if and only if" connective. Take the following example:

30. The dryer will get the clothes dry if and only if the toddler leaves it alone.

We can represent example 30 symbolically by using the double arrow:

31. P ↔ Q

In example 31, P represents "The dryer will get the clothes dry," Q represents "the toddler leaves the dryer alone," and ↔ symbolizes the connective "if and only if."

Like the "if . . . then" connective, there are stylistic variants for the "if and only if" connective. For example, "The dryer will get the clothes dry *just in case* the toddler leaves it alone" and "The dryer will get the clothes dry *just as long as* the toddler leaves it alone" are equivalent ways of expressing example 30.

Equivalence rule ME is concerned with the double arrow. It tells us that we can move back and forth from claims of the form P ↔ Q to claims of the form (P → Q) · (Q → P) and back and forth from claims of the form P ↔ Q to claims of the form (P · Q) ∨ (~P · ~Q).[8]

Table 2.4.2 summarizes our ten equivalence rules. It does so using the double colon: ::. This indicates that we can move back and forth from statements of the form symbolized on the left to statements of the form symbolized on the right. Where the rule has multiple forms, those forms appear on separate lines.

TABLE 2.4.2
Equivalence Rules

DN	Comm	Re	Cont
P :: ~~P	P v Q :: Q v P	P :: P v P	P → Q :: ~Q → ~P
	P · Q :: Q · P	P :: P · P	

As	Ex	MI
P v (Q v R) :: (P v Q) v R	(P · Q) → R :: P → (Q → R)	P → Q :: ~P v Q
P · (Q · R) :: (P · Q) · R		

Dist	DeM	ME
P · (Q v R) :: (P · Q) v (P · R)	~(P · Q) :: ~P v ~Q	P ↔ Q :: (P → Q) · (Q → P)
P v (Q · R) :: (P v Q) · (P v R)	~(P v Q) :: ~P · ~Q	P ↔ Q :: (P · Q) v (~P · ~Q)

Two additional rules of indirect proof need to be introduced to complete our list of rules. Before introducing these, let's do a few practice exercises using our equivalence rules. Try these:

32.

~P v Q

Q → P

So P ↔ Q

33.

~(P v Q)

R

So (R · ~P) · ~Q

34.

(P · Q) v (P · Q)

P → (Q → R)

So R

As with the exercises employing our implication rules, here again it will be helpful to start with the conclusion and work backward.

In example 32, the conclusion has a double arrow. We know from ME that we can prove a double arrow if we can prove that arrows point in each direction. In other words, here we can prove P ↔ Q if we can prove P → Q and Q → P. The first premise is logically equivalent to P → Q by the rule of MI. And the second premise gives us Q → P. We can use the implication rule of Conj to conjoin these as (P → Q) · (Q → P). We can then apply ME to get our conclusion. Written out formally, our proof is:

35.

1.	~P ∨ Q	[premise]
2.	Q → P	[premise]
3.	P → Q	from 1 by MI
4.	(P → Q) · (Q → P)	from 2,3 by Conj
5.	P ↔ Q	from 4 by ME

Notice that we couldn't apply ME to lines 2 and 3 together. Indeed, ME, like all other equivalence rules, can be applied only to a single line at a time. Thus we had to conjoin lines 2 and 3 in order to apply ME.

Move to example 33. Here the conclusion is a conjunction that has a conjunction as one of its conjuncts. Claims of this kind can be manipulated using the rule As. This rule allows us to move the parentheses in such claims freely. Thus if there were a way to prove that each of the conjuncts of example 33 is true, then we could use As, if necessary, to move the parentheses to match this conclusion. Here's how we can prove each conjunct of example 33. Premise 2 gives us R. And premise 1, by DeM, is equivalent to ~P · ~Q. We simply need to apply DeM to premise 1 and conjoin the result with premise 2. Then we can use As. Here's our proof:

36.

1.	~(P ∨ Q)	[premise]
2.	R	[premise]
3.	~P · ~Q	from 1 by DeM
4.	R · (~P · ~Q)	from 2,3 by Conj
5.	(R · ~P) · ~Q	from 4 by As

Finally, let's look at example 34. Here the conclusion is R, which we find in premise 2. From premise 2, we can tell that if we could prove P and Q, we could prove R. In fact, if we wished, we could replace premise 2 with (P · Q) → R by Ex and then use P · Q, if we could prove the latter. And, as it turns out, we can prove P · Q from premise 1 by Re. Putting this together, we get:

37.

1.	(P · Q) ∨ (P · Q)	[premise]
2.	P → (Q → R)	[premise]
3.	(P · Q) → R	from 2 by Ex
4.	P · Q	from 1 by Re
5.	R	from 3,4 by MP

For both examples 33 and 34, there are alternative ways you might prove the conclusion, though many of these alternatives will take more steps than are used in examples 36 and 37. Generally speaking, this is often the case: what you can prove in few steps you can prove in a different way in more steps.

Before moving on to introduce the rules of indirect proof, we conclude our discussion of equivalence rules with the following observation about how their use can differ from the use of implication rules: whereas implication rules cannot be applied only to parts of lines in a proof, equivalence rules can. Thus, for example, using the equivalence rule of Re we could replace just the antecedent of:

38. (P ∨ P) → R

By doing so, we would get:

39. P → R

By contrast, we cannot use Ad to replace the antecedent of example 39 so that we get:

40. (P ∨ Q) → R

The reason for this difference is this: while what is logically equivalent to a given symbolized statement must stand in all the same logical relations as that statement, not every implication of that statement must stand in the same logical relations as that statement. To refer back to our examples here, given that P is related to R so as to make P → R true, we can conclude that anything equivalent to P, such as P ∨ P, also stands in this relation to R; however, we cannot conclude that implications of P, such as P ∨ Q, are related to R in this way. Thus to avoid making mistakes we must apply only equivalence rules, and not implication rules, to parts of lines in a proof.

Thus far we've introduced the implication rules and equivalence rules that can be used to construct proofs. The final two rules we need to discuss are the rules for indirect proofs. The **rules of indirect proof** are *rules that allow us to prove something not directly on the basis of preceding premises but instead on the basis of an assumption that we will temporarily introduce into the proof before then discharging.*

The first rule of indirect proof is **CP**, for "conditional proof." This rule allows us to prove conditionals, or "if . . . then" statements. It does so by allowing us to assume the antecedent of the conditional we aim to prove and then offering a proof of the consequent of the conditional given this assumption.

When we successfully prove the consequent of the conditional within the scope of assuming its antecedent, we then discharge our assumption, close off our conditional proof, and write that we have proven the conditional in question using the justification of CP.

Let's pose an example to illustrate. In the following argument we can use CP to prove the conclusion.

41.

$$Q$$
$$\sim P \lor R$$
$$\text{So } P \rightarrow (Q \cdot R)$$

In using CP to give a proof of example 41, we assume the antecedent of the conclusion: P. We then attempt to show that, given the assumption of P, we can prove the consequent of the conclusion: $Q \cdot R$. Let's think briefly about how to prove $Q \cdot R$ given the assumption that P. First, observe that premise 1 gives us Q. Thus all we need is to prove R, and then we can conjoin Q and R. Next, notice that our assumption, P, together with premise 2, will allow us to prove R. One way to use these claims to prove R is to apply MI to premise 2 to get $P \rightarrow Q$ and then to apply MP to this claim and the assumption P to get R. Here's how this all looks when we write it out formally:

42.

1.	Q	[premise]
2.	$\sim P \lor R$	[premise]
3.	P	[assume for CP]
4.	$P \rightarrow R$	from 2 by MI
5.	R	from 3,4 by MP
6.	$Q \cdot R$	from 1,5 by Conj
7.	$P \rightarrow (Q \cdot R)$	from 3–6 by CP

Notice four features of proof 42. First, we set our conditional proofs apart in our list of justifications with a bracket. The bracket begins with the step where we take our assumption on board and ends where we discharge that assumption and draw our conditional conclusion. Second, the justification for the first step of a conditional proof is "assume for CP." Third, the justification for the last step of a conditional proof lists all the premises in the conditional proof and then says "by CP." Fourth, each other step in the conditional proof must be justified by either a premise, a claim already proven, or an assumption, together with our rules. Thus, for example, notice that claim 4 is justified by premise 2 and MI, while claim 5 is justified in part by the assumption made in claim 3.

The second rule for indirect proof is **RAA**, after the Latin *reductio ad absurdum* (reduction to absurdity). Here we assume the opposite of what we intend to prove and then show that a contradiction follows from this assumption. A **contradiction** is *a claim of the form P · ~P—that is, a conjunction of a statement and its negation*. Notably, we can use RAA to prove both negations and statements that are not negations. Use of RAA differs from use of CP in terms of what is assumed, what we aim to prove given our assumption, and what we are thereby licensed to conclude. But in all other respects, it works just like CP.

Let's look at an example.

43.

$$P \rightarrow (Q \rightarrow R)$$
$$\sim R \cdot Q$$
$$\text{So } \sim P$$

For example 43 we can attempt to prove the conclusion using RAA. To do this, we'll assume the opposite of the conclusion—P—and attempt to prove a contradiction given this assumption. Here how it works: first, assuming P, it follows by MP from premise 1 that $Q \rightarrow R$. Premise 2 gives us Q as one of its conjuncts. So by another application of MP, we could prove R. However, premise 2 gives us ~R as its other conjunct. Thus given our assumption of P, we can prove R · ~R, which is a contradiction. When we write it out formally, it looks like this:

44.

1. $P \rightarrow (Q \rightarrow R)$ [premise]
2. $\sim R \cdot Q$ [premise]
3. P   [assume for RAA]
4. $Q \rightarrow R$ from 1,3 by MP
5. Q   from 2 by Simp
6. R   from 4,5 by MP
7. $\sim R$ from 2 by Simp
8. $R \cdot \sim R$ from 6,7 by Conj
9. $\sim P$ from 3–8 by RAA

Again, notice that the only difference between CP and RAA concerns the justification we write for the first step of RAA ("assume for RAA"), the kind of conclusion we aim to prove within RAA (a contradiction), the kind of conclusion we reach when we conclude the RAA (the opposite of what we assumed), and the justification we give for this conclusion ("by RAA").

There are some important ways in which CP and RAA are flexible. First, neither CP nor RAA has to be used at the outset of a proof in the way they are in examples 42 and 44. They can in principle begin anytime during the proof other than the last two steps. Second, it is sometimes helpful to use CP or RAA to prove a claim other than the conclusion of an argument. We used each to prove the conclusion above, but sometimes we might use them to prove a step on our way toward the conclusion. Third, a single proof can use both CP and RAA, and they can each be used multiple times within proofs. Indeed, they can be used within each other. For example, part of the proof of an RAA might involve a CP (we'll look at an example in a moment). Finally, CP and RAA can be used to prove claims without any premises at all—or what we call a logical theorem. A logical **theorem** is *a statement that can be proven without any premises.*

To illustrate how CP and RAA can be combined together as part of a proof and how they can be employed to construct proofs of theorems, consider this claim:

45. $(P \to (Q \to R)) \leftrightarrow ((P \cdot Q) \to R)$

Notice that example 45 is a statement of the equivalence rule Ex. We can prove this rule from no premises and without appealing to Ex itself by using a combination of CP and RAA. To do this, we'll use CP to prove each direction of the double arrow. And as part of our proof of one of these directions, we'll use RAA. Here's a proof of example 45 that proceeds in this way:

46.

1.	$P \to (Q \to R)$	[assume for CP]
2.	$P \cdot Q$	[assume for CP]
3.	P	from 2 by Simp
4.	$Q \to R$	from 1,3 by MP
5.	Q	from 2 by Simp
6.	R	from 4,5 by MP
7.	$(P \cdot Q) \to R$	from 2–6 by CP
8.	$(P \to (Q \to R)) \to ((P \cdot Q) \to R)$	from 1–7 by CP
9.	$(P \cdot Q) \to R$	[assume for CP]
10.	P	[assume for CP]
11.	$\sim(Q \to R)$	[assume for RAA]

12. ~(~Q ∨ R)	from 11 by MI
13. ~~Q · ~R	from 12 by DeM
14. ~~Q	from 13 by Simp
15. Q	from 14 by DN
16. P · Q	from 10,15 by Conj
17. R	from 9,16 by MP
18. ~R	from 13 by Simp
19. R · ~R	from 17,18 by Conj
20. Q → R	from 11–19 by RAA
21. P → (Q → R)	from 10–20 by CP
22. ((P · Q) → R) → (P → (Q → R))	from 9–21 by CP
23. (P → (Q → R)) ↔ ((P · Q) →R)	from 8,22 by ME

To say the very least, example 46 is a complicated proof! Please do not feel discouraged if you couldn't come up with this proof on your own. The example is used simply to illustrate how multiple instances of CP and RAA can be employed to give a proof and how these can be employed within the scope of one another. When giving a proof calls for the use of CP and RAA in

Key Ideas for Review

The **Proof Method** is a method used to determine that an argument is valid by constructing a proof of the argument's conclusion where each step of the proof is justified by an implication rule, an equivalence rule, or an indirect proof rule.

A **conjunct** is the statement on one side of "and" in a conjunction.

A **proof** of an argument is a set of symbolic statements that begins with symbolized representations of the argument's premise(s) and ends with a symbolized representation of its conclusion, where each other statement in the set is justified by a rule of implication, equivalence, or indirect proof.

The **rules of implication** are **MP**, **MT**, **DS**, **HS**, **CD**, **Simp**, **Conj**, and **Add**. For statements of these rules, see table 2.4.1. The application of these rules will often cite multiple lines, but they

must be applied to *whole* lines and not mere *parts* of lines of a proof.

The **rules of equivalence** are **DN**, **Comm**, **Re**, **Cont**, **As**, **Ex**, **MI**, **Dist**, **DeM**, and **ME**. For statements of these rules, see table 2.4.2. The application of these rules can cite only single lines, and these rules can be applied to either whole lines or parts of lines in a proof.

The **rules of indirect proof** (**CP** and **RAA**) are rules that allow us to prove something not directly on the basis of preceding premises but instead on the basis of an assumption that we will temporarily introduce into the proof before then discharging.

A **contradiction** is a claim of the form P · ~P— that is, a conjunction of a statement and its negation.

A logical **theorem** is a statement that can be proven without any premises.

this way, it is important to follow the conventions used here. Each instance of CP or RAA gets its own bracket in the section where we write justifications. When the uses of CP or RAA are nested (that is, when one occurs within the scope of another), we write additional sets of brackets outside our original set(s) in the way done above.

If you're unsure of your ability to use CP or RAA effectively, have no fear! Try out some of the practice exercises in 2.4.C below. As a help to remember CP and RAA, consult table 2.4.3.

TABLE 2.4.3

Rules of Indirect Proof

CP	RAA (options 1 and 2)	
P	P	~P
Q	Q · ~Q	Q · ~Q
P → Q	~P	P

2.4.3 Summary

This section has introduced the Proof Method, a method whereby we determine that an argument is valid by constructing a proof of its conclusion using rules of implication, equivalence, or indirect proof. These rules have been introduced and their use has been illustrated. We must stress that the Proof Method is for complex arguments and that skill in using this method requires practice.

Exercise 2.4

A. Proofs with Rules of Implication. Construct proofs of the following symbolized arguments using the rules of implication.

1.

  P
  (P ∨ R) → S
  So S

2.

  P · ~Q
  Q ∨ R
  So R

3.

  (P · Q) → R
  R → S
  P
  Q
  So S

4.

P → Q
~Q
~P → R
S → T
So R v T

5.

(P → Q) · (R v T)
~T
So R · ~T

6.

~P
Q → P
So ~Q · ~P

7.

P · ~Q
(~Q v R) → S
P → T
So T v S

8.

(P · ~Q) → R
Q → S
~S · P
So R

9.

(P v Q) → (R · S)
(R · S) → T
Q
So T

10.

(P → Q) → R
S → Q
P → S
So R · (P → S)

B. Proofs with Rules of Implication and Equivalence. Construct proofs of the following symbolized arguments using the rules of implication or the rules of equivalence.

1.

P → Q
(~Q → ~P) → (R v R)
So R

2.

(P · Q) v (P · R)
(Q v R) → (S · T)
So T

3.

(P · Q) · R
(Q · R) ↔ S
~(T · S)
So ~T

4.

~R · P
P → (Q → R)
So ~Q

5.

P ↔ Q
~(P · Q)
So ~P · ~Q

6.

P v Q
Q → ~P
So ~P ↔ Q

7.

P v Q

P → R

So ~Q → (R v R)

8.

~(P · Q) v S

~T → ~S

P · Q

So T v R

9.

~(P → Q)

So P ↔ ~Q

10.

(P v Q) → R

P v (S · Q)

R ↔ T

So T

C. Indirect Proofs. The following are either arguments or theorems. For the arguments, construct proofs using the rules of implication, equivalence, or indirect proof. For the theorems (the examples with only one line), give a proof of the theorem from no premises.

1.

P → (Q · R)

~R v T

So P → T

2.

P ↔ Q

So ~(P · ~Q)

3.

~(P · Q)

(R → Q) v (~R v Q)

So R → ~P

4. (P v Q) → ~(~P · ~Q)

5. (~P v Q) → (~(Q → P) v
   (P ↔ Q))

6.

P · ~Q

So ~ (P ↔ Q)

7.

~(P v Q)

R → Q

So ~R

8. (P · (Q v R)) → (~R → (P ↔ Q))

9.

~P v (R v (S · T))

~(T v U)

So P → R

10. (P · ~P) → Q

D. Proving English Arguments. Symbolize the following arguments for purposes of using the Proof Method. Then construct proofs of them using any of the rules covered in this section.

1. Either God foreknows what you will do or God is not omniscient. If God foreknows what you will do, then what you will do was settled long ago. And if what you will do is up to you, then what you will do was

not settled long ago. So if God is omniscient, then what you will do is not up to you.

2. If there are reasons for paying our taxes on time and reasons for not paying our taxes on time, then the weight of these reasons should determine whether we should pay the taxes on time. It isn't the case that there aren't reasons for paying taxes on time. So if it isn't the case that the weight of the reasons should determine whether we pay the taxes on time, then it isn't the case that there are reasons for not paying our taxes on time.

3. God is metaphysically simple if and only if God does not have parts. If God has parts, then God is divisible. Either God is not divisible or God can be destroyed. So it is not the case that God both can be destroyed and is metaphysically simple.

4. Many conservative voters think democracy is problematic because it allows ignorant, uninformed people to play a significant role in the political process. But it is a problem for ignorant, uninformed people to play a significant role in the political process if and only if it is a problem for ignorant, uninformed people to determine the distribution of wealth through making free decisions about how to spend their money. And if it is a problem for ignorant, uninformed people to play a significant role in the political process if and only if it is a problem for ignorant, uninformed people to determine the distribution of wealth through making free decisions about how to spend their money, then if many conservative voters think democracy is problematic because it allows ignorant, uninformed people to play a significant role in the political process, then many conservative voters should think that capitalism is problematic. So many conservative voters should think that capitalism is problematic.

5. You are quite possibly mistaken about what is ultimately good for you. But if you are quite possibly mistaken about what is ultimately good for you and you reject belief in God on the basis of your views of what is ultimately good for you, then your rejection of belief in God is not well-founded. So either your rejection of belief in God is not well-founded, or you do not reject belief in God on the basis of your views about what is ultimately good for you.

6. There are evils for which no created persons are responsible if there are evils for which created persons are responsible. Either there is no free will or there are evils for which created persons are responsible. So if there is free will, then there is free will if and only if there are evils for which no created persons are responsible.

7. Theologians need philosophical training just in case theology requires careful reasoning and philosophical training helps one engage in careful reasoning. If theology does not require careful reasoning, then theology should not be studied. So if theology should be studied and philosophical training helps one engage in careful reasoning, then theologians need philosophical training.

8. God cannot be blamed for allowing too much evil in the world if there is no minimum amount of evil necessary for accomplishing God's purposes. There is a minimum amount of evil necessary for accomplishing God's purposes only if there is some amount of evil such that God's purposes could not have been accomplished with any less evil than it. It is not the case that there is some amount of evil such that God's purposes could have been accomplished with any less evil than it. So there is no minimum amount of evil necessary for accomplishing God's purposes, and God cannot be blamed for allowing too much evil in the world.

9. If I don't volunteer, then somebody else will volunteer and there won't be too many volunteers. If somebody else volunteers and I volunteer, there will be too many volunteers. So if somebody else volunteers, then there are not too many volunteers if and only if I do not volunteer.

10. You forgive your offender if and only if you cultivate good will for your offender. To love all people is to cultivate good will for all people; if to love all people is to cultivate good will for all people, then if you love your offender, you cultivate good will for your offender. So either you don't love your offender, or you forgive your offender.

2.5 Expanded Proof Method with Predicates and Quantifiers

This section introduces an Expanded Proof Method that builds on the Proof Method introduced in the previous section. The **Expanded Proof Method** is *a method used to determine that an argument is valid by constructing a proof of its conclusion using the rules of the Proof Method together with the additional rules of implication, indirect proof, and equivalence unique to the Expanded Proof Method.* The basic strategy of the Expanded Proof Method remains the same as the basic strategy of the Proof Method: to employ a set of rules of inference in order to determine that an argument is valid by constructing a proof of its conclusion. The rules used in the Expanded Proof Method are simply expanded, thus enabling us to successfully determine more arguments to be valid than we are able to determine by using the Proof Method alone.

To see the value of the Expanded Proof Method, consider the following argument, which cannot be shown to be valid using the Proof Method:

1. Thomas is a toddler, and Thomas likes Dora the Explorer; Sam is a toddler, and Sam likes Dora the Explorer. If any person is both a toddler and likes Dora the Explorer, he also will be very excited when Dora comes to visit the library. So Thomas and Sam will be very excited when Dora comes to visit the library.

If we attempted to evaluate the argument of example 1 using the proof method, we would get something like the following symbolization, for which no proof can be constructed using the Proof Method:

2.

$(P \cdot Q) \cdot (R \cdot S)$
$T \rightarrow U$
So $V \cdot W$

Yet the argument of example 1 is clearly valid. If its premises are true, then its conclusion must be true as well. The Proof Method is not the only method we've discussed thus far that cannot be employed to successfully evaluate the argument of example 1: we can't determine its validity by using the Famous Forms Method or Venn Diagram Method either. Thankfully, the Expanded Proof Method can help us.

2.5.1 New Symbols of the Expanded Proof Method

In order to employ the Expanded Proof Method, we must learn some additional vocabulary and inference rules that this method combines with the symbols and inference rules of the Proof Method. The new vocabulary is used to symbolize quantifiers, variables, constants, and predicates.

Look back at example 1. Notice that while its second premise doesn't repeat any of the statements from its first premise (and this is why there aren't any letters repeated in the first two premises of the symbolized argument in example 2 above), it does repeat *something* from its first premise. More specifically, what is repeats are two **predicates**—*expressions referring to properties or features of something*. The predicates are "is a toddler" and "likes Dora the explorer." These predicates are simply applied to different things in the first two premises of the argument. Premise 1 applies them to "Thomas" and "Sam," while premise 2 applies them to "person" and "he." We will call terms that function the way "Thomas" and "Sam" do here **constants**, because they are *terms that refer to the same entities throughout an argument*. Terms that function like "person" and "he" do here are, by contrast, **variables**—*terms the referent of which is left unspecified*. You have already been introduced to quantifiers—terms that specify how much of a subject they are concerned with. The English quantifier employed in example 1 is "any."

For the Expanded Proof Method, we will use italicized capital letters to represent predicates, italicized lowercase letters from w to z to symbolize variables, and italicized lowercase letters from a to d to symbolize constants. In any statement used in a proof constructed using the Expanded Proof Method, a sentence that affirms some predicate of a constant or variable will be represented with a symbol for the predicate followed by a symbol for the constant or variable. For example, using P to symbolize "is a toddler" and a to symbolize "Thomas," we might symbolize "Thomas is a toddler" as:

3. Pa

Since Pa is a statement, it can be combined with other statements using symbols already familiar from the Proof Method. For example, using Q to symbolize "likes Dora the Explorer," we can use the dot symbol to symbolize "Thomas is a toddler, and Thomas likes Dora the Explorer" as:

4. $Pa \cdot Qa$

If we let the constant b symbolize "Sam," then we can symbolize the entirety of the first premise in example 1 as:

5. $(Pa \cdot Qa) \cdot (Pb \cdot Qb)$

The only vocabulary items that remain to be introduced are those used to symbolize quantifiers. Following a common convention, we will use the backward-E symbol, ∃, to symbolize particular statements and the upside-down-A symbol, ∀, for universal statements. The ∃ symbol is called an **existential quantifier**, which is *a quantifier (represented by the ∃ symbol) that tells us that* there is *something such that an expression following the ∃ symbol is true of it*. The ∀ symbol is called a **universal quantifier**, which is *a quantifier (represented by the ∀ symbol) that tells us that* for anything *there is, the expression following the ∀ symbol is true of it*.

Each time the ∀ or ∃ symbol is used correctly, it will be followed by a variable and a statement that uses the vocabulary of the Expanded Proof Method. For example, using the variable x, the predicate R for "will be excited when Dora comes to the library," and the predicates P and Q as before, we might symbolize the second statement of example 1 as:

6. $\forall x((Px \cdot Qx) \rightarrow Rx)$

When you read example 6, you should read it as asserting "For anything, x, if the predicate P and the predicate Q both apply to x, then the predicate R applies to x." Notice that the term x here is used as a variable both immediately after the $\forall$ and within the parentheses following the $\forall$. Notice also these parentheses themselves. Our convention will be to enclose any statement within the scope of a quantifier within parentheses. The **scope** of a quantifier is *the part of an expression to which a quantifier applies*. If instead of example 6 we had $\forall x(Px \cdot Qx) \rightarrow Rx$, this would be read as "If it is the case that for anything, x, both P and Q apply to x, then R applies to ____." We use a blank here because technically Rx—and indeed $\forall x(Px \cdot Qx) \rightarrow Rx$—is not a statement. Both expressions use a letter we use only to symbolize variables—x—but do so outside the scope of any quantifier. This is something the vocabulary of the Expanded Proof Method does not permit. Only the letters a–d can be used in this way, and they are used for constants rather than variables.

Let's do an example using the existential quantifier. Using the same symbols for predicates as we did previously, try to symbolize this statement:

7. There is someone who will be very excited when Dora comes to the library but is not a toddler.

The correct symbolization for example 7 is:

8. $\exists x(Rx \cdot {\sim}Px)$

Example 8 should be read as "There is someone, x, to which both the predicate R and the predicate $\sim P$ apply."

Sometimes we must use both the $\forall$ and the $\exists$ to symbolize a statement. For example, consider:

9. For every mother there is a toddler that likes Dora the Explorer.

Letting P symbolize "is a mother," Q symbolize "is a toddler" and R symbolize "likes Dora the Explorer," we could symbolize example 9 as:

10. $\forall x(Px \rightarrow \exists y(Qy \cdot Ry))$

We read example 10 as "For anything, x, if P applies to x, then there is something, y, to which both Q and R apply. Likewise, using the same symbols for the same English terms, we might symbolize example 11 with example 12:

11. If there is a toddler who likes Dora the Explorer, then it is not the case that everything is a mother.

12. $\exists x(Qx \cdot Rx) \rightarrow \sim\forall y(Py)$

Notice that in each of these cases, when we need a new variable because we have introduced a new quantifier, our convention is to introduce a new letter from the end of the alphabet.

We close this subsection on vocabulary by showing that with just the $\exists$ and $\forall$ symbols, we are able to symbolize all four of the kinds of statements we symbolized in a different way for using the Venn Diagram Method. Consider the following examples:

13. All mice are nocturnal creatures.
14. No mice are nocturnal creatures.
15. Some mice are nocturnal creatures.
16. Some mice are not nocturnal creatures.

These are the four types of statement we discussed when evaluating categorical syllogisms. Example 13 is a universal affirmative statement; example 14 is a universal negative statement; example 15 is a particular affirmative statement; and example 16 is a particular negative statement. Using P for "is a mouse" and Q for "is a nocturnal creature," we can symbolize these statements respectively as:

17. $\forall x(Px \rightarrow Qx)$
18. $\forall x(Px \rightarrow \sim Qx)$
19. $\exists x(Px \cdot Qx)$
20. $\exists x(Px \cdot \sim Qx)$

With this new vocabulary in hand, we are ready to introduce the new rules of inference that will enable us to use this new vocabulary in the construction of proofs.

2.5.2 New Inference Rules of the Expanded Proof Method

The Expanded Proof Method adds five new rules to the rules of the Proof Method: two implication rules, an equivalence rule (in four forms), and a rule of indirect proof (in two forms). All of them are concerned with inferences involving the quantifiers $\forall$ or $\exists$.

We'll start with the **rules of implication**, which are the most intuitive. The first rule, **∀-elimination**, allows us to eliminate a universal quantifier and replace the variable that falls in its scope uniformly with a constant. This rule will allow us to prove that the argument in example 1 is valid. Recall that we symbolized the second premise of example 1 as:

6. $\forall x((Px \cdot Qx) \rightarrow Rx)$

Applying ∀-elimination to this premise and selecting a for our constant, we get:

21. $(Pa \cdot Qa) \rightarrow Ra$

We can apply ∀-elimination to the premise in example 6 a second time, using the constant b, to get $(Pb \cdot Qb) \rightarrow Rb$. Notice than in each of these two applications of ∀-elimination, we eliminated the ∀ symbol along with the first occurrence of a variable following it, and we replaced that variable everywhere within the scope of the quantifier with the relevant constant. We also eliminated the outermost pair of parentheses.

Once we've proved the foregoing two statements by ∀-elimination, we can construct a proof of the conclusion of example 1 using the inference rules of the Proof Method. Here is how we write the proof:

22.

1.	$(Pa \cdot Qa) \cdot (Pb \cdot Qb)$	[premise]
2.	$\forall x((Px \cdot Qx) \rightarrow Rx)$	[premise]
3.	$(Pa \cdot Qa) \rightarrow Ra$	from 2 by ∀-elimination
4.	$(Pb \cdot Qb) \rightarrow Rb$	from 2 by ∀-elimination
5.	$(Pa \cdot Qa)$	from 1 by Simp
6.	$(Pb \cdot Qb)$	from 1 by Simp
7.	Ra	from 5,3 by MP
8.	Rb	from 6,4 by MP
9.	$Ra \cdot Rb$	from 7,8 by Conj

Example 22 gives us our first example of a proof using the Expanded Proof Method.

The second implication rule is **∃-introduction**. This rule allows us to introduce a statement that uses the ∃ symbol followed by a variable, and then followed by a statement that is the same as a statement already affirmed in the argument except that a constant in that statement is here replaced by the relevant variable. For example, consider again the statement:

21. $(Pa \cdot Qa) \rightarrow Ra$

By applying ∃-introduction, we would get:

23. $\exists x((Px \cdot Qx) \rightarrow Rx)$

∃-introduction is especially helpful when we are proving a conclusion that is more general than some of its premises. For example, consider the argument:

24. Thomas is a toddler, but Thomas does not like Dora the Explorer. If anyone is a mom, she is not a toddler. So there is someone who is not a mom that doesn't like Dora the Explorer.

Using a for "Thomas," P for "is a toddler," Q for "likes Dora the Explorer," and R for "is a mom," try to give a proof of argument 24. Doing so will require you to use ∃-introduction. Here's one way to construct the proof:

25.
1.	$Pa \cdot {\sim}Qa$	[premise]
2.	$\forall x(Rx \rightarrow {\sim}Px)$	[premise]
3.	$Ra \rightarrow {\sim}Pa$	from 2 by ∀-elimination
4.	Pa	from 1 by Simp
5.	${\sim}{\sim}Pa$	from 4 by DN
6.	${\sim}Ra$	from 3,5 by MT
7.	${\sim}Qa$	from 1 by Simp
8.	${\sim}Ra \cdot {\sim}Qa$	from 6,7 by Conj
9.	$\exists x({\sim}Rx \cdot {\sim}Qx)$	from 8 by ∃-introduction

Notice here that we used both of our implication rules.

Move next to the **rules of indirect proof**. Each of these rules is a rule of indirect proof because its correct application involves taking on board an assumption and later discharging it. The first rule is called **indirect ∃-introduction** because it involves an indirect proof of a statement that introduces the ∃ symbol. In the first step of indirect ∃-introduction, we remove from a previous line of the proof the ∃ symbol along with the first instance of the variable that immediately succeeds it, and we replace all the other instances of that variable in the line with an arbitrarily chosen constant. By saying that the constant must be chosen arbitrarily, what should be emphasized is that the constant must not be chosen intentionally to be identical to a constant already employed in the argument. We will ensure this does not happen by requiring that the constant chosen has not already been employed in the proof. To illustrate this first step of indirect ∃-introduction, we could change the premise from example 26 to that of example 27 provided that *c* has not already been employed in a previous line of the proof:

26. $\exists x(\sim Rx \cdot \sim Qx)$

27. $\sim Rc \cdot \sim Qc$

Thus far we have described only how to engage in the first step of indirect ∃-introduction. At this step, we take on board an assumption: we assume that the particular constant we have identified is one of the constants to which the replaced statement applies. For example, in the move from example 26 to example 27, we assume of the constant *c* that it is one of the constants to which ~R and ~Q apply. Example 26 tells us that there is at least one such constant. Our assumption is that *c* is among those constants. This is why it is inappropriate to use a constant that has already appeared in the argument: while it may be controversial that the statement in question applies to a constant already employed in the argument, it is not controversial that it applies to *something or other* for which we arbitrarily select a name.

Once we've taken on board this assumption about our arbitrarily chosen constant, we can engage in further reasoning concerning what follows given this claim about the constant in question. For example, if we had the additional premise that $\forall x(\sim Rx \rightarrow Sx)$ with the premise in example 26, then we could prove that *Sc*. This in turn would allow us to prove $\exists x(Sx)$. Yet we would not have been able to prove this without indirect ∃-introduction. Here's what the proof would look like:

28.
1. $\exists x(\sim Rx \cdot \sim Qx)$ [premise]
2. $\forall x(\sim Rx \rightarrow Sx)$ [premise]
3. $\sim Rc \cdot \sim Qc$ — from 1; assumption for indirect ∃-introduction
4. $\sim Rc$ — from 3 by Simp
5. $\sim Rc \rightarrow Sc$ — from 2 by ∀-elimination
6. Sc — from 5,4 by MP
7. $\exists x(Sx)$ — from 3–6 by indirect ∃-introduction

The argument in example 28 illustrates the correct application of indirect ∃-introduction. Notice how this application proceeds. First, we replace the variables of an existentially qualified statement that has appeared in the argument using an arbitrarily selected constant (claim 3). Then we prove something else regarding this constant, given our assumption regarding it (claims 4–6). Finally, we conclude that there is something to which what we have now proven of our constant applies (claim 7). In providing justifications for this proof, we draw a bracket in the same way we did when using the indirect proof rules of the Proof Method. We justify our first step in the bracket by citing the premise to which we have applied ∃-elimination and saying "assumption for indirect ∃-introduction," while we justify our final step by citing all other claims in the bracket and saying "by indirect ∃-introduction."

Try applying this strategy to the following argument:

29. Some preachers do not have revisable opinions. Anyone who is well-educated has revisable opinions. So some preachers are not well-educated.

Let P stand for "is a preacher," Q stand for "has revisable opinions," and R stand for "is well-educated." We can use indirect ∃-introduction to provide a proof of this argument, as follows:

30.
1. $\exists x(Px \cdot \sim Qx)$ [premise]
2. $\forall x(Rx \rightarrow Qx)$ [premise]
3. $Pc \cdot \sim Qc$ — from 1; assumption for indirect ∃-introduction
4. $\sim Qc$ — from 3 by Simp
5. $Rc \rightarrow Qc$ — from 2 by ∀-elimination
6. $\sim Rc$ — from 4,5 by MT
7. Pc — from 3 by Simp
8. $Pc \cdot \sim Rc$ — from 7,6 by Conj
9. $\exists x(Px \cdot \sim Rx)$ — from 3–8 by indirect ∃-introduction

The second rule of indirect proof is **indirect ∀-introduction**, so named because it involves an indirect proof of an ∀-introduction. For the first step of indirect ∀-introduction, we perform ∀-elimination: we eliminate the ∀ symbol and its immediately succeeding variable from a statement already employed in the argument and then replace all other instances of this variable in the statement with an arbitrarily selected constant. Again, what is most relevant is that the constant selected is not one that has been employed previously in the argument. So, for example, we might replace the premise in example 31 with that in example 32 provided that *a* has not been employed previously in the argument:

31. $\forall x(\sim Px \lor Qx)$

32. $\sim Pa \lor Qa$

We next attempt to prove something else of our arbitrarily chosen constant. For example, if in addition to the premise in example 31, we had $\forall x(Qx \to Rx)$, then we could prove $Px \to Rx$. Indirect $\forall$-introduction would then allow us to prove $\forall x(Px \to Rx)$. The formal proof would look like this:

33.

1. $\forall x(\sim Px \lor Qx)$ [premise]
2. $\forall x(Qx \to Rx)$ [premise]
3. $\sim Pa \lor Qa$ from 1; assumption for indirect $\forall$-introduction
4. $Pa \to Qa$ from 3 by MI
5. $Qa \to Ra$ from 2 by $\forall$-elimination
6. $Pa \to Ra$ from 4,5 by HS
7. $\forall x(Pa \to Ra)$ from 3–6 by indirect $\forall$-introduction

The strategy employed here is very similar to the strategy employed for indirect $\exists$-introduction. We assume of some arbitrarily chosen constant *a* that a previous universally quantified statement in the argument is true of it. We next prove that another statement is true of *a*, using this assumption along with our other premises and rules. We then use $\forall$-introduction on the proven statement. The justifications for the proof are similar to those used for indirect $\exists$-introduction. But for the first step of the indirect proof we write "assumption for indirect $\forall$-introduction," and for the last step we write "by indirect $\forall$-introduction."

Try to prove the following example using indirect $\forall$-introduction:

34. Anything that is round and red is colored. Nothing that is colored is invisible. So nothing that is round and red is invisible.

Let *P* symbolize "is round," *Q* symbolize "is red," *R* symbolize "is colored," and *S* symbolize "is invisible." You can then construct the following proof using indirect $\forall$-introduction:

35.

1. $\forall x((Px \cdot Qx) \to Rx)$ [premise]
2. $\forall x(Rx \to {\sim}Sx)$ [premise]
3. $(Pa \cdot Qa) \to Ra$ ⌐ from 1; assumption for indirect $\forall$-introduction
4. $Ra \to {\sim}Sa$ | from 2 by $\forall$-elimination
5. $(Pa \cdot Qa) \to {\sim}Sa$ | from 3,4 by HS
6. $\forall x((Px \cdot Qx) \to {\sim}Sx)$ ⌐ from 3–5 by indirect $\forall$-introduction

Notice that each of the previous two examples in which we used indirect $\forall$-introduction were examples where this enables us to prove a universally quantified statement from other universally quantified statements. Indeed, this is one very common use for indirect $\forall$-introduction.[9]

The final new rule for the Expanded Proof Method is the **rule of quantifier equivalence**. The rule comes in four forms and allows us to move back and forth from statements that employ the $\forall$ symbol to equivalent statements that employ the $\exists$ symbol. The four forms of the rule are:

36. $\forall x\mathbf{P} :: {\sim}\exists x{\sim}\mathbf{P}$
37. $\forall x{\sim}\mathbf{P} :: {\sim}\exists x\mathbf{P}$
38. $\exists x\mathbf{P} :: {\sim}\forall x{\sim}\mathbf{P}$
39. $\exists x{\sim}\mathbf{P} :: {\sim}\forall x\mathbf{P}$

In these statements, the bold capital letter **P** stands for any statement of the Expanded Proof Method.[10] When we read the statements correctly, it should be clear why they are true. Example 36 should be read as "'for all x, P' is equivalent to 'there is not an x such that ${\sim}$P.'" Example 37 should be read as "'for all x, ${\sim}$P' is equivalent to 'there is not an x such that P.'" Example 38 should be read as "'there is an x such that P' is equivalent to 'it is not the case that for all x ${\sim}$P.'" Example 39 should be read as "'there is an x such that ${\sim}$P' is equivalent to 'it is not the case that for all x, P.'"

These rules of quantifier equivalence can sometimes be helpful in proving arguments. Consider, for example:

40. Some philosophers are welders. Nothing that is a welder is completely useless in navigating practical affairs. So it is not the case that if anything is a philosopher, then it is completely useless in navigating practical affairs.

Let's let P symbolize "is a philosopher," Q symbolize "is a welder," and R symbolize "is completely useless in navigating practical affairs." We can construct a proof of example 40 as follows:

41.

1. $\exists x(Px \cdot Qx)$ [premise]
2. $\forall x(Qx \rightarrow \sim Rx)$ [premise]
3. $Pa \cdot Qa$ from 1; assumption for indirect $\exists$-introduction
4. $Pa \rightarrow Ra$ assumption for RAA
5. Pa from 3 by Simp
6. Ra from 4,5 by MP
7. $\sim\sim Ra$ from 6 by DN
8. $Qa \rightarrow \sim Ra$ from 2 by $\forall$-elimination
9. Qa from 3 by Simp
10. $\sim Ra$ from 8,9 by MP
11. $Ra \cdot \sim Ra$ from 6,10 by Conj
12. $\sim(Pa \rightarrow Ra)$ from 4–11 by RAA
13. $\exists x(\sim(Px \rightarrow Rx))$ from 3–12 by indirect $\exists$-introduction
14. $\sim\forall x(Px \rightarrow Rx)$ from 13 by quantifier equivalence

Example 41 is no simple proof. It combines the use of several difficult rules, including an application of quantifier equivalence for its last step, all in one proof. Notice that when we justify the final step we simply write "by quantifier equivalence."

Let's discuss the proof in example 41 briefly in more detail. In attempting to construct proofs of arguments like example 40, it is often helpful to begin with the conclusion, as we saw with some of the examples for which we used the Proof Method. Here the conclusion is a negated universally quantified statement. With our knowledge of the rule of quantifier equivalence, specifically the rule stated in example 39 above, we know that this is equivalent to an existentially quantified negation. Specifically, using symbols, the existentially quantified negation to which our conclusion is equivalent is $\exists x(\sim(Px \rightarrow Rx))$. This claim cannot be inferred immediately from the premises, and it has an existential quantifier. Thus to prove it we need to introduce the $\exists$ symbol, and we do this by using indirect $\exists$-introduction. Specifically, we need to perform indirect $\exists$-introduction where the penultimate line of our indirect proof is what we would get if we applied $\exists$-elimination to $\exists x(\sim(Px \rightarrow Rx))$. Using a as our constant, what we want the last line of our indirect $\exists$-introduction to say is $\sim(Pa \rightarrow Ra)$.

We know that in order to perform indirect $\exists$-introduction, we need to begin by performing $\exists$-elimination. And we have to do this on premise 1, since it is our only premise that contains an $\exists$ symbol. The result is claim 3 above: $Pa \cdot Qa$. Our task now is to prove $\sim(Pa \rightarrow Ra)$ given this assumption and our premises. The approach taken above is to use RAA. Often when what we need to prove is a negation, this approach can be helpful. To complete it successfully, we begin by assuming the opposite of what we aim to prove, and we then attempt to derive a contradiction. Thus above we assumed $Pa \rightarrow Ra$ and derived the contradiction $Ra \sim Ra$.

With the rules of ∀-elimination, ∃-introduction, indirect ∃-introduction, indirect ∀-introduction, and quantifier equivalence now introduced, we are ready to begin using the Expanded Proof Method. As is the case with the Proof Method in section 2.4, here again practice is essential.

2.5.3 Summary

This section has introduced the Expanded Proof Method with predicates and quantifiers. The Expanded Proof Method can be used to determine that an argument is valid by constructing a proof of its conclusion using the rules of the Proof Method together with the additional rules of ∀-elimination, ∃-introduction, indirect ∃-introduction, indirect ∀-introduction, and quantifier equivalence. The latter rules, along with the unique vocabulary of the Expanded Proof Method, have been introduced in this section.

Exercise 2.5

A. New Vocabulary. Symbolize the following statements using the symbols of the Proof Method and the new symbols introduced for the Expanded Proof Method. Pick your own symbols for predicates, variables, and constants within the parameters set by this section.

1. Some churches are closed on Mondays.
2. Nothing that lives forever should fear death.
3. Not every vigilante is a hero.
4. Brad Pitt is an actor and a philanthropist.
5. If there is something that is green and round, then not everything that is round is blue.
6. Either there is a necessary being or it is not the case that every dependent being has an explanation.
7. Augustine was either a writer or a pastor, but not both.
8. There is a solution to the paradox if and only if someone has found a solution to the paradox.
9. If every stick stuck in water is bent, then no stick that is seen is a material object.

Key Ideas for Review

The **Expanded Proof Method** is a method used to determine that an argument is valid by constructing a proof of its conclusion using the rules of the Proof Method together with the additional rules of implication, indirect proof, and equivalence unique to the Expanded Proof Method.

A **predicate** is an expression referring to a property or feature of something.

A **constant** is a term that refers to the same entity throughout an argument.

A **variable** is a term the referent of which is left unspecified.

An **existential quantifier** is a quantifier (represented by the ∃ symbol) that tells us that *there is* something such that an expression following the ∃ symbol is true of it.

A **universal quantifier** is a quantifier (represented by the ∀ symbol) that tells us that *for anything there is*, the expression following the ∀ symbol is true of it.

The **scope** of a quantifier is the part of an expression to which a quantifier applies.

The following schemas represent correct applications of the unique **rules of implication** of the Expanded Proof Method. Here *P* stands for a predicate, *a* for a constant, and *x* for a variable:

∀-elimination	∃-introduction
∀x(Px)	Pa
So Pa	So ∃x(Px)

The following schemas represent correct applications of the unique **rules of indirect proof** of the Expanded Proof Method. Here *P* and *Q* stand for predicates, *a* for an arbitrarily chosen constant, and *x* for a variable:

Indirect ∃-introduction	Indirect ∀-introduction
∃x(Px)	∀x(Px)
Pa	Pa
Qa	Qa
So ∃x(Qx)	So ∀x(Qx)

The following schemas represent correct applications of the unique **rule of quantifier equivalence** of the Expanded Proof Method (where **P** stands for a statement of the Expanded Proof Method, *x* stands for a variable, and :: stands for logical equivalence):

$$\forall x\mathbf{P} :: {\sim}\exists x{\sim}\mathbf{P} \quad \exists x\mathbf{P} :: {\sim}\forall x{\sim}\mathbf{P}$$
$$\forall x{\sim}\mathbf{P} :: {\sim}\exists x\mathbf{P} \quad \exists x{\sim}\mathbf{P} :: {\sim}\forall x\mathbf{P}$$

10. Either it is not the case that all the parking spots are taken, or if there is a spot for our car, it is on another street.

B. Proofs for Symbolized Arguments. Provide a proof for each of the following symbolized arguments using the Expanded Proof Method.

1.
$Pa \cdot ({\sim}Pa \vee Qb)$
So $\exists x(Qx)$

2.
$\forall x(Px \cdot (Px \leftrightarrow Qx))$
So Qa

3.
$\forall x({\sim}Px \rightarrow (Qx \vee Rx))$
$(Pa \rightarrow Sa) \cdot {\sim}(Sa \vee Qa)$
So Ra

4.

$\exists x(Px) \to \forall x(Qx)$

$\forall x(Px \lor Rx)$

$\sim Ra$

So $\forall x(Qx)$

5.

$\forall x(Px \leftrightarrow Rx)$

$\exists x(Rx)$

So $\exists x(Px)$

6.

$\sim\exists x(Px \cdot \sim Qx)$

$\sim Qc$

So $\exists x(\sim Px)$

7.

Pa

$\forall x((Qx \lor Rx) \to \sim Px)$

So $\sim\forall x(Rx)$

8.

$\sim\exists x(Px \leftrightarrow Qx) \lor \forall x(\sim Rx)$

$Pa \cdot Qa$

So $\sim\exists x(Rx)$

9.

$\forall x(Px \to (Qx \to Rx))$

$\exists x(Qx)$

So $\exists x(Px \to Rx)$

10.

$\sim\forall x(Px \lor Qx) \to Ra$

So $\sim Pb \to (\sim Qb \to \exists x(Rx \lor Sx))$

C. Proofs for English Arguments. Symbolize each of the following English arguments using the symbols of the Proof Method and the Expanded Proof Method. Then provide a proof.

1. John Locke was a Christian and a brilliant philosopher. So it is not the case that no brilliant philosophers are Christians.

2. No infinite collection is assembled through finite additions. If the universe did not have a beginning, then the universe's past is an infinite collection that is assembled through finite additions. So the universe had a beginning.

3. Any trait that is a virtue is a trait that makes its possessor better as a person. The tendency to underestimate one's valuable features doesn't make its possessor better as a person if there is someone who can accurately estimate her valuable features without harming herself or others. Some saints can accurately estimate their valuable features without harming themselves or others. So the tendency to underestimate one's valuable features isn't a trait that is a virtue.

4. If there is an experience that is best explained by a miracle, then there is a reason to believe in God. Some mystical experiences are experiences that are best explained by a miracle. So it is not the case that there is no reason to believe in God.

5. For any claim, if it is very important whether that claim is true, and it isn't the case that progress in determining the truth of that claim cannot

be made by investigating it, then it is important to investigate the public evidence for the claim. It is very important whether the claim "there is a God" is true. So if it isn't the case that progress in determining the truth of the claim "there is a God" cannot be made by investigating it, then it is important to investigate the public evidence for it.

6. Some exercises of virtue cannot occur in the absence of evil. Some evils are permissible if not every exercise of virtue can occur in the absence of evil. So some evils are permissible.

7. Nothing that is a consequence of past facts or laws of nature is something that anyone can do anything about. Everything anyone does is a consequence of past facts or laws of nature. So your working on this logic exercise is not something that anyone can do anything about.

8. Any case of unfair treatment of visitors is a failure of hospitality. Every case of denying legal foreign workers the same benefits as legal domestic workers is a case of unfair treatment of visitors. So if there is a case of denying legal foreign workers the same benefits as legal domestic workers, there is a case of failure of hospitality.

9. There are some wrong acts that are perpetrated against victims who go to heaven but are not forgiven by these victims before they go to heaven. Any wrong act that is perpetrated against a victim who goes to heaven but is not forgiven by that victim before she goes to heaven is either never forgiven or forgiven in heaven. There is no wrong act that is perpetrated against a victim who goes to heaven but is never forgiven. So some wrong acts are forgiven in heaven.

10. Either everyone in hell is there by choice or anyone in hell is there unfairly. There is no one in hell who is there unfairly. So either there is no one in hell or everyone who is in hell is there by choice.

3

▶ ▶ ▶ ▶ ▶

Inductive Logic

In chapter 2 our focus was on learning methods that can be employed to determine if an argument is valid or invalid. These methods can help us to determine for quite a lot of arguments whether they are good in one particular way or whether they fail to be good in a particular way. But in chapter 1 we saw that being valid is not the only way for an argument to be good. Some invalid arguments can be good in a different way: by being strong. Our focus in this chapter will be on learning methods that can be used to determine that an argument is strong.

Consider, for example, the following argument:

1. Ninety-five percent of those who have taken on the super-duper giant cheeseburger challenge have failed to eat the entire cheeseburger. Sam took on the super-duper giant cheeseburger challenge. So Sam failed to eat the entire cheeseburger.

The truth of the premises of this argument doesn't *guarantee* its conclusion in the way required for the argument to be valid. Even if 95 percent of those who have taken on the challenge have failed and Sam has taken on the challenge, it is *possible* that Sam is among those who didn't fail. Nonetheless, in the absence of certain further information, example 1 appears to present a strong argument. If all the information you have to go on to determine whether Sam had or had not failed the challenge is the information provided in example 1, the safe bet for you would be to conclude that Sam had failed.

Example 1, then, seems to provide a strong argument—or at least it is an example of an argument that, as we just suggested, is strong *in the absence of certain further information.* This is because, in the absence of certain further information, the premises of example 1 make its conclusion likely, though they do not guarantee it. Given only the facts that 95 percent of those who have taken on the challenge have failed and that Sam took on the challenge, it is likely that Sam failed.

We've suggested that the argument in example 1 is strong only in the absence of certain further information. But it is possible that there is some further information that, when combined with the information provided by the premises of example 1, would prevent us from concluding that it is strong. Imagine, for instance, that the following claim is true: Sam is a world-champion competitive eater, and 80 percent of world-champion competitive eaters who have taken the challenge have succeeded. Given the information provided by the premises of example 1 *and* this further information, we can no longer conclude that the conclusion of example 1 is more likely than not.

What we have just pointed out about example 1 generalizes. Although the information provided by the premises of an argument can make its conclusion more likely than not *in the absence of certain additional information,* it can nonetheless be that *given* this additional information, the premises do not any longer make the conclusion more likely than not. Accordingly, given our definition of what it is for an argument to be strong—namely, that its conclusion is more likely than not, given its premises—an argument can be strong in the absence of certain additional information but not strong given that further information.

This fact about strength marks an important difference between strength and validity. While the strength of an argument can depend on the presence or absence of additional information, the validity of an argument cannot. If an argument is valid, then regardless of any additional information that can be given, the argument will remain valid. Logicians sometimes use the terms monotonic and non-monotonic to denote this fact. To claim that validity is **monotonic** is *to claim that for any valid argument "P. So Q," the argument "P. R. So Q" is also valid, where P and Q are the same statements in each quotation and R is any statement whatsoever.* To claim that strength is **non-monotonic** is *to claim that it is not the case that for any strong argument "P. So Q," any argument "P. R. So Q" is strong, where P and Q are the same statements in each quotation and R is any statement whatsoever.*

In this chapter we will pay special attention to the non-monotonicity of argument strength. Each of the five sections will introduce a distinct famous strong argument form. A **famous strong argument form** is *an argument form that is such that any argument with this form is strong in the absence of certain* *additional information.* However, given the non-monotonicity of argument strength, for each of these arguments it is also the case that, given certain further information, we cannot conclude that the argument is strong. Thus our approach will be to learn to determine when an argument uses one of these famous forms and then to learn to evaluate what kind of additional information would prevent us from concluding that an argument with one of these forms is strong and what kind of additional information would not prevent us from doing so.

3.1 Statistical Syllogism

The first famous strong argument form is **statistical syllogism**. This argument form looks like this:

2.
> x% of A are B.
> Y is an A.
> So Y is a B.

In example 2, x is a number, A and B are categories, and Y is an individual. To be an instance of a statistical syllogism, the number used for x must be greater than 50 and less than 100.

Thus example 1 from the introduction to this chapter is an example of a statistical syllogism. In example 1, the number used for x is 95, category A is the category of those who have attempted the super-duper cheeseburger challenge, category B are those who had failed the challenge, and Y is Sam. The following subsections discuss in more detail how to identify statistical syllogisms and what kind of additional information does and does not threaten their strength.

3.1.1 Identifying Statistical Syllogisms

There are four features to look for when attempting to determine whether an argument is an instance of statistical syllogism. First, as we said earlier, the number used for x must be greater than 50 and less than 100. If the number used for x is equal to 50, equal to 100, or less than 50, then the argument is not a statistical syllogism. By definition, a statistical syllogism presents an argument that is strong in the absence of certain additional information. But an argument with the form of example 2 that uses a number for x that is equal to 50 or less than 50 is not a strong argument in the absence of certain additional information. Imagine that instead of example 1 we had:

3. Fifty percent of those who have taken on the super-duper giant cheese-burger challenge have failed to eat the entire cheeseburger. Sam took on the super-duper giant cheeseburger challenge. So Sam failed to eat the entire cheeseburger.

The premises of example 3 do not make the conclusion more likely than not in the absence of certain additional information. So we cannot conclude that example 3 is strong in the absence of certain additional information.

The reason an argument with the form of example 2 that uses a number for x equal to 100 is not strong is that such an argument is valid. Its premises guarantee its conclusion. Since no valid argument is strong, an argument with the form of example 2 that uses a number for x equal to 100 is not a statistical syllogism.

The second feature to look for when determining whether an argument is a statistical syllogism is that the number used for x can be imprecise. In other words, x can be a *range* of numbers, such as 60–80, as long as the numbers within this range are all greater than 50 and less than 100. Alternatively, an expression that can be *formulated* as a range of percentages between 50 and 100 can be used in place of $x\%$ in an argument with the form of example 2. For example, if instead of example 1 we had example 4, we would still have a statistical syllogism:

4. Most of those who have taken on the super-duper giant cheeseburger challenge have failed to eat the entire cheeseburger. Sam took on the super-duper giant cheeseburger challenge. So Sam failed to eat the entire cheeseburger.

"Most" can be formulated as "more than 50 percent and less than 100 per-cent." Other expressions such as "A majority of" can be used in a similar way to construct statistical syllogisms.

The third feature to look for when identifying statistical syllogisms is that their categories are used uniformly throughout. Compare example 1 with example 5:

5. Ninety-five percent of those we observed taking the super-duper giant cheeseburger challenge have failed to eat the entire cheeseburger. Sam took on the super-duper giant cheeseburger challenge. So Sam failed to eat the entire cheeseburger.

At first glance, you might think that example 5 and example 1 are equivalent. But the form of argument used in example 5 is actually quite different from that of example 1. The term used in place of letter A from the argument form of example 2 in the first premise of example 5 is "those *we observed* taking the super-duper giant cheeseburger challenge," whereas in premise 2 the term used in place of A is "those who *took* the super-duper giant cheeseburger challenge." A is not replaced consistently throughout example 5, whereas A *is* replaced consistently throughout example 1 with the same term: "those who took the super-duper giant cheeseburger challenge."

In some cases, it is reasonable to expect that all members of a category are members we have observed. But in many cases it is not. Depending on who the "we" represents in example 5, there may be quite a bit of difference between the categories of those who have attempted the challenge and those who "we" observed attempting it. If "we" is a group that is aware of only a very small percentage of those who have taken the challenge, then example 5 is quite different from example 1.

This is not to say that arguments with the form of example 5 cannot be strong. In section 2 we will learn how to use the information in the premises of example 5 to construct a more complex argument for its conclusion that we can conclude to be strong given certain restrictions. The point here is simply that arguments with the form of example 5 are not statistical syllogisms. This is because they replace the letters of the argument form of example 2 inconsistently.

The fourth feature to look for when discerning whether an argument is a statistical syllogism is that the categories employed by an argument may be complex categories. For example, consider this argument:

6. Most politicians are politicians who will alter their policy-making only to please those who can vote for them. Elana is a politician. So Elana is a politician who will alter her policy-making only to please those who can vote for her.

Here the category that stands in place of letter B in the argument form of example 2 is a complex category: the category of politicians who will alter their policy-making only to please those who can vote for them. As you attempt to discern whether arguments are statistical syllogisms, be on the lookout for complex categories like this.

3.1.2 *Evaluating Statistical Syllogisms for Strength*

Once we've determined that an argument has the form of a statistical syllogism, we can conclude that *in the absence of certain further information,* the argument is strong. What this suggests is that when evaluating statistical syllogisms, it is very important for us to consider whether such further information is available. If such information is available, then we cannot conclude that the argument in question is strong.

What kind of additional information can prevent us from concluding that a statistical syllogism is strong? We saw one prominent example in the chapter introduction. There we imagined that in addition to having the information that 95 percent of those who have taken the cheeseburger challenge have failed and Sam has taken the challenge, we had the further information that Sam is a world-champion competitive eater and 80 percent of world-champion competitive eaters who have taken the challenge have succeeded. We cannot conclude that the argument of example1 is strong given this further information.

Notice the structure that this information takes. The information tells us that Sam, the subject of the argument's conclusion, belongs to a category not named in the argument, and that a percentage that is at least as much as 50 percent of the members of this new category are not members of the category of those who have failed the challenge. More generally, we cannot conclude that a statistical syllogism with the form

x% of A are B.

Y is an A.

So Y is a B.

is strong if we have the additional information that

Y is a C, and at least 50% of C are ~B.

The "at least" here is important. If we know that at least 50 percent of world-champion competitive eaters who have taken the cheeseburger challenge did not fail, this implies that it is not the case that *more* than 50 percent of world-champion competitive eaters who have taken the cheeseburger challenge failed. At *most* 50 percent may have failed. And if at most 50 percent failed, then we cannot conclude in the absence of further information that it is more likely than not that Sam failed. It is at most equally likely. If the percentage of world-champion competitive eaters who have taken the cheeseburger challenge and did not fail is more than 50 percent, then in the absence of further information it is more likely than not that Sam succeeded—not more likely than not that he failed. The same holds more generally for other instances of Y and C plugged in to the schema above.

There are other ways to learn this same kind of information that may initially seem as if they involve learning a different kind of information that could challenge a statistical syllogism. Imagine that we had the information provided by example 1 and then learned that all the challenge-takers who failed were less than six feet tall and that Sam is not less than six feet tall. At first glance it may seem we aren't learning something about a category to which Sam belongs such that most of its members were not members of the category of failed contestants. We've just learned that Sam is a member of the category of those less than six feet tall. We don't know what percentage of those less than six feet tall failed the challenge. Very few people less than six feet tall may have taken the challenge.

Nonetheless, while the information does differ in this way from the information provided in our original challenge to the argument of example 1, this new information can also be made to fit the schema above. What it tells us is that Sam is a member of the complex category of *challenge-takers who are not less than six feet tall* and that all members of this category are members of the category of those who did not fail the challenge. Thus if we learned this information, it would challenge the strength of the argument in example 1 in the same basic way we saw earlier: by showing that the individual in question is a member of a category of which at least 50 percent of the members are not members of the category in the predicate of the conclusion. Indeed, the only kind of information that can prevent us from concluding that a statistical syllogism is strong is information that can be made to fit this schema. In the absence of such information, a statistical syllogism is strong.

Let's think through what kind of information might be provided to challenge the strength of the argument of example 6. Given our schema above, if we are to identify information that, when combined with the information provided by example 6, would not render its conclusion more likely than not, what we need is information fitting our schema above. That is, we need information that implies that Elana is a member of a category at least 50 percent of the members of which are not politicians who will alter their policy-making only to please those who can vote for them. Can you think of any category that would plausibly work here? Perhaps the category of "politicians who are immigrants" would be a good candidate. If those who were themselves immigrants can be expected to be more sensitive to the needs of other immigrants, and many immigrants cannot vote, then perhaps politicians who are immigrants can be expected to be sensitive to the needs of some who cannot vote—even sensitive enough to alter their policies for them. So here is an example of some information that could very well be true, and that, if true, would present a challenge to the strength of the argument of example 6:

7. Elana is a politician who is an immigrant, and at least 50 percent of politicians who are immigrants are not politicians who will alter their policy-making only to please those who can vote for them.

Key Ideas for Review

To claim that validity is **monotonic** is to claim that for any valid argument "P. So Q," the argument "P. R. So Q" is also valid, where P and Q are the same statements in each quotation and R is any statement whatsoever.

To claim that strength is **non-monotonic** is to claim that it is not the case that for any strong argument "P. So Q," any argument "P. R. So Q" is strong, where P and Q are the same statements in each quotation and R is any statement whatsoever.

A **famous strong argument form** is an argument form that is such that any argument with this form is strong in the absence of certain additional information.

A **statistical syllogism** is a famous strong argument form with the following form, where x is a number or range of numbers greater than 50 and less than 100, A and B are categories, and Y is an individual:

x% of A are B.
Y is an A.
So Y is a B.

We cannot conclude that a statistical syllogism with the above form is strong given further information of the form:

Y is a C and at least 50% of C are ~B.

Given the information provided by example 7, the argument of example 6 would not be strong. Thus when evaluating an argument like example 6, it is valuable to consider whether information like that provided by example 7 can be found. In the absence of information of this kind, arguments like example 6 are strong; however, given such information, we cannot conclude that they are.

3.1.3 Summary

In this section, we introduced the famous strong argument form of statistical syllogism. We explained how to identify statistical syllogisms, and we learned what kind of information can present a challenge to the strength of statistical syllogisms.

Exercise 3.1

A. Identifying Statistical Syllogisms. Determine whether the following arguments are statistical syllogisms. If an argument is not a statistical syllogism, explain why it is not. If an argument is a statistical syllogism, identify the terms used for x, A, B, and Y. If a statistical syllogism uses a word or phrase that can be formulated using a range of numbers for x, give the range.

1. One hundred percent of graduating students in the philosophy department have studied logic. Felicia is a graduating student in the philosophy department. So Felicia has studied logic.

2. Sixty percent of smokers eventually get lung cancer. Edward is a smoker. So Edward will eventually get lung cancer.

3. Eighty percent of restaurants in town that are open for lunch either close at 5:00 p.m. or do not allow children for dinner. Bennie's is a restaurant in town that is open for lunch. So Bennie's either closes at 5:00 p.m. or does not allow children for dinner.

4. Most syllabi for philosophy classes include few readings by female authors. The syllabus for Contemporary Moral Issues is a syllabus for a philosophy class. So the syllabus for Contemporary Moral Issues includes few readings by female authors.

5. Fifty percent of vegetarians are vegans. Noel is a vegetarian. So Noel is a vegan.

6. Sixty percent of stars thus far measured are larger than our sun. Polumbo is a star. So Polumbo is larger than our sun.

7. There are more bikers who are drinkers than bikers who are not drinkers, though not all bikers are drinkers. Richard is a biker. So Richard is a drinker.

8. Though some gun owners have not had accidents with their guns, at least as many gun owners have had accidents with their guns as have not had accidents with their guns. Priscilla is a gun owner. So Priscilla has had an accident with her gun.

9. Fifty-one percent of travelers have gotten a prohibited item past the Transportation Security Administration (TSA) unintentionally. Stella is a traveler. So Stella has gotten a prohibited item past TSA unintentionally.

10. Eighty to ninety percent of college applicants will change their intended major. James is a college applicant. So James will change his intended major.

B. Evaluating Statistical Syllogisms. For each of the following statistical syllogisms, identify a further item of information that could well be true and that is such that, given its truth, we cannot conclude that the syllogism is strong.

1. Most of the original twelve disciples gave their lives out of loyalty to Jesus. Judas was one of the original twelve disciples. So Judas gave his life out of loyalty to Jesus.

2. Seventy-five percent of philosophy departments that have recently hired a new staff member have hired a female. The philosophy department at Philosophy of Science Forever University is a philosophy department that recently hired a new staff member. So the philosophy department at Philosophy of Science Forever University hired a female.

3. A majority of events that were once attributed to a supernatural agent can now be explained adequately without appealing to a supernatural agent. The origin of the universe was once attributed to a supernatural agent. So the origin of the universe can now be explained adequately without appealing to a supernatural agent.

4. Most people who bought a house last year got an income tax refund. The people who bought the large house down the street bought a house last year. So the people who bought the large house down the street got an income tax refund.

5. Fifty-one percent of people who claim that someone rose from the dead are insane. Peter claimed that someone rose from the dead. So Peter was insane.

6. Eighty to ninety percent of people who live within two miles of the university cycle to work on sunny days. Max lives within two miles of the university. So Max cycles to work on sunny days.

7. More than 50 percent of newspaper articles in the United Kingdom that mention a Muslim are negative press, though not all are. The article "Imam Saves Puppy" is a newspaper article in the United Kingdom that mentions a Muslim. So the article "Imam Saves Puppy" is negative press.

8. Nearly all humans have sinned. Jesus was a human. So Jesus sinned.

9. Ninety-five percent of lawyers will earn more money this year than they did last year. Philip is a lawyer. So Philip will earn more money this year than he did last year.

10. Most religions have a message that contains false claims. Christianity is a religion. So Christianity has a message that contains false claims.

3.2 Induction by Enumeration

This section introduces a second famous strong argument form: **induction by enumeration**. Arguments that exhibit this form employ the following pattern:

1.

$x\%$ of a sample of A are B.
So $x\%$ of A are B.

Here x is any number or range of numbers between zero and one hundred, inclusive, and A and B are categories.

The following arguments each exhibit the form of induction by enumeration:

2.
> Fifty percent of smokers studied in a recent survey were also drinkers.
> So fifty percent of smokers are drinkers.

3.
> Zero percent of Christian students recently polled support going to war.
> So zero percent of Christian students support going to war.

4.
> Eighty to one hundred percent of the first five exams the professor graded received a ninety percent or above.
> So eighty to one hundred percent of the exams the professor graded received a ninety percent or above.

3.2.1 Key Features of Induction by Enumeration

Several features of arguments that exhibit induction by enumeration are worth pointing out. First, the pattern of reasoning used in an argument that employs induction by enumeration involves drawing a conclusion about an entire class or category of things on the basis of a claim about a sample, or subset, of items within that category. For example, the argument in example 2 draws a conclusion about the entire category of smokers on the basis of a claim about the subset of smokers who were studied in a recent survey. Example 3 draws a conclusion about the entire population of Christian students on the basis of a claim about a sample of those students recently polled. This kind of argument can be very useful because it allows us to extrapolate wider-ranging claims from limited sets of data.

Second, notice that unlike in the argument form of statistical syllogism, the argument form of induction by enumeration uses a percentage in both its premise and its conclusion. Moreover, this percentage must be the same in the premise and in the conclusion. As with a statistical syllogism, the percentage may be imprecise. For example, in example 4 the percentage is a range between eighty and one hundred. Similarly, terms that represent a range of percentages can be employed in arguments that use induction by enumeration. Thus we might have replaced example 2 with:

5.
> Exactly as many smokers studied in a recent study were drinkers as were not drinkers.
> So exactly as many smokers are drinkers as are not drinkers.

Example 5 has the same meaning as example 2 and is an example of induction by enumeration.

Third, as examples 2–4 make quite clear, the number (or phrase) used for x is less restricted than it was in the case of statistical syllogism. It can be anywhere between zero and one hundred, inclusive—meaning that any number that is either zero, one hundred, or between zero and one hundred is acceptable.

Fourth, it should be emphasized again that what is substituted not only for x but also for A and B must be substituted uniformly throughout an argument if the argument is to be an example of induction by enumeration. Imagine that instead of example 2 we had:

6.

> Fifty percent of smokers studied in a recent survey reported that they are also drinkers.
>
> So fifty percent of smokers are drinkers.

Example 6 is very similar to example 2, and one might easily conclude that they are the exact same argument. But drawing this conclusion would be a mistake. Example 2 uniformly substitutes "drinkers" for letter B in the argument form of example 1, while example 6 does not. Example 6 replaces letter B in the premise of the argument form of example 1 with "people who reported being drinkers," while it replaces letter B in the conclusion of the argument form of example 1 with "drinkers." This failure to replace letter B uniformly creates a significant difference between example 2 and example 6. It very well could be that the percentage of smokers who will report that they are drinkers is not equivalent to the percentage of smokers who are drinkers. Perhaps for certain psychological reasons, people will shy away from reporting truthfully that they are drinkers, for example. Thus it is important when identifying arguments as instances of induction by enumeration that we take care to ensure that they uniformly replace the letters in the argument form of example 1.[1]

When we keep these four features of arguments that employ induction by enumeration in mind, such arguments will not be difficult to identify as instances of this famous strong argument form.

3.2.2 Evaluating Induction by Enumeration for Strength

As we have seen, to say that induction by enumeration is a strong argument form is to say that in the absence of certain further information, we may conclude that arguments that exhibit this form are strong. Thus we may conclude that in the absence of certain further information, the arguments in examples 2–4 are strong. Yet, as we saw also with statistical syllogisms, further information can prevent us from concluding that arguments with the form of induction by enumeration are strong.

Return to example 3, the argument about Christian students who overwhelmingly do not support going to war. Suppose that in addition to the information provided by the premise—that 0 percent of the Christian students recently polled support going to war—we also had the following item of information: the students who were polled were exclusively Christian students who are members of the Christian Pacifists Club. It is plausible that we could not reasonably conclude that the argument in example 3 is strong given this further information, since it is plausible that the percentage of Christian students who are members of the Christian Pacifists Club who support going to war is lower than the percentage of Christian students generally who oppose going to war. The sample of Christian students who were polled—a sample that included only members of the Christian Pacifists Club—is plausibly not a sample that is representative of the whole group in question. The sample is likely to differ from the entire group with respect to the feature with which the argument is concerned—support for the war. If so, then we cannot conclude that the argument in example 3 is strong given this further information.

Similarly, take example 2 about the smokers and drinkers. Suppose that, in addition to the information provided by the premise of this argument, we learned that the population of smokers surveyed included only smokers who were carrying brown paper bags outside convenience stores. Plausibly, we could not conclude that example 2 was a strong argument given this further information, for, plausibly, the subgroup of smokers who carry brown paper bags outside convenience stores is not representative of the whole group of smokers with respect to whether they are drinkers. Indeed, plausibly, smokers seen carrying a brown paper bag outside a convenience store are more likely than other smokers to be drinkers. Thus it would be problematic to conclude that example 2 is a strong argument given this further information.

Finally, consider again example 4 about the first five student exams. Imagine that, in addition to the information provided by the premise of this argument, we learned that the instructor has employed the practice of grading his students' exams following the order in which they are turned in. Thus the first five exams he grades are the first five exams turned in. Imagine, moreover, that we learn that earlier exams are more likely to score high than later exams—perhaps because the students who complete them have mastered the requisite skills and are confident in their answers, leading them to turn in the exams earlier. We could not conclude that example 4 was a strong argument given this further information. Again, the sample of exams with which the premise is concerned is unlikely to be representative of the whole stack of exams with respect to the relevant feature, their score.

The above examples of information that can undermine the strength of an argument have something in common. In each case, the additional information provides reason for thinking that the sample selected in the first premise of the relevant argument is not a representative sample. That is, with respect to the relevant category substituted for B in the argument form of example 1, the percentage of the sample that belongs to this category is likely to differ significantly from the percentage of the total group that belong to this category. In our example involving the argument from example 3 (about Christian students who oppose war), the information provided reason to think the percentage of the sample likely to belong to the relevant category was significantly *lower* than the percentage of the whole group likely to belong to the category. In our example involving the argument from example 4 (about student exam scores), the percentage of the sample likely to belong to the relevant category was significantly *higher* than the percentage of the total group likely to belong to this category. Thus, generally speaking, we can identify information that presents a challenge to the strength of an argument that employs the form of induction by enumeration if the information provides reason for thinking that the sample identified in the premise of the argument is not a representative sample.

Not just any information about a difference between a sample and a total group will show that the sample is not representative, however. Imagine that in addition to the information provided by the premise of example 2, we also learned that all the smokers studied were people who sit rather than stand when working at an office computer. If we don't have any further information that provides reason to think that those who sit when working at an office computer are any more or less likely to be drinkers than those who stand when working at an office computer, then this additional information will not present any challenge to the strength of the argument in example 2. Without such further information, the additional information provided will not provide a reason to think that the sample is not representative. Given only this additional information, that the members of the sample in example 2 sit when working at an office computer, the argument in example 2 remains strong. What is necessary in order to present a challenge to the strength of an argument that employs induction by enumeration, then, is information that provides reason for thinking that the sample identified by the premise of the argument is not representative of the whole population with respect to the category used by the argument in place of letter B in the argument form of example 1.

It is sometimes thought that in addition to information that provides reason to think that a sample is not representative, information about the size of the sample employed in an argument that uses induction by enumeration can present a challenge to the strength of this argument. Imagine that in addition to the information provided by example 3, we learned that of the entire population of three thousand Christian students, the size of the sample referenced in the premise of example 3 was only five students. All five students did not support going to war. Sometimes it is thought that we cannot conclude that an instance of induction by enumeration is strong if we learn that the sample size is only such a small proportion of the total population. Here, for example, we cannot conclude that the argument of example 3 is strong given this information that the sample size is only five students out of three thousand.

Learning that a sample size cited in an instance of induction by enumeration is small does provide important information that can be quite relevant for determining whether the argument is strong. It would be a mistake to overlook such information in our evaluation of the strength of instances of induction by enumeration when it is available. However, we must be careful about inferring directly that an instance of induction by enumeration is not strong given such additional information. Indeed, it would be a mistake to conclude that given only this information about sample size and no further information beyond it, an instance of induction by enumeration is not strong. It is only when this information about sample size is combined with additional information that provides reason to think the sample is not representative that a challenge to the argument's strength has been identified.

To see why this is so, consider again the example just introduced. Imagine that all we know is that there is a group of three thousand Christian students, and that five members—about which we know nothing further—of the group were recently surveyed and all do not support going to war. This is *all* the information we have to go on. And imagine that we must make a bet on whether the entire population does not support going to war. We propose here that if we dutifully exclude any additional information, the safer bet would be that the entire population does not support going to war.

You might be tempted to disagree. However, our suggestion here is that any temptation to disagree is likely driven by an unnoticed temptation to include additional information beyond the information stated in the previous paragraph when assessing the strength of the argument. For example, you might be tempted, when evaluating the argument, to include your background knowledge of the fact that in a large population, regardless of how similar the members are, there is almost certainly going to be disagreement about whether to support going to war. We grant that we cannot conclude that the argument of example 3 is strong given *this* additional information. However, this information was not included in the information supplied in the previous paragraph. It is information that goes beyond the mere fact about the small sample size introduced there.

The point is this: information that a sample size is small does not all by itself present a challenge to the strength of an instance of induction by enumeration. Given only such information and no further information, we are still in a position to judge that the argument is strong. That is, its conclusion is more likely than not given its premises—even if it is only slightly more likely than not. However, when further information is introduced—even information that might seem obvious, like the information cited in the previous paragraph—we can then be in a position to no longer conclude that the argument is strong. But this occurs only if the additional information provides reason to think that the sample (whatever its size) is not representative. Thus, quite plausibly, the only way to present a challenge to the strength of an instance of induction by enumeration is to identify information that provides reason to think that the sample is not representative. In the exercises below, when asked to identify information that is such that we cannot conclude that an argument is strong given this information, the information you should provide is information that provides reason to think that the sample cited in the argument is not representative.

3.2.3 Combining Induction by Enumeration and Statistical Syllogism

We conclude this section by showing how arguments can combine instances of induction by enumeration and statistical syllogism in an interesting way. To see this, return to an example used in the previous section:

7. Ninety-five percent of those we observed taking the super-duper giant cheeseburger challenge have failed to eat the entire cheeseburger. Sam took on the super-duper giant cheeseburger challenge. So Sam failed to eat the entire cheeseburger.

We said in the previous section that example 7 is not an instance of a statistical syllogism because the category substituted for letter A in the argument form for statistical syllogisms is not substituted uniformly throughout the argument. In premise 1, the category substituted for letter A is "those we observed taking the super-duper giant cheeseburger challenge," while in premise 2 the category is "those who took on the super-duper giant cheeseburger challenge." Nonetheless, we suggested there that arguments of this form can be strong, given certain restrictions. We can see how by restating the information of example 7 with a combination of induction by enumeration and statistical syllogism.

Notice that the first premise in example 7 is concerned with a sample of those who have attempted the cheeseburger challenge. Thus given what we've learned in this chapter, we could employ this premise to construct an argument for a conclusion about the entire population of those who have taken on the cheeseburger challenge using induction by enumeration. It would look like this:

8.

> Ninety-five percent of those we observed taking the super-duper giant
> cheeseburger challenge have failed to eat the entire cheeseburger.
> So ninety-five percent of those who have taken the super-duper giant
> cheeseburger challenge have failed to eat the entire cheeseburger.

Since the conclusion of example 8 offers us information about the entire
population of those who have taken on the cheeseburger challenge, and since
example 7 tells us that Sam is a member of this population, the conclusion
of example 8 can be employed alongside the information from example 7 to
construct an instance of statistical syllogism, as follows:

9.

> Ninety-five percent of those who have taken the super-duper giant cheese-
> burger challenge have failed to eat the entire cheeseburger.
> Sam took the super-duper giant cheeseburger challenge.
> So Sam failed to eat the entire cheeseburger.

We can combine examples 8 and 9 in such a way that we get two conclusions. The first of the two we call a **subconclusion**, because it is *a conclusion
in an argument that is itself used as a premise in defense of another conclusion*. The resulting argument would be:

10.

> Ninety-five percent of those we observed taking the super-duper giant
> cheeseburger challenge have failed to eat the entire cheeseburger.
> So ninety-five percent of those who have taken the super-duper giant
> cheeseburger challenge have failed to eat the entire cheeseburger.
> Sam took the super-duper giant cheeseburger challenge.
> So Sam failed to eat the entire cheeseburger.

In example 10, we use an instance of induction by enumeration to defend
a subconclusion about the entire population of those who have taken on
the cheeseburger challenge. We then employ this subconclusion to present a
statistical syllogism defending the conclusion that Sam failed the challenge.

Arguments with the form of example 10 are strong given three requirements.
First, with respect to the argument employed to defend the subconclusion of
such arguments, the kind of information that would challenge the strength of
these arguments must not be present. More specifically, information that provides reason to believe that the sample in question is not representative of the

entire population cannot be present. Second, with respect to the part of these arguments that employs the subconclusion to defend the main conclusion, the kind of information that threatens the strength of statistical syllogisms cannot be present. That is, there cannot be reason to think that the individual in question belongs to an unnamed category that is at most 50 percent likely to belong to the relevant category. Here, for example, there cannot be information that provides reason to think that Sam belongs to a category whose members are at most 50 percent likely to have failed the challenge.

Thus far these requirements have introduced nothing new beyond what we have learned earlier in discussing statistical syllogism and induction by enumeration. A third requirement, however, does introduce something new. The third requirement is that the result of multiplying the likelihood of the subconclusion given the first premise by the likelihood of the main conclusion given the subconclusion *and* last premise is not 50 percent or lower. This requirement is important because there can be cases where the subconclusion is more than 50 percent likely given the first premise, and where the main conclusion is more than 50 percent likely given the subconclusion and last premise, but where the argument is not strong because the conclusion is not more likely than not given the premises.

The general problem at work here is known as the **problem of dwindling probabilities**. One way to state this problem is that *in any argument that employs a subconclusion, and in which the premises offer merely probabilistic support for the subconclusion and the main conclusion, the probability of the main conclusion given the premises that are not subconclusions is lower than the probability of the subconclusion given those premises used to defend it.* As we work our way through the argument, the probability of each conclusion dwindles, even though every conclusion drawn throughout the argument is drawn on the basis of a strong argument.

Consider the following example:

11.

A fair six-sided die was tossed.
So it landed on a number between 1 and 4.
So it landed on a number between 1 and 3.

In example 11, the first premise makes the subconclusion more likely than not. Given that the die really is fair, and so there's an equal chance for each of the numbers 1–6 to turn up, it is more likely than not that the number that turns up is between 1 and 4. Likewise, the main conclusion is more likely than not given the subconclusion. Given that the die lands on a number between 1 and 4, it is more likely than not that it lands on a number between 1 and 3. Yet the conclusion of example 11 is *not* more likely than not given the premises of the argument that are not subconclusions. That is, given only that a far six-sided die was tossed, it is not more likely than not that it landed on a number between 1 and 3. It is equally likely that it did and that it didn't. The argument from "A fair six-sided die was tossed" to "So it landed on a number between 1 and 3" is not strong.

Again, the problem here is that when we attempt to determine the precise probability of the conclusion given the premises in arguments like examples 10 and 11, we must do so by *multiplying* two other probabilities. Specifically, we multiply the probability of the subconclusion given the premises on which it is based by the probability of the main conclusion given the subconclusion and any other premises used to defend the main conclusion. In example 11, these probabilities are 66 percent, or .66, and 75 percent, or .75. When we multiply .66 and .75, we get .5, or 50 percent. Thus in example 11, even though both the subconclusion and the main conclusion are more probable than not given the claims on which they are immediately based, the main conclusion is not more probable than not given those premises of the argument that are not also subconclusions. For this reason, the argument in example 11 is not strong.

Similarly, in assessing the argument of example 10, we must ask what the result is of multiplying the probability of the subconclusion given those premises on which it is based by the probability of the main conclusion given the subconclusion and the last premise. Notably, this requirement highlights in a different way than we noted earlier the importance of sample size. Earlier we proposed that in the absence of any additional information, knowledge that a sample size is very small does not render an instance of induction by enumeration weak. At most, it will show that its conclusion is only slightly more probable than not given its premises. However, this fact can be important if induction by enumeration is employed as part of a more complex argument like example 10. Imagine that in example 10 the sample size of those cheeseburger-eating contestants we have observed is an extremely small percentage of the total. Thus the probability of the subconclusion given the first premise, while higher than 50 percent, may not be *much* higher. Suppose it is 51 percent. And suppose that we accept that given the subconclusion and the final premise, the probability of the conclusion is 95 percent. In order to determine whether the argument of example 10 is strong in this case, we'll need to multiply 95 percent, or .95, by 51 percent, or .51. The result is .48, or 48 percent, which yields a weak argument. In this way, while small sample sizes do not by themselves present a challenge to the strength of instances of induction by enumeration, they can lead to problems for complex arguments that use induction by enumeration to defend subconclusions.

Key Ideas for Review

Induction by enumeration is a strong argument form employing the following pattern of reasoning, where x is any number between 0 and 100, inclusive, and A and B are categories:

x% of a sample of A are B.
So x% of A are B.

Any argument that employs induction by enumeration is strong in the absence of information that provides reason to think that the sample of A it cites is not representative of the entire population of A with respect to category B. A sample of A is not representative of the entire population of A with respect to category B when the likelihood that a member of the sample of A is a member of B differs from the likelihood that a member of A is a member of B.

Complex arguments can be formed that employ both an instance of induction by enumeration and an instance of a statistical syllogism. Even if each conclusion in such an argument is defended by a strong argument, we cannot conclude that the argument itself is strong if the result of multiplying the probability of its subconclusion given the premises on which it is based by the probability of the main conclusion given the premises on which it is based is at most 50 percent.

A **subconclusion** is a conclusion in an argument that is itself used as a premise in defense of another conclusion.

The **problem of dwindling probabilities** is a problem in which in any argument that employs a subconclusion, and in which the premises offer merely probabilistic support for the subconclusion and the main conclusion, the probability of the main conclusion given the premises that are not subconclusions is lower than the probability of the subconclusion given those premises used to defend it.

3.2.4 Summary

This section introduced the argument form induction by enumeration. We identified characteristic features of arguments that employ induction by enumeration, and we learned that instances of induction by enumeration are strong in the absence of information that provides reason for thinking that the samples they reference are not representative samples. We further saw how instances of induction by enumeration can be combined with statistical syllogisms to form complex arguments that are strong given three requirements, the last of which concerned the problem of dwindling probabilities.

Exercise 3.2

A. Identifying Induction by Enumeration. For each of the following arguments, determine whether the argument is an instance of induction by enumeration. If it is, identify the number, or phrase, employed for x and the categories employed for A and B.

1.

   Zero percent of terrorist attacks recently studied were religiously motivated.
   So zero percent of terrorist attacks are religiously motivated.

2.

   Twenty-five percent of reported extraterrestrial sightings occurred in Nevada.
   So twenty-five percent of extraterrestrial sightings occurred in Nevada.

3.

   Fifty percent of humans aged 25 are female.
   So fifty-one percent of humans aged 26 are female.

4.

   One hundred percent of elephants in this year's circus have scars.
   So one hundred percent of elephants have scars.

5.

   Seventy-five percent of philosophy professors have a PhD.
   So seventy-five percent of professors have a PhD.

6.

   Eighty percent of students whose last names begin with the letters A–K passed the exam.
   So eighty percent of students whose last names begin with the letters L–Z passed the exam.

7.

   No more than eighty percent of ancient manuscripts attributed to Herodotus were written by the author to whom they were attributed.
   So no more than eighty percent of ancient manuscripts were written by the author to whom they were attributed.

8.

   Most pregnant women recently surveyed had late-night cravings.
   So most pregnant women have late-night cravings.

9.

   Most participants in this year's clinical research trial reported anxiety.
   So most participants in clinical research trials experience anxiety.

10.

   Of the personal trainers who were recently surveyed, as many preferred working weekends rather than weekdays as preferred working weekdays rather than weekends, and all had one preference or the other.
   So fifty percent of personal trainers prefer working weekends rather than weekdays.

B. Evaluating Induction by Enumeration. For each of the following arguments, identify an item of further information that is such that it could well be true, and such that we cannot conclude that the argument is strong given that this information is correct.

1.

Ninety percent of philosophy professors studied logic.
So ninety percent of professors studied logic.

2.

One hundred percent of nonbiblical sacred writings are fallible.
So one hundred percent of sacred writings are fallible.

3.

Ten percent of extreme sports cyclists ride without a helmet.
So ten percent of cyclists ride without a helmet.

4.

Eighty percent of people in North America have heard the gospel.
So eighty percent of people in the world have heard the gospel.

5.

Seventy percent of divinity school students who graduate do not believe in the historicity of the resurrection.
So seventy percent of divinity school students do not believe in the historicity of the resurrection.

6.

One hundred percent of observed entities can be seen.
So one hundred percent of all entities can be seen.

7.

Ninety-five percent of events that were attributed to supernatural causation in 500 BC have nonsupernatural explanations.
So ninety-five percent of events that are attributed to supernatural causation have nonsupernatural explanations.

8.

One hundred percent of hot drinks at the local café are served with caffeine.
So one hundred percent of hot drinks are served with caffeine.

9.

Twenty percent of recent superhero movies have a lead protagonist with no obvious major moral failings.
So twenty percent of superhero movies have a lead protagonist with no obvious major moral failings.

10.

Ten percent of video-game players in 1995 were female.

So ten percent of video-game players are female.

C. Complex Arguments. Each of the following arguments can be transformed into an argument that employs one instance of induction by enumeration and one instance of statistical syllogism. First, transform each argument so that it fits this pattern. Second, highlight three items of further information that are such that we cannot conclude that the argument is strong given that this information is true.

1.

Ninety percent of self-supporting foreign missionaries take more than a year to gain facility in the language of the people group they have joined.

Alexandra is a foreign missionary.

So Alexandra took more than a year to gain facility in the language of the people group she joined.

2.

Seventy percent of recovering alcoholics recently surveyed had succumbed to the temptation to drink.

Joe is a recovering alcoholic.

So Joe has succumbed to the temptation to drink.

3.

One hundred percent of previously studied ancient copies of the book of Matthew exhibit a standard deviation from one another of 1 percent or less.

The recently discovered text is an ancient copy of the book of Matthew.

So the recently discovered text exhibits a standard deviation from other ancient copies of the book of Matthew of 1 percent or less.

4.

Eighty percent of philosophers with a permanent academic job do not believe in God.

John is a philosopher.

So John does not believe in God.

5.

One hundred percent of those who played the lottery by placing their bets at the corner store did not win.

Stephen played the lottery.

So Stephen did not win.

3.3 Arguments from Authority

This section introduces a third strong argument form, the argument from authority. This argument form is exactly what it sounds like: an **argument from authority** is *an argument that concludes that something is true because an authority on the subject has asserted that it is*. The argument form of argument from authority can be stated as follows, where X is an authority on whether P is true, and P is a statement:

1.

    X asserts P.

    So P.

Arguments from authority are very commonly employed and can be quite useful in the process of seeking the truth. Below we discuss three key features of arguments from authority, identify two ways that the strength of an argument from authority can be challenged, and identify one way in which arguments from authority can be combined with other famous strong argument forms to form complex argument forms that are strong given certain requirements.

3.3.1 Authorities, Assertion, and What Is Asserted

There are three key features of arguments from authority. The first is that in order for an instance of the argument form of example 1 to be an argument from authority, the person substituted for X must be an authority on whether P is the case. What is required for a person to be an authority may be less than you would expect. An **authority** about a statement P is *someone who is more likely than not to have a true belief about whether P is true*. To be an authority on whether P is the case, it is simply required that a person is more likely to have a true belief about whether P is the case than to not have a true belief about whether P is the case. The reason for this is that, plausibly, if someone who is more likely to have a true belief about P than not asserts that P is the case, then in the absence of additional information, it is more likely than not that P is the case. We might describe a person who is an authority about whether P is the case as being well-positioned to believe the truth about P. When a person who is well-positioned to believe the truth about P asserts that P is the case, it is more likely than not that P is the case in the absence of

124

any additional information. Betting that P is the case given only this information has better odds than betting that P is not the case.

It's worth pointing out that this somewhat minimal description of what it takes for someone to be an authority may help to explain the widespread use, and indeed the widespread usefulness, of arguments from authority. For example, given this minimal account of what it is to be an authority, all of us are quite plausibly authorities on a wide range of matters—everything from what we ate for breakfast this morning to facts about our family life to facts about the fields in which we work. Arguments from authority that are strong in the absence of further information can therefore be generated by citing what we have asserted about such matters. For example, if you've asserted that you ate a bagel for breakfast, we could construct the following argument from authority:

2.

> You asserted that you ate a bagel for breakfast.
>
> So you ate a bagel for breakfast.

In the absence of further information, we should conclude that this argument from authority is strong.

While there is a wide range of matters about which each of us is more likely to have a true belief than not, there are also matters about which we are not more likely than not to have a true belief. For example, I personally have very little knowledge of the most popular "boy bands" of today. So if I were to assert something about the most popular boy bands of today, you would not succeed in constructing an argument from authority by appealing to what I had said. By substituting me for X and a claim about the most popular boy bands of today for P in example 1, you would not get an argument from authority, because I am not an authority on these boy bands. I am not more likely than not to have a true belief about them. This mistake is often called the fallacy of an **appeal to an unqualified authority**, which is *an informal fallacy that employs the form of an argument from authority but substitutes someone for X who is not an authority about whether P is the case.*

A second feature of arguments from authority is that the authority selected must have asserted that P. To **assert** that P is *to present P as if it is true*. Many times when we make statements, this is precisely what we do: present the statements we are making as true. But sometimes this is not what we are doing. Knowing what you do about my knowledge of boy bands, for instance, imagine that I said, "Sally asserted of me that I know everything there is to know about today's most popular boy bands." It would be a mistake to conclude from this that I had *asserted* that I know everything there is to know about today's most popular boy bands. It's true that what I asserted contained this statement as a component. However, I did not assert *this* statement; rather, I asserted the larger statement that contains it—a statement about what Sally (mistakenly) asserted.

What this example illustrates is that we must be careful when claiming that an authority has asserted something. While it is often the case that statements we utter are assertions, sometimes the statements we utter are not assertions; we are not presenting them as true. Unfortunately, the kind of example just cited, where an utterance is taken out of context and attributed to an authority as if he had asserted it, occurs all too commonly in our contemporary political discourse.

A final, related feature of arguments from authority is that what the authority is cited as asserting must match what is concluded to be the case. As an illustration of the importance of this feature, imagine that Fred, an expert on today's most popular boy bands, asserted, "It's unclear whether any of today's most popular boy bands will be involved in the charity concert." Imagine further that someone attempted to construct an argument from authority appealing to Fred's assertion as follows:

3.

Fred asserted that it is unclear whether any of today's most popular boy bands will be involved in the charity concert.

So none of today's most popular boy bands will be involved in the charity concert.

While the form of example 3 resembles the form of example 1, example 3 is not an argument from authority since the statement substituted for P in the premise of example 3 does not match the statement substituted for P in the conclusion. The statement substituted for P in the premise is "it is unclear whether any of today's most popular boy bands will be involved in the charity concert," whereas the statement substituted for P in the conclusion is "none of today's most popular boy bands will be involved in the charity concert." These statements are not equivalent. Indeed, if one of the bands wanted to keep their involvement a secret, and if Fred was suspicious of this, we might easily imagine Fred asserting, "It is unclear whether any of today's most popular boy bands will be involved in the charity concert, but this is just what we should expect given the penchant these bands have for surprise." And this assertion would provide evidence against the conclusion of example 3. The moral here is that when constructing arguments from authority, we must be careful to conclude only what the authority has said—not something similar but not equivalent to what the authority has said.

3.3.2 *Evaluating Arguments from Authority*

Once we've identified an argument from authority, the next step is to evaluate it for strength. As with other instances of strong argument forms, any argument from authority is strong in the absence of certain further information. Our aim in this section is to identify the form that additional information must take if it is to present a challenge to the strength of an argument from authority.

One kind of further information that can present a challenge to an argument from authority is information that provides reason to think that the authority's assertion is not aimed at providing true information. Sometimes, even though an authority presents something as true, the authority does not do so with the aim of providing truthful information to the intended audience. More specifically, the authority does not do so with the aim of providing *what has been asserted* as truthful information to the intended audience.

Imagine that in addition to the information provided by the premise of example 2, we learn that you have just been invited to grab a bagel for lunch, that you very much do not like bagels, and that in order to get out of eating things that you don't like, you very frequently falsely claim that you have just eaten the food item that you don't want to eat. It would be a mistake for us to conclude that example 2 is a strong argument given this further information. This further information provides reason for us to think that while you *presented* the claim that you ate a bagel for breakfast as true, in doing so you did not aim to provide this claim to us as truthful information. Indeed, you aimed to provide it to us as false information that we would believe and on the basis of which we would perhaps search for a different lunch option. While you are an authority on whether you ate a bagel for breakfast, and while you asserted that you ate a bagel, given this further information about your dislike of bagels and your tendency to make false assertions about what you've recently eaten, we cannot conclude that it is more likely than not that you ate a bagel for breakfast.

As we've suggested, this example provides an illustration of a more general phenomenon—namely, that sometimes we can have reason to think that a person is not making an assertion with the aim of providing what is asserted as truthful information to the intended audience. One way in which this can occur, as in the previous example, is if we have reason to think that the authority is aiming to provide the asserted statement as false information. There are other ways too. An authority might not be aiming to provide the assertion as information at all but may be motivated to make the assertion for a reason that has nothing to do with intentions to provide information. For example, if one is an authority on a particular matter and is threatened by someone powerful to make an assertion about that matter, the authority might make this assertion without aiming to provide what is asserted as truthful information. One can imagine many such cases in which the information cited provides reason to think that the authority did not make the assertion with the intention of providing what was asserted as truthful information.

We might call the kind of information provided by the first type of challenge to the strength of an argument from authority an undercutting defeater for the argument. An **undercutting defeater** is *any information that undercuts the support that the premises of an argument provide for its conclusion without providing direct support for the denial of the conclusion.* In the above example, that an assertion was made under duress undercuts an argument from authority that appeals to this assertion, but this fact doesn't provide direct support for the denial of the conclusion. Perhaps what the authority asserts under duress is what the authority would have asserted if aiming to provide truthful information freely as well.

Another, distinct kind of challenge to arguments from authority provides what we might call a rebutting defeater to them. A **rebutting defeater** is *any information that challenges the support an argument's premises provide for its conclusion by directly providing support for the denial of that conclusion.* One interesting form this kind of challenge can take when applied to arguments from authority is when the information provided itself comes in the form of a competing argument from authority. Imagine that in addition to the information provided by example 2, we learned that your friend Sue, who was present with you during breakfast and is a competent judge of breakfast foods, has asserted that you ate an English muffin rather than a bagel. With this information we might construct the following competing argument from authority:

4.

Sue asserts that you ate an English muffin rather than a bagel for breakfast.

So you ate an English muffin rather than a bagel for breakfast.

Example 4 is an argument from authority that, in the absence of other information, provides support for the denial of the conclusion of example 2. When we are faced with competing arguments from authority of this kind, in the absence of further information, we cannot conclude that either argument is strong. Here, we cannot conclude that example 2 is a strong argument given the availability of example 4, and we cannot conclude that example 4 is a strong argument given the availability of example 2.

Sometimes information becomes available that enables us to break the tie between two competing arguments from authority. If we learned, for example, that while both you and Sue are more likely than not to have a true belief about what you ate for breakfast, but that you are significantly more likely than Sue is to have a true belief about this, then the tie between the arguments in examples 2 and 4 would be broken in favor of example 2. In the absence of such additional information, however, when we have available information provided by a competing argument from authority, we are put in a position where we can no longer conclude that the argument we are evaluating is strong. This is because we have direct support for the denial of that argument's conclusion, and we do not have reason to think that the support is weaker than the support provided in favor of the conclusion by the original argument from authority.

Other kinds of information can supply a rebutting defeater for an argument from authority. Generally speaking, for any argument from authority for a claim P, the availability of any information that can be used to construct a sound argument for not-P, or an argument for not-P that is cogent in the absence of the information provided by the argument from authority in question, presents a challenge to the strength of the argument from authority. We cannot conclude that the argument is strong given this further information. For example, if in addition to the information provided by example 2, we learned that you ate breakfast in your kitchen and that there were no bagels in your kitchen when you ate breakfast, then we could not conclude that example 2 is a strong argument since we would have a sound argument for the denial of its conclusion.

Any information that can be used to challenge the strength of an argument from authority will be of one of the two forms highlighted here. Either it will be information that provides reason to think that what the authority asserted was not asserted with the aim of providing truthful information to the intended audience (an undercutting defeater), or it will be information that provides support for a denial of the argument's conclusion (a rebutting defeater).

3.3.3 Complex Arguments Using Arguments from Authority

Arguments from authority can be combined with other argument forms to compose complex arguments that are strong given certain requirements. For example, return to an argument we discussed briefly in the previous section:

5.

Fifty percent of smokers studied in a recent survey reported that they are also drinkers.

So fifty percent of smokers are drinkers.

129

We observed in the previous section that this argument is not an instance of induction by enumeration because the category to which 50 percent of smokers recently surveyed are said to belong in the premise is not the same category as the category to which 50 percent of smokers are said to belong in the conclusion. The premise is concerned with the category of those who *reported* that they are drinkers, while the conclusion is concerned with the category of drinkers.

The relationship between these two categories should immediately catch our attention given that we have just discussed arguments from authority, since arguments from authority are precisely concerned with drawing inferences from what people report or assert to what is in fact the case. Thus arguments from authority can be employed in order to reconstruct arguments like example 5 into arguments that are strong given certain requirements.

Let's think about how to transform example 5 in a useful way. If we assume, as seems reasonable, that the smokers studied in the recent survey are more likely than not to have true beliefs about whether they are drinkers, then it follows that these smokers are authorities about whether they are drinkers. Thus we can employ assertions or reports of theirs to generate an argument from authority for the conclusion that they are drinkers. Since 50 percent asserted that they were drinkers, we can form an argument from authority for the conclusion that 50 percent of the smokers recently surveyed are drinkers. Once we've gotten this conclusion, we can then employ it as a premise in an instance of induction by enumeration to argue for the conclusion that 50 percent of the entire population of smokers are drinkers—since the claim about smokers recently surveyed is a claim about a subset of smokers more generally. When we apply both maneuvers to example 5, we get the following, more complex argument:

6.

> Fifty percent of smokers studied in a recent survey asserted that they are also drinkers.
>
> So fifty percent of smokers studied in a recent survey are also drinkers.
>
> So fifty percent of smokers are also drinkers.

In example 6, we have transformed the information provided by example 5 so that we now have an argument that is strong given certain requirements. It is an argument that employs an argument from authority to defend a subconclusion and then employs this subconclusion in an instance of induction by enumeration. Example 6 thereby combines the use of two strong argument forms.

In a very similar way, we can combine arguments from authority with statistical syllogisms. Consider the following example:

7.

> Ninety-five percent of cheeseburger challenge contestants asserted that they did not eat the entire cheeseburger.
>
> Sam was a cheeseburger challenge contestant.
>
> So Sam did not eat the entire cheeseburger.

Example 7, as it is currently stated, is not a statistical syllogism, an instance of induction by enumeration, or an argument from authority. However, in much the same way we transformed the information provided by example 5 into an argument that employed two strong argument forms, we can do the same here. Yet here the result will be an argument that employs one instance of argument from authority and one instance of statistical syllogism. It will look like this:

8.

> Ninety-five percent of cheeseburger challenge contestants asserted that they did not eat the entire cheeseburger.
>
> So ninety-five percent of cheeseburger challenge contestants did not eat the entire cheeseburger.
>
> Sam was a cheeseburger challenge contestant.
>
> So Sam did not eat the entire cheeseburger.

Assuming that the cheeseburger challenge contestants are authorities about whether they completed the challenge, which seems reasonable, the argument from the first premise of example 8 to its subconclusion is an argument from authority. The argument from this subconclusion and the final premise to the main conclusion is a statistical syllogism.

We can conclude that complex arguments with a form like example 6 or 8 are strong in the absence of certain further information. First, the kind of information discussed earlier in this section that can challenge the arguments from authority employed in these complex arguments cannot be present. Second, the kind of information discussed in sections 3.1 and 3.2 that can be used to challenge the strength of statistical syllogisms or induction by enumeration cannot be present. Third, as we observed in the previous section, the argument cannot succumb to the problem of dwindling probabilities: the result of multiplying the probability of its subconclusion given the premises on which it is based by the main conclusion given the premises on which it is based cannot be 50 percent or less. In the absence of information of these types, complex arguments like examples 6 and 8 are strong.[2] They illustrate how arguments from authority can be usefully combined with instances of other strong argument forms.

3.3.4 Summary

This section has introduced the strong argument form of argument from authority. It has highlighted important features of arguments that exhibit this form and identified two kinds of challenges that can be offered to the strength of arguments from authority. Moreover, we have seen how to combine arguments from authority with other kinds of strong arguments to generate complex arguments that are strong given certain requirements.

Exercise 3.3

A. Identifying Arguments from Authority. For each of the following arguments, determine whether it is an argument from authority. Assume that the persons cited in the premises are authorities concerning the claim attributed to them. If the argument is an argument from authority, identify what stands for X and what stands for P.

1.

Stephanie has been quoted as saying "I do not like green eggs and ham" as part of a larger statement.

So Stephanie does not like green eggs and ham.

2.

Jesus asserted that he is the way, the truth, and the life.

So Jesus is the way, the truth, and the life.

3.

The president asserted that his cabinet did not have a meeting last Thursday.

So the president's cabinet did not have a meeting last Thursday.

4.

The pastor asserted that he was not inclined to think that the budget is empty.

So the budget is not empty.

5.

Jesus asked Peter, "Who do you think that I am?"

So Jesus did not know who Peter thought he was.

B. Evaluating Arguments from Authority. For each of the following arguments from authority, identify two items of additional information, each of which could very well be true and each of which is such that we cannot conclude that the argument is strong given the truth of this information.

1.

Comedian Jimmy Fallon asserted that he was recently spending time with a political figure.

So Jimmy Fallon was recently spending time with a political figure.

2.

The first-term president asserted that his cabinet did not meet in secret last Thursday.

So the first-term president's cabinet did not meet in secret last Thursday.

3.

Philosopher Bertrand Russell asserted that there is insufficient evidence to conclude that God exists.

So there is insufficient evidence to conclude that God exists.

4.

Spy James Bond asserted that he does not know where the nuclear launch codes are.

So James Bond does not know where the nuclear launch codes are.

5.

Biblical scholar Bart Ehrman asserts that the best explanation for the New Testament evidence concerning Jesus's supposed resurrection is not that Jesus rose from the dead.

So the best explanation for the New Testament evidence concerning Jesus's supposed resurrection is not that Jesus rose from the dead.

C. Complex Arguments. Transform the information provided in each of the following arguments into a complex argument that employs one instance of an argument from authority and one instance of either a statistical syllogism or induction by enumeration. For each of the resulting arguments, identify one item of further information that is such that we cannot conclude that the argument in question is strong given the truth of this information.

1.

Fifteen percent of philosophers with a permanent academic job report that they do believe in God.

So fifteen percent of philosophers do believe in God.

2.

Seventy-five percent of architects of new commercial structures report that they have not designed a building with a rectangular shape.

Nathan is an architect of a new commercial structure.

So Nathan did not design a building with a rectangular shape.

3.

Sixty-five percent of attendees at the Methodist revival reported sensing God's presence.

So sixty-five percent of revival attendees sense God's presence.

4.

Eighty percent of office workers report experiencing frustration with their coworkers.

Alison is an office worker.

So Alison experiences frustration with her coworkers.

5.

Seventy-five percent of the members of First Baptist Church, Woodstone, reported that they bring their own Bibles with them to church.

So seventy-five percent of Baptist church members bring their own Bibles with them to church.

3.4 Arguments from Analogy

Another kind of argument that is strong in the absence of certain information is argument from analogy. An **argument from analogy** is *a kind of argument in which we identify an analogy between two different individuals or groups— a way or range of ways in which the two individuals or groups compared are alike—and then conclude that because one of the two has some further feature, the other does as well.* Because the two individuals or groups are analogous in certain respects, we conclude that they are analogous in this further respect as well.

3.4.1 Identifying Arguments from Analogy

We can characterize the form of argument employed by an argument from analogy as follows, where X and Y are individuals or groups, R_1–R_n are ways in which X and Y are alike, and P is a feature:

1.

> X is like Y in respects R_1–R_n.
>
> Y has P.
>
> So X has P.

Equally, an argument with a form that switches the placement of X and Y in example 1 is an argument from analogy.

Here are two examples of arguments from analogy:

2.

> Philosophers are like mathematicians in that their profession often requires constructing formal proofs.
>
> Mathematicians can easily find work in secondary educational institutions.
>
> So philosophers can easily find work in secondary educational institutions.

3.

> Ian and Vanessa both work at the cell phone store and enjoy playing games.
>
> Vanessa spends more money per month on apps for her phone than she does on eating out.
>
> So Ian spends more money per month on apps for his phone than he does on eating out.

Notice that two groups are compared in example 2, whereas two individuals are compared in example 3. Likewise, notice that the two compared items in example 2 are said to be alike in only one respect, whereas the two compared items in example 3 are said to be alike in multiple respects. Nonetheless, given the way we specified the form of an argument from analogy, examples 2 and 3 both qualify as arguments from analogy.

Arguments from analogy are very similar to combined arguments that employ one instance of induction by enumeration and one instance of a statistical syllogism. For instance, if we have no further information beyond what is provided by example 3, then we could use the information it provides to construct the following argument:

4.

One hundred percent of a sample of those who work at the cell phone store and enjoy playing games also spend more money per month on apps for their phones than on eating out.

So one hundred percent of those who work at the cell phone store and enjoy playing games also spend more money per month on apps for their phones than on eating out.

Ian works at the cell phone store and enjoys playing games.

So Ian spends more money per month on apps for his phone than on eating out.

Example 4 employs an instance of induction by enumeration to defend its subconclusion and an argument with a structure very similar to statistical syllogism to defend its main conclusion.[3] To see why it is acceptable to represent the information provided by example 3 as we have in example 4, assuming we have no further information, notice that *Vanessa herself is a sample* of those who work at the cell phone store and enjoy playing games. Thus we can say that 100 percent of *this* sample—the sample that is just Vanessa—spends more money on apps than on eating out. And since we don't have any further information about any potential ways that Ian or others might depart from Vanessa in this respect, we can conclude via induction from enumeration that 100 percent of the total population that works at the cell phone store and enjoys playing games spends more money on apps than on eating out. Then all we need to do is affirm, as example 3 does, that Ian belongs to this population. And by using an argument with a structure much like statistical syllogism, we can conclude that he spends more money on apps than on eating out.

The point of the foregoing observation is this: reasoning using arguments from analogy is much like complex reasoning using small sample sizes. Where the analogy is between individuals, we reason that because 100 percent of a sample that consists of a single individual with certain features R_1–R_n has some further feature P, another individual that likewise possesses R_1–R_n has P. Where the analogy is between groups, we reason that because 100 percent of a sample that consists of a single group with certain features R_1–R_n has some further feature P, another group that likewise possesses R_1–R_n has P. Just as complex reasoning of this kind using small sample sizes generates arguments that are strong in the absence of further information, so does reasoning using arguments from analogy.

3.4.2 Evaluating Arguments from Analogy

While arguments from analogy are strong in the absence of further information, there are two types of further information that can challenge their strength. We cannot conclude that an argument from analogy is strong given the presence of either of these types of further information.

The first kind of information that can challenge the strength of an argument from analogy is information that provides reason to think that the respect or respects in which the compared items are alike are irrelevant. If two items are similar in respect R, this similarity is **relevant** to their possession of P if *it is more likely than not that if something possesses R, it possesses P*. If two items are similar in respect R, this similarity is **irrelevant** to their possession of P if *it is* not *more likely than not that if something possesses R, it possesses P*.

As applied to example 1, this first kind of information provides reason to think that it is not more likely than not that something that has R_1–R_n has P. By saying that such information provides reason to think that the respects are irrelevant, what we mean is that it provides reason for thinking that they are not relevant in the right way to the possession of feature P. In other words, it is not the case that their presence makes it more likely than not that the thing that possesses them also has P.

For instance, imagine that in addition to the information provided by the premises of example 3, we learned that Ian and Vanessa have twenty total other colleagues, and that nineteen of them enjoy playing games but spend less money per month on apps for their phones than on going out to eat. This further information makes it clear that the respects in which Ian and Vanessa are alike are irrelevant. That is, these respects in which they are alike are not such that it would be more likely than not that those who possess them spend more money per month on apps for their phones than on eating out. Given only the data provided by the argument and the data we have just noted, what we know is that nineteen of twenty-one people who are alike in these respects do *not* spend more money per month on apps than on going out to eat. Thus these features are irrelevant to the property substituted for P in example 3—the property of spending more money on apps than on going out to eat. Indeed, quite the opposite is true. Possessing these features is relevant to *not* spending more money on apps than on eating out.

At a minimum, in order for information to challenge the strength of an argument from analogy in this first way, it must provide reason for thinking that the likelihood that things that possess R_1–R_n also possess P is not greater than 50 percent. And as in the illustrative example of the previous paragraph, it is possible for the information to go further than this, providing reason for thinking that possessing R_1–R_n makes it more likely than not that something does *not* have P.

It is important to point out that when an argument from analogy employs multiple respects of likeness, it will not be enough to challenge the strength of the argument if we have information that bears on the relevance of only *one* of these respects of likeness. For instance, imagine that in addition to the information provided by example 3, we had the additional information that most people who work at the cell phone store do not spend more money on apps than on going out to eat. This information does not yet present a successful challenge to the strength of the argument in example 3. While it shows that merely working at the cell phone store is not relevant to spending more money on apps than on eating out, this by itself does not challenge the idea that working at the store *and* enjoying playing games is relevant to spending more money on apps than on eating out. Without a challenge to this, we haven't yet gotten a challenge to the strength of the argument in example 3.

As we've just observed, the first kind of challenge to arguments from analogy challenges these arguments by identifying reason for thinking that the respects of similarity identified in them are irrelevant to the additional feature with which they are concerned. To use some terminology introduced in the previous section, this kind of challenge can be thought of as presenting an undercutting defeater for arguments from analogy. It aims to undercut the support that the premises of these arguments supply for their conclusions and can do so without providing direct support for the negation of the conclusions of these arguments.

A second kind of information that can be employed to challenge the strength of an argument from analogy provides a rebutting defeater to the argument. Such information challenges the strength of an argument from analogy by providing direct support for the negation of its conclusion. Applied to example 1, such a challenge provides reason for thinking that it is not the case that X has P.

Such information can come in many forms. Regardless of what form it takes, it will be information that can be employed in order to construct an argument for the denial of the conclusion of the argument from analogy in question that is either sound or cogent in the absence of further information. Imagine that in addition to the information provided by example 2, we learned that philosophers cannot easily find employment *anywhere* (not to be confused with the claim that those who *study philosophy as undergraduates* cannot easily find employment anywhere—something that, at least at the time of the writing of this book, is quite far from the truth). Given this claim, the negation of the conclusion of example 2 follows directly. Indeed, supposing this additional information were true, we could construct a sound argument for the negation of the conclusion of example 2 and thus could not conclude that example 2 is a strong argument given this additional information. Its conclusion is not more likely than not given its premises once we factor in this further information that philosophers cannot easily find employment anywhere.

Among the most interesting forms that challenges of this second kind take is when the information provided identifies a **relevant disanalogy** between the two items compared in the argument in question. There is a disanalogy between X and Y with respect to some feature P if either X possesses P and Y doesn't or Y possesses P and X doesn't. *If X and Y are disanalogous with respect to P, this disanalogy between them is relevant to their possession of Q if there is a difference between the likelihood that something possesses Q given that it possesses P and the likelihood that something possesses Q given that it doesn't possess P.* Put more simply, a disanalogy between two items is a relevant disanalogy to their possession of a feature P if this disanalogy makes a difference for how likely it is that they possess P. Relevant disanalogies can be employed to provide rebutting defeaters for arguments from analogy. In particular, a relevant disanalogy can be employed to rebut an argument with the form of argument from analogy if it identifies either a feature Q that X has and Y does not have, where possessing Q makes something more likely than not to not possess P, or it identifies a feature Q that Y has and X does not have, where not possessing Q makes something more likely than not to not possess P.

For instance, imagine that, in addition to the information provided by example 2, we learned that while mathematics is a subject standardly taught in secondary educational institutions, philosophy is not. Imagine, moreover, that we learned that when a subject is not standardly taught in secondary educational institutions, it is not easy for persons who are practitioners of that subject to find employment in secondary educational institutions. By learning this additional information, we would be learning that there is a relevant dissimilarity between philosophers and mathematicians. They are dissimilar in that the subject of which mathematicians are practitioners is standardly taught in secondary educational institutions, whereas the subject of which philosophers are practitioners is not standardly taught in secondary educational institutions. The property of being a group of practitioners whose subject is standardly taught in secondary education institutions is possessed by mathematicians but not by philosophers. Moreover, it is more likely that if one's group does not possess this property of having its subject standardly taught, then it is not easy for one's group to find employment in secondary educational institutions. To use the letters we introduced in the previous paragraph, the form this example has taken is to identify a feature, Q, which is possessed by mathematicians but not philosophers, and which is such that something's not possessing it makes it more likely than not that it doesn't possess P. The information regarding this disanalogy that has been revealed is information that could be used to construct an argument for the denial of the conclusion of argument 2 that is either sound or cogent in the absence of further information.

Let's apply the same technique to example 3. Imagine that in addition to the information provided by example 3, we learned that the games Ian likes to play are games that are most fun to play in public, not games on his phone, whereas the games that Vanessa likes to play are games on her phone, not games that are most fun to play in public. Imagine, moreover, that we learned that most people who enjoy playing games that are most fun to play in public, not games on their phones, do not spend more money per month on apps for their phones than on eating out. This information would identify a relevant dissimilarity between Vanessa and Ian and enable us to construct an argument directly opposing the conclusion of example 3 that is cogent in the absence of further information. The relevant dissimilarity in question is a feature that Ian possesses but Vanessa does not, which makes it more likely than not that its possessor does not have the property substituted for P in example 1—the property of spending more money per month on apps than on eating out.

The foregoing are the only two ways for information to challenge the strength of an argument from analogy. Either the information provides reason to think that the respects in which the compared items are similar are not relevant to the additional property with which the argument is concerned, or the information can be employed to construct an argument for the denial of the argument's conclusion that is either sound or cogent in the absence of further information. Information that identifies a relevant disanalogy is a common kind of information that challenges the strength of an argument from analogy in the second of these two ways.

3.4.3 Summary

This section introduced arguments from analogy. Arguments that employ this argument form are strong in the absence of certain further information. Information that can challenge the strength of an argument from analogy can come in two forms. Either it challenges the relevance of the similarities between the two items compared, or it provides information that constitutes a rebutting defeater to the conclusion of the argument from analogy in question.

Exercise 3.4

A. Identifying Arguments from Analogy. Determine whether the following arguments are arguments from analogy. If an argument is an argument from analogy, identify what has been substituted for X, Y, R_1–R_n, and P.

1.
> Fetuses are like newborns in terms of their visible resemblance to larger humans, abilities, and inner material constitution.
> It is morally problematic to kill newborns.
> So it is morally problematic to kill fetuses.

2.
> Edward compares books.
> Books contain paragraphs.
> So paragraphs contain books.

3.
> God is like a good father with respect to how he loves his children.
> A good father celebrates when a delinquent child returns.
> So God celebrates when a delinquent child returns.

4.

Both the establishment candidate and the candidate who is a political outsider campaigned in Ohio.

The establishment candidate will also campaign in Nebraska.

So the candidate who is a political outsider will also campaign in Nebraska.

5.

The kingdom of heaven is like a fine pearl in terms of how one should go about pursuing it.

A fine pearl is such that it is reasonable to sacrifice all one has to obtain it.

So the kingdom of heaven is such that it is reasonable to sacrifice all one has to obtain it.

B. Evaluating Arguments from Analogy. For each of the following arguments from analogy, identify one further item of information that, if true, would challenge the strength of the argument.

1. Both the chicken noodle soup and the soup of the day served in this restaurant are soups. The chicken noodle soup served in this restaurant is not suitable for vegetarians. So the soup of the day served in this restaurant is not suitable for vegetarians.

2. A very difficult decision is like a coin flip in that it could equally go one way or the other. The outcome of a coin flip isn't up to anyone. So the outcome of a very difficult decision isn't up to anyone.

3. God, like Fred, has good fatherly qualities. Fred, in addition to being a father, also has a father. So God, in addition to being a father, also has a father.

4. A romantic relationship is like a battlefield in that there are conflicts that must be navigated well. In a battlefield, it is permissible to use deadly weapons. So in a romantic relationship, it is permissible to use deadly weapons.

5. Like a person who doesn't intervene to save a drowning child when she can easily do so, God doesn't stop very bad things from happening when doing so would not be difficult for him. A person who doesn't intervene to save a drowning child is morally imperfect. So God is morally imperfect.

6. The Father, Son, and Spirit in the Trinity, like the three leaves of a three leaf clover, are three distinct entities that are united. The three leaves of a three leaf clover are parts of a larger whole (the clover). So the Father, Son, and Spirit are parts of a larger whole (God).

7. Like a screwdriver in the hand of a carpenter, a human is a tool God can use to accomplish God's purposes. A screwdriver in the hand of a carpenter cannot reasonably demand to be treated by its user (the carpenter) in any particular way. So a human cannot reasonably demand to be treated by its user (God) in any particular way.

8. The Father, Son, and Spirit in the Trinity, like the solid, liquid, and gas forms of water, are distinct from one another but are of the same substance. The solid, liquid, and gas forms of water are just three ways that something else (H_2O) can be. So the Father, Son, and Spirit are just three ways that something else (God) can be.

9. Immigrants are like rodents in one's house in that they are searching for a comfortable place to live and provide for their kin, but the place they have chosen already has occupants. It is permissible to forcibly remove rodents from one's house. So it is permissible to forcibly remove immigrants.

10. God, like the world's greatest artist, has created something (the world) with expert skill. The world's greatest artist wouldn't intervene to act on what he's made once he's completed it. So God wouldn't intervene to act on what he's made once he's completed it.

3.5 Inference to the Best Explanation

The final argument form we will discuss is inference to the best explanation. In arguments exhibiting this form, we conclude that a proposed explanation for some datum is true because it is the best explanation for that datum available to us. The form of **inference to the best explanation** is as follows, where D is a datum and H is a hypothesis:

1.
> H is the best available explanation for why D.
> So H.

Below, we will highlight some of the key features of inferences to the best explanation, and we will identify one way in which the strength of arguments that employ inference to the best explanation can be challenged.

3.5.1 Key Features of Inferences to the Best Explanation

Some clarifying remarks concerning the meaning of key terms in example 1 should be helpful. First, we should clarify what kinds of things D and H are supposed to be. D is supposed to be a datum. For our purposes, a datum will consist in a statement. Thus the statement "Carlos is wearing a striped tie" could be substituted for D. Moreover, while we will speak of D as a datum (instead of the plural data), it is perfectly acceptable for D to be a complex datum consisting of a complex statement. Thus the more complex statement, "Carlos is wearing a striped tie or everyone who has observed his tie has either been hallucinating or has lied about what they have seen," could be substituted for D. Put more simply, any statement can be substituted for D.

In the context of an inference to the best explanation, it is assumed that the statement substituted for D is true. Sometimes this assumption is left implicit in the context in which inferences to the best explanation are presented because it is assumed that for anything to be explained it must be the case. In other words, it is assumed that the only things that can be explained are true statements. Thus if H provides the best available explanation for D, then D must be true. When we evaluate instances of inference to the best explanation below, we will make this assumption.

The term H will also consist in a statement. More specifically, H will consist in a statement that is a *candidate* explanation for D. In other words, it is possible that H is what explains D. Furthermore, H is a candidate explanation for D that is available—available to the audience of the argument. Precisely what is required in order for a candidate explanation to be available to an audience is a matter of controversy, but for our purposes it involves the audience being aware of the explanation. We will think of H as a claim that the audience is aware of and that could explain D. In short, *H is an* **available explanation** *for D if the audience of the inference to the best explanation is aware of H as a candidate explanation for D.*

The premise of an inference to the best explanation claims not merely that H is one candidate explanation of D among others that is available to the audience but that H is the best candidate explanation of D available to the audience—that there is no other candidate explanation of D available to the audience that is as good as or better than H. This explanation of what it means for H to be the best available explanation of D employs the idea of an explanation being *good* and, indeed, the idea that the goodness of an explanation can be compared with the goodness of other explanations in such a way that at times two candidate explanations are equally good, while at other times one is better than the other. In short, *H is the* **best explanation** *for D if there is no other explanation for D that is as good as or better than H.*

This raises the important question: What is necessary for a candidate explanation to be a good explanation? It is probably best to approach this question somewhat indirectly. Rather than asking what is necessary for an explanation to be a good one, we can ask what kinds of features contribute to the goodness of an explanation—that is, what features an explanation can possess that improve the quality of that explanation, other things being equal.

While the answer to this question remains controversial among philosophers, we will identify a few features here that have commonly been claimed to improve the quality of explanations that have them, other things being equal.

The first feature is *explanatory power*, the extent to which the candidate explanation renders the datum in question predictable. Does the candidate explanation have the power necessary to explain the datum in question? Other things being equal, the more predictive power an explanation has, the better the explanation is.

Imagine we were comparing two candidate explanations for why Carlos wore a striped tie. One candidate explanation is that Carlos prefers striped ties to plain ties, and the other candidate explanation is that Carlos is wearing a plain jacket and always wears a striped tie when he wears a plain jacket. In this case, the second candidate explanation has greater explanatory power since it renders more highly expectable, or predictable, that Carlos will wear a striped tie. Whereas the first candidate explanation fits equally well with alternative outcomes, the second candidate explanation does not fit equally well. The claim that Carlos prefers striped ties to plain ties fits just fine, for example, with the idea that Carlos prefers ties with dots above all other kinds of ties and so wore a tie with dots. The second explanation does not cohere as well with this alternative outcome. Thus the second explanation renders the actual outcome—the datum that Carlos wore a striped tie—more expectable than does the first explanation. In other words, the second explanation exhibits greater explanatory power.

This is not to say that, all things considered, the second explanation is better than the first. It is simply to say that, with respect to the one particular feature of explanatory power, the second explanation is better. In other words, if the explanations were in all other respects equally good, then the second would be preferable to the first because it has greater explanatory power.

The second feature that contributes to the goodness of explanations is *coherence with background knowledge*. Other things being equal, a candidate explanation of the datum in question is better to the extent that it coheres well with our background knowledge—that is, with other things we know.

Imagine that we're again comparing the two explanations for why Carlos wore a striped tie. And imagine that part of our background knowledge is that Carlos wears no jacket about as often as he wears plain jackets and that when he wears no jacket, he almost always wears a plain tie. This item of background knowledge does not fit particularly well with the claim that, generally speaking, Carlos prefers striped ties to plain ties. If he did have this preference, one would expect that he would wear striped ties more frequently when not wearing a jacket. At the very least, that he frequently wears plain ties when not wearing a jacket, despite his preference for striped ties over plain ties, cries out for further explanation. It leaves something unexplained. But this item of background knowledge does not conflict in this same way with the second candidate explanation. There is not any apparent conflict between the claims that Carlos wears no jacket about as often as he wears a plain jacket, that when he wears no jacket he almost always wears a plain tie, and that when he wears a plain jacket he always wears a striped tie. Combining these claims together does not leave us scratching our heads and feeling as if something surprising has been left unexplained. Thus the second explanation coheres better with this item of background knowledge than the first. If the explanations are in all other respect equally good, then this fact will imply that the second explanation is better than the first.

A third and final feature that contributes to the goodness of explanations is *simplicity*. Other things being equal, an explanation that posits fewer entities, or fewer kinds of entities, is better than one that posits more.

Imagine that we compare the second explanation for why Carlos wore a striped tie with a very similar but slightly modified candidate explanation. The slightly modified explanation proposes that Carlos wore a striped tie because he wore a plain jacket, he always wears a striped tie when he wears a plain jacket, *and* he was specifically instructed by a scary ghost this morning to wear a striped tie. This latter explanation is more complex than the earlier explanation since it posits in addition to the entities posited by the former explanation—Carlos's jacket and his pattern of tie-wearing behavior—an additional entity of a very different kind: a scary ghost. This latter explanation seems needlessly complex since adding the bit about the ghost is not necessary for the explanation to render it expectable that Carlos is wearing a striped tie. The earlier explanation already renders this datum expectable without appealing to the ghost, so the latter explanation is unnecessarily complex. Thus if the two explanations are in all other ways on par, the earlier explanation is better than the later, modified explanation.

The foregoing are three features that are commonly thought to improve the quality of explanations. Other things being equal, explanations that have these features—explanatory power, coherence with background knowledge, and simplicity—are better than explanations that do not have these features.[4]

3.5.2 Evaluating Inferences to the Best Explanation

In this subsection we will identify one way—the only way—in which an argument with the form of example 1 can fail to be strong. This occurs if we have information that provides reason to think that candidate explanation H is not sufficiently good. In other words, even if the premise of the argument in question is correct in claiming that H is the best explanation among our candidate explanations, H may nonetheless not be sufficiently good as to be more likely than not. This situation is sometimes described as the problem of the bad lot. The idea is that while H is the best among our candidate explanations, H is merely the best among a bad lot—or a group of explanations of which none is sufficiently good as to be more likely than not.

In order for it to be the case that some information provides reason to think that a candidate explanation is not sufficiently good, this information must provide reason to think that the candidate explanation does not perform sufficiently well with respect to one or more features that improve the quality of explanations. If we assumed that the only features that improve the quality of explanations are those identified in the previous subsection, then this would imply that any information of the kind in view here would have to target one or more of those features. It would have to be information that provides reason for thinking that the explanation in question is not sufficiently explanatorily powerful, does not cohere sufficiently well with our background knowledge, or is not sufficiently simple.

Information provides reason to think that an explanation is not *sufficiently* good when the information provides reason to think that the explanation is not good enough as to be more likely than not. But this raises the question: How poorly must an explanation perform with respect to those features that improve the quality of explanations to provide reason to think that the explanation is not more likely than not? We cannot answer this question precisely here. All we can say is that the worse an explanation is shown to be with respect to those features that improve the quality of explanations, the less likely it is to be more likely than not. Certainly, if a candidate explanation performs very poorly with respect to all of these features, then it is not good enough to be more likely than not. Thus what we end up with here is a kind of strategy for challenging the strength of arguments that employ inference to the best explanation. The strategy is to argue that while the explanations in question may be the best among our candidate explanations, they do not perform well with respect to those features that improve the quality of explanations. It's not clear just how poorly they must be shown to perform for this strategy to be successful, but the worse an explanation performs with respect to these features, the less likely it is that the explanation is more likely than not, and so the less likely it is that the argument in question is strong.

Let's think through how this strategy could be applied to an example. Consider the following inference to the best explanation:

2. The best available explanation for why Carlos wore a striped tie is that Carlos prefers striped ties to plain ties. So Carlos prefers striped ties to plain ties.

Imagine that, together with the information provided by the premise of example 2, we also had the further information identified in the previous subsection that Carlos wears no jacket about as frequently as he wears a plain jacket and that he always wears a plain tie when he wears no jacket. Imagine, however, that we don't have the further information that when he wears a plain jacket he always wears a striped tie. Given only this information, we might challenge the strength of the argument in example 2 in the way highlighted above. We could grant that the best available explanation for why Carlos wore a striped tie is that he prefers striped ties to plain ties. (Remember, we're supposing here that the candidate explanation that he always wears striped ties when wearing a plain jacket isn't available—we aren't aware of what kind of tie Carlos wears when he wears a plain jacket.) However, we might argue that this explanation that appeals to Carlos's preferences is merely the best of a bad lot. While it is better than our alternative explanations, it isn't very good.

To do this, we will need to show that this candidate explanation does not perform well with respect to features that improve the quality of explanations. For example, as we highlighted in the previous subsection, we might note that this candidate explanation doesn't have very great explanatory power. It doesn't render very expectable that Carlos will wear a striped tie. Moreover, and perhaps even more significant, this candidate explanation doesn't cohere very well with the further item of background knowledge identified above regarding Carlos's habits when he wears no jacket. The claim that Carlos generally prefers striped ties to plain ones doesn't fit well with our background knowledge that he always wears plain ties when wearing no jacket. While these claims aren't strictly inconsistent, they leave us puzzled as to why Carlos would act this way.

Arguing in this way, we will have shown that the proposed best available explanation cited in example 2 doesn't perform very well with respect to two of the features the previous subsection identified as improving the quality of explanations. Are these facts sufficient to imply that the explanation in question, despite being the best available, is not good enough that it is more likely than not? It's hard to say. Nonetheless, it is clear that they should decrease our confidence that it is more likely than not. In this way, by challenging the goodness of this best available explanation we can offer reason for decreasing our confidence that an inference to the best explanation is strong.

3.5.3 Summary

This section introduced inference to the best explanation. Arguments with this form conclude that a candidate explanation is true because it provides the best available explanation for some datum. The strength of such arguments

---

Key Ideas for Review

An **inference to the best explanation** uses the following argument form, where D is a datum and H is a hypothesis:

> H is the best available explanation for why D.
> So H.

H is an **available explanation** for D if the audience of the inference to the best explanation is aware of H as a candidate explanation for D.

H is the **best explanation** for D if there is no other explanation for D that is as good as or better than H.

The extent to which an explanation H is a good explanation is determined by how well H performs with respect to those features that improve the quality of explanations. Three features that improve the quality of explanations are *explanatory power, coherence with background knowledge,* and *simplicity*.

The only strategy for challenging the strength of an inference to the best explanation is to argue that the best available explanation H is not a sufficiently good explanation to be more likely than not.

---

can be challenged by information that provides reason to think that the candidate explanation cited as the best available explanation is not sufficiently good. Such information provides reason for thinking that the explanation does not perform sufficiently well with respect to one or more features that improve the quality of explanations.

Exercise 3.5

A. Identifying Inferences to the Best Explanation. Determine whether the following arguments are inferences to the best explanation. If they are, identify D and H.

1. The best explanation for why the current financial crisis occurred is that the Fed lowered interest rates too soon. So the Fed lowered interest rates too soon.

2. The best available explanation for why the biblical data regarding the empty tomb and postmortem sighting of Jesus contains the evidence it does is that Jesus rose from the dead. So Jesus rose from the dead.

3. As good an explanation as any for why the snack food in the kitchen is lacking is that the teenagers ate it. So the teenagers ate it.

4. The best available explanation for why the sirens were running but then stopped is that an emergency vehicle that had been en route to its destination arrived at its destination. So an emergency vehicle that had been en route to its destination arrived at its destination.

5. The best available explanation for why I seem to have hands is that I have hands. So at least one human exists.

B. Evaluating Inferences to the Best Explanation. Present a challenge to the strength of each of the following inferences to the best explanation, making reference to the feature of explanatory power, the feature of coherence with background knowledge, or the feature of simplicity. If presenting the challenge requires specifying some further information not provided in the argument itself, identify that information.

1. The best available explanation for why violence has been perpetrated in the name of religion is that religions teach that violence is good. So religions teach that violence is good.
2. The best available explanation for why you've gained weight is that you've eaten more sweets lately. So you've eaten more sweets lately.
3. The best available explanation for why God does not provide more compelling evidence of his existence is that there is no God. So there is no God.
4. The best available explanation for why the candidate won't release his tax information is that it contains something embarrassing. So it contains something embarrassing.
5. The best available explanation for why the top-ranked team lost is that its star player was injured. So its star player was injured.
6. The best available explanation for why God doesn't work more miracles to prevent very bad events is that God either doesn't care or is unable to do anything. So God either doesn't care or is unable to do anything.
7. The best available explanation for why the prospective employers have not returned my call is that they do not intend to hire me. So they do not intend to hire me.
8. The best available explanation for why Elliot sinned is that Elliot is not a Christian. So Elliot is not a Christian.
9. The best available explanation for why the tornado hit that particular town rather than another nearby town is that that town is more morally corrupt than other nearby towns and God sent the tornado as judgment. So that town is more morally corrupt than other nearby towns, and God sent the tornado as judgment.
10. The best available explanation for why the prosecution presented that evidence to the jury is that the defendant is guilty. So the defendant is guilty.

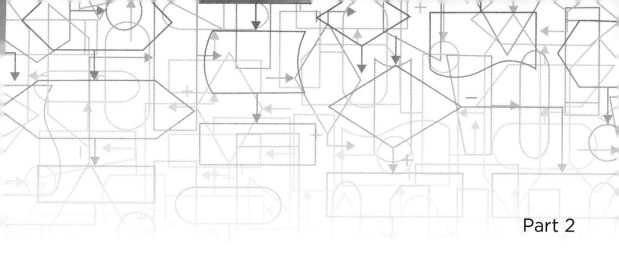

The Virtues of Inquiry

Part 1 introduced you to a set of skills that can help you to improve your reasoning abilities. In particular, the skills introduced in part 1 help you to identify and evaluate arguments. Living a life of cognitive excellence is not entirely a matter of possessing and utilizing such skills, however. A person may be skilled in evaluating arguments but not care to do so. He may be skilled in identifying well-supported conclusions but fail to believe those conclusions. He may sufficiently evaluate those arguments he encounters but be disposed to consider only a highly selective subset of the relevant available arguments. When a person fails in these ways—not caring about the truth, not believing what is warranted, attending only selectively to relevant evidence—he fails in a particularly bad way. He fails as an inquirer.

Part 2 is devoted to the virtues of inquiry. It is not enough for living a life of cognitive excellence to acquire a certain set of skills in reasoning. We must exercise these skills virtuously. We must develop the kind of intellectual character that will guide us in the proper application and utilization of these skills. We must learn to conduct our inquiries with wisdom.

Not that long ago philosophers paid little attention to virtues—intellectual and moral. Following the Enlightenment, philosophers' focus was on the evaluation of actions and beliefs. The important questions were whether actions were morally right or wrong and whether particular beliefs were justified or known.

But a dramatic change took place in the late twentieth century. First, in the sphere of action and then in the sphere of belief, there was a revival of interest in the virtues.[1] Of course it is important to evaluate actions and beliefs. Of course it is important that we develop theories that can explain what it is for an action to be morally right or morally wrong and theories that can explain what it is for a belief to be rational. But just as important is evaluating *persons*, constructing theories that can explain what it is for a *person* to be loving, friendly, courageous, or generous—theories that can explain what it is for a person to be morally and intellectually virtuous.

Part 2 will challenge you with some of the most important results from this revival of interest in virtues—in particular, *intellectual* virtues. In the following chapters we will explore several specific intellectual virtues. These virtues are united in being conceived of as habits or dispositions of inquiry that orient us toward achieving good intellectual ends. They are, we might say, excellent ways of being for good intellectual goals[2]—goals such as obtaining true beliefs, believing responsibly, and achieving knowledge and understanding. Intellectual virtues are traits that make persons and their communities good at accomplishing these valuable intellectual goals. They are stable features of our character that help us to carry out the task of inquiry with excellence.[3]

It is a basic assumption of part 2 that these intellectual virtues can be acquired and strengthened. Those who don't have them can gain them through practice, and those who have them to some degree can have them in greater measure. The purpose of the following chapters is to lead you toward the acquisition, maintenance, and deepening of these intellectual virtues.

4

▶ ▶ ▶ ▶ ▶

Internal Virtues

We begin our investigation of the intellectual virtues by looking at four internal virtues: love of intellectual excellence, intellectual courage, intellectual caution, and introspective vigilance. These are called "internal virtues" because it is possible for one to practice them privately in one's mental life even in the absence of interaction with other persons. This will not be the case for the other two sets of virtues we will investigate in chapters 5 and 6—virtues displayed characteristically when we depend on others in our inquiries or when they depend on us in theirs.

As will become clear, possessing and exercising the internal virtues will no doubt have a significant impact on the way one interacts with others. The intellectually courageous person, for example, will surely respond differently to criticisms of her work than will the intellectually cowardly person. Similar things may be said of the one who loves intellectual excellence or the introspectively vigilant person. So while internal virtues can be practiced privately in one's mental life, their fullest expression plausibly has consequences for how one interacts in a community of inquirers.

In each of the following sections, an internal virtue will be defined, contrasted with its contrary vices, and illustrated. You will then have an opportunity through practice exercises to reflect on the consequences the virtue or its contrasting vices would have for real-life inquiry. We begin with the virtue of loving intellectual excellence.

4.1 Love of Intellectual Excellence

Many philosophers who have contributed to the revival of interest in the intellectual virtues agree that at the center of the life of the intellectually virtuous person lies a certain virtuous motivation—a motivation to pursue what is intellectually good, accomplish intellectual goals, and live a life of intellectual excellence.[1] Here we will characterize this virtuous motivation as the love of intellectual excellence.

Love is often said to have two primary components: a benevolence component and a unitive component. When one person loves another, the person desires the good for the other. This is the benevolence component of love. The lover wills to see the beloved have a life filled with all that is good. Second, the lover desires union with the beloved. This union will be different for different kinds of relationships. Spouses who love each other desire a different kind of union than would be appropriate for parents and children who love each other. Yet in every loving relationship, those who love each other desire some kind of union appropriate to their relationship.

This unitive component of love is primarily in view when we speak of loving intellectual excellence. The one who loves intellectual excellence wants union with what is intellectually excellent. The sort of union appropriate to this relationship is for the inquirer and his community to *possess* intellectual excellence. It is for the inquirer and his community to achieve the goals of inquiry and to achieve them in excellent ways. The one who loves intellectual excellence desires to attain knowledge, understanding, and wisdom, and to attain these in ways that manifest intellectual responsibility.

We would have an impoverished conception of the virtue of loving intellectual excellence if we characterized it merely as a *desire* for attaining intellectual goods in a responsible manner. The person who loves excellence does not merely desire these things but is disposed to behave in a manner that manifests this desire. The motivation to attain intellectual goods responsibly regulates the inquirer's own processes of inquiry. The **love of intellectual excellence**, then, is *a disposition to conduct inquiries in a way that displays a deep motivation for achieving intellectual goods responsibly.*

In a certain way, the love of intellectual excellence has a root in all of us. As Aristotle stated, "All people by nature desire to know." The baby's practice of putting everything—yes, everything—in her mouth reveals that we are naturally explorers of the world. There is a sense of satisfaction that comes to us when we are able to distinguish between things, to understand, and even to be acquainted with something new. To some extent or other, we all want this. Yet while there is an innate curiosity in each of us, this inborn thirst for what is intellectually excellent needs to be formed in us in ways that will make us more excellent inquirers. In some of us, this natural motivation needs to be recovered, as it may have been suppressed. In others, it needs to be redirected. In still others, it needs to be sculpted and refined. What is in view when we talk about the love of intellectual excellence, then, is more than a natural appetite for intellectual goods; it is a refined and mature forming of this appetite that regulates the process of responsible inquiry. It is not an indiscriminate love of using one's belief-forming faculties but a discriminating love—a love that wants those intellectual goods that are significant, relevant, and worthy of attention. As Christian philosophers Robert Roberts and Jay Wood write, the one who loves intellectual excellence wants

> true perceptions and beliefs, not false ones; she wants well-grounded beliefs, not vagrant, floating ones; she wants significant rather than trivial, relevant rather than irrelevant, knowledge; she wants deep rather than shallow understanding; and she wants knowledge that ennobles human life and promotes human well-being rather than knowledge that degrades and destroys; she wants to know important truths.[2]

This mature love of intellectual excellence is extolled in the Scriptures as well. The author of Proverbs is fond of praising the great value of excellent intellectual accomplishments. He urges the reader, "Call out for insight and raise your voice for understanding," "seek it like silver and search for it as for hidden treasures" (Proverbs 2:3–4). He offers similar remarks about wisdom: "Wisdom is better than jewels, and all that you may desire cannot compare with her" (Proverbs 8:11). The discriminating love of intellectual excellence is also found in the New Testament. Consider the admonition of the apostle Paul: "Whatever is true, whatever is honorable, whatever is just, whatever is pure, whatever is lovely, whatever is commendable, if there is any excellence, if there is anything worthy of praise, think about these things" (Philippians 4:8). According to the Scriptures, it is clear that intellectual excellences are to be highly prized and pursued.

In the remainder of this chapter, we will seek to clarify the nature of the central motivational virtue of loving intellectual excellence in two ways. First, we will examine four imperatives that are followed by the possessor of this virtue. Second, we will contrast the virtue of loving intellectual excellence with those vices that oppose it. Along the way, we will consider some illustrative examples. The goal of this discussion is to attain a deeper acquaintance with what it is like to love intellectual excellence.

4.1.1 The Imperatives of Loving Intellectual Excellence

The first imperative followed by the person who loves intellectual excellence is to love intellectual excellence sacrificially. It is clear to us that in our loving relationships with other persons, love requires sacrifice. No loving relationship works without sacrifices of some kind—whether those are sacrifices of time, career, other relationships, or material possessions. The same goes when it comes to the love of intellectual excellence. The intellectually virtuous person loves intellectual excellence with a sacrificial love, being willing to sacrifice time, energy, money, reputation, and even relationships to attain it.

A person who loves what is intellectually excellent may have the direction of her life radically changed because of it. She may end up pursuing a career that provides her with less material goods but more intellectual accomplishments. She may end up endorsing views that put her at odds with friend, family, and even employers. She may end up suffering ridicule for her love of the truth. In the most dire cases—like those of Socrates or Jesus—she might be called to stand for the truth to the point of suffering extreme harm or death. The one who loves intellectual excellence is willing to sacrifice for intellectual goods.

A second imperative followed by the one who loves intellectual excellence is to take an interest in that which is most intrinsically valuable. Some objects of inquiry are simply more worthy of inquiry than are others, because they are intrinsically more valuable than others. Someone who contemplates the nature of human beings or the origins of the universe contemplates objects of inquiry far more worthy than that which is contemplated by someone who wants to count the grains of sand on the sea shore. The virtuous inquirer tends to gravitate toward those objects of inquiry that are most intrinsically valuable.

Of course, the example of counting grains of sand is extreme. Few of us are tempted to spend our time counting grains of sand. But many of us are tempted to spend inordinate amounts of time and resources learning about things that are of very little value. Far too many people today spend their very best intellectual efforts learning about the details of the latest Hollywood gossip or engrossing themselves in the lives of reality TV stars. Learning about these things is not necessarily bad in itself, as it can provide a much-needed distraction from more demanding intellectual tasks. But when learning about these things becomes the obsessive focus of a person's intellectual activities, a mind has been wasted.

The intellectually virtuous person, as one who loves what is intellectually excellent, tends to gravitate toward objects of inquiry that are most intrinsically valuable. Here the Christian has something unique to contribute. For the Christian—or the theist more generally—the highest object of intellectual inquiry is God. The Christian, or theist, might very reasonably maintain that the ultimate intellectual goal of life is to seek what understanding may be had of the glorious and magnificent Being who is the source of all we have and are.

The third imperative is closely related to the second. Those who love intellectual excellence take an interest in that which is explanatorily more ultimate.

Such people tend to invest their intellectual resources in addressing deeper and deeper "why" questions. As we saw previously, some objects of inquiry are less valuable than others. Whatever the truth is about how many grains of sand there are on the sea shore, this truth is a rather trivial truth in comparison to others. Part of what makes some truths more important than others is the intrinsic worthiness of what they are about, as we saw above. Another element of what makes some truths more important than others is their explanatory role. Imagine, for instance, that the truth about the number of grains of sand on the sea shore is that there are $10^{10,000}$ grains of sand. Knowing this would be interesting, but it would help us explain little else. The claim that there are $10^{10,000}$ grains of sand just doesn't tell us much about why anything else in the world is the way it is.

But knowing other claims *does* help us to explain why things are the way they are in the world. When scientists uncovered the nature of HIV and its behaviors, they were able to explain why certain people were all sharing similar symptoms of illness. When psychologists come to understand the truth about a mental illness, they are better able to explain and correct the behaviors of their patients. When philosophers attain clearer insight into the nature of a foundational concept like causation, this contributes to a deep understanding of the way the entire world is constructed. When theologians uncover something about God's purposes in the world, they are better able to explain the unfolding of history.

Some claims bear more of an explanatory load than others. They answer more "why" questions than others do. The one who loves intellectual excellence, as someone who has a matured and refined appetite for understanding, will gravitate toward taking an interest in those areas of inquiry that promise to answer our most fundamental questions about why things are as they are.

The final imperative of the one who loves intellectual excellence is to endeavor to ensure that the attitudes formed toward claims are adequately supported. Some beliefs may require different kinds or degrees of support than others. Scientific beliefs may require support from verifying scientific experiments. Beliefs about persons in one's community may require testimonial support. Beliefs about philosophical questions may require support from widely shared intuitions about basic concepts. Beliefs about the divine may require a critical sensitivity to the inner testimony of the Spirit or the appropriate application of interpretive techniques to authoritative sources from Scripture and Christian tradition. Regardless of what one is inquiring about, the one who loves intellectual excellence will display a concern to ensure that his attitudes receive the kind and degree of support they should.[3] In whatever way a belief about some subject requires support for it to be held appropriately, the one who loves intellectual excellence will demand that his own beliefs meet those requirements.

Ensuring that beliefs are adequately supported requires the exercise of the virtue of introspective vigilance (the focus of section 4.3). The inquirer who loves intellectual excellence will have to be willing to examine the explanatory history of her own beliefs, asking, "Why do I believe what I believe?" Through such introspection, the inquirer will be better equipped to monitor her belief system to ensure that it meets the demands of rationality she treasures as a one who loves intellectual excellence. Doing so will also better equip her to effectively share her reasons for belief with other members of her community.

Loving intellectual excellence in this way may lead the virtuous inquirer to ask questions where others would not. Others may caution him not to ask questions about why something is believed but just to believe it. But as someone whose appetite for what is intellectually excellent has been refined, he will not uncritically accept this demand. By scouring the foundations of those beliefs he shares with his community, he may break new ground and contribute innovative and creative discoveries to his community's stock of intellectual achievements. His loyalty to accomplishing intellectual goals properly may in many cases trounce his loyalty to some particular way of viewing the world.

The one who loves intellectual excellence follows the imperatives we have discussed: loving intellectual goods sacrificially, taking an interest in that which is intrinsically worthy of investigation and that which is explanatorily fundamental, and carefully monitoring one's belief system and that of one's community to ensure that beliefs that are held and maintained are adequately supported. We attain a positive portrait of the life of the one who loves intellectual excellence by attending to these guiding principles. We can also attain deeper insight by examining those vices that are contrary to the virtue of loving intellectual excellence. To these we now turn.

4.1.2 Vices of Intellectual Motivation

At least four intellectual vices contrast with the virtue of loving intellectual excellence. The first is being inadequately concerned to believe the truth. Some inquirers lack intellectual virtue because they are not strongly motivated to hold true beliefs as opposed to false ones. This is usually because they are motivated more strongly to hold beliefs with some other quality. For example, some inquirers are so strongly concerned to hold beliefs that are common within their community and will lead to their own acceptance in that community that they are willing to sacrifice the truth of their beliefs for this other goal. They make it their intellectual goal to believe what will gain them acceptance rather than to believe what is true. Acceptance within a community is deeply valuable for our flourishing as humans, but the goal of a virtuous inquirer is not to hold beliefs that will gain him acceptance but to attain as far as is possible an accurate and detailed view of the way the world really is. Those who are more concerned with being accepted than with believing the truth sacrifice this intellectual goal too readily.

There are other ways of displaying inadequate concern for believing the truth. Some inquirers are afraid of revising their beliefs. They are so strongly concerned with maintaining beliefs that keep them comfortable that they miss out on making valuable discoveries that contribute to their excellence as inquirers. They forego believing the truth to maintain their own comfort. In some, this vice can become so severe that it is not only an inadequate concern to believe the truth but also a thoroughgoing opposition to inquiry. Some inquirers become so afraid of having their views challenged that they would rather remain blissfully ignorant of the evidence for or against these views. They insulate and disengage their intellectual lives from the outside world. They refuse to inquire.

At times in the history of Christianity, this vice has tempted the church. In the face of perceived opposition to their beliefs based on scientific discoveries in the mid-1800s, many members of the church decided to restrict the evidence they were willing to consider to the Bible alone, refusing to consider any other sources of information. In doing so they displayed a willful lack of concern for believing what is true as opposed to believing what they were comfortable believing. Thankfully, a very different view has been advocated by many of the greatest minds in Christian history—thinkers like the early church apologist Justin Martyr. Justin is well-known for his claim, "All truth is God's truth wherever it is found." For Justin, and for those who love intellectual excellence, truth is not something to be afraid of but something to love. The intellectually virtuous person, as someone who loves intellectual excellence, will have a concern to believe the truth that will not permit her to remain willfully opposed to inquiry. She will instead maintain a loyalty to the truth that prompts her to pursue thorough and passionate consideration of relevant evidence for her beliefs.

A second vice that opposes loving intellectual excellence is intellectual complacency. The intellectually complacent person has not so much an inadequate concern for truth as an inadequate concern for intellectual accomplishments. He would be more than happy to believe the truth if someone would simply make it easy for him to do so, but he is unwilling to put forth the effort required to attain intellectual achievements of his own. He is unwilling to do what it takes to *discover*, to *know*, to *understand*. He fails to appreciate that part of what it is to live a life of intellectual excellence is not simply to believe the truth but also to understand why what one believes is the truth—that part of what it is to live a life of intellectual excellence is to find out the truth for oneself.

A weak form of this vice might help to explain the experience of some undergraduate students when they first encounter an intellectually demanding discipline like philosophy. These students find it unusual that the professor is not simply telling them what to think. Instead, the professor introduces them to a variety of arguments and views, often has something to say both for and against these, and asks the students for their own thoughts on these matters. Many students are left speechless. Some students meet this encounter as they ought—treating it as a new challenge, doing the hard thinking they are being encouraged to do, reading beyond what is required for their course, and engaging in dialogue outside class with their peers and instructor. But others find this task daunting and simply give up. It is as if they have never been challenged to think for themselves. They are tempted to respond by saying that one can't really *know* anything in this discipline. But in responding in this way, they betray their own misunderstanding of knowledge as something that is attainable only by believing the testimony of an authoritative expert. They overlook the possibility that knowledge may be something they can personally attain with hard work. While this is work that they could do, they refuse to do it because they are intellectually complacent.

The one who loves intellectual excellence will not stand for this sort of complacency. She *loves* discovery. She *loves* that flash of insight that leads to understanding. She *loves* to achieve—yes, *achieve*—knowledge. She appreciates the value of holding beliefs in such a way that one appropriately receives credit for getting those beliefs right. She prizes hard-nosed, excellent inquiry. This is what she, as an inquirer, lives for.

The one who loves intellectual excellence is not only dramatically different from those who have an inadequate concern for believing the truth or for attaining intellectual accomplishments, but also different from those who care for such intellectual goods but in the wrong way. Virtuous love of excellence is opposed to a viciously *misdirected* concern for the intellectual goods.

Some inquirers view intellectual goods instrumentally. They treat attaining knowledge or believing the truth as merely good for the sake of some other good it enables the inquirer to obtain. Again, this perspective is often represented among college students. Many attend class simply to get a good grade and desire good grades simply to get a good job. This perspective is not entirely the students' fault. Their institution likely markets its educational product in ways geared toward producing such thinking. And this way of thinking isn't strictly incompatible with a love of intellectual excellence. Those who love intellectual excellence may also desire a good job as an outcome of their process of inquiry. They may recognize that knowledge is power, that gaining understanding and acquiring intellectual skills can contribute to their flourishing as a human being by helping them to find a place of meaningful and gainful employment. But what is incompatible with the love of intellectual excellence is seeking knowledge *only* for instrumental reasons—viewing true belief, knowledge, and understanding as *only* of instrumental value, that is, merely valuable for the sake of something else.

The one who loves intellectual excellence, by contrast, appreciates the intrinsic value of intellectual goods. He takes the courses of his major not principally to get a good job but because it is satisfying as an inquirer to discover the significant truths attainable through focused study of a discipline. Even if he doesn't get a job in his field right away, pursuing these studies will have been of immense value.

College students are not the only ones tempted by the vice of misdirected concern for intellectual goods, of course. Professionals, even professional academics, can display this same vice quite remarkably. A scholar might work on a project merely because it will get funding from the National Endowment for the Humanities. The goal is not to appreciate the intrinsic value of coming to understand the subject but to investigate the subject for the sake of something else. But such misdirected goals fail to display a deep love of intellectual excellence. The one who loves intellectual excellence is able to recognize both the intrinsic and the instrumental value of a given object of inquiry.

Finally, the love of intellectual excellence stands opposed to the vice of being recklessly concerned with intellectual goods. Like many virtues, the virtue of loving intellectual excellence is a kind of mean between extremes. On the one hand, the one who loves intellectual excellence is opposed to intellectual complacency. On the other hand, the one who loves intellectual excellence is opposed to too extreme of a concern for truth and intellectual accomplishments that leads one to pursue these at the expense of other important values. The one who loves intellectual excellence is not reckless.

There are many people whose fascination with discovery—whose dominating desire to know—has taken them to places they should never have gone and led them to do things they should never have done. For example, reckless concern for the truth sometimes leads people to disrespect the privacy of others. Reckless interest in visual and mental stimulation might partially explain the appalling disrespect for personal privacy exhibited by paparazzi, gossip peddlers, and even Peeping Toms. The one who loves intellectual excellence is opposed to this sort of reckless concern for intellectual goals. She instead recognizes that some information should be pursued only by certain individuals and that all knowledge must be pursued in a way consistent with respect for human well-being.

An extreme example of reckless concern for intellectual accomplishments is supplied by totalitarian regimes that use their power over certain segments of their populations to conduct revolting experiments. The Nazis who performed experiments on prisoners at concentration camps did have an interest in attaining knowledge of diseases and their treatments. But their concern for these intellectual goals was deeply reckless and destructive of human well-being in the process. This sort of extreme recklessness in the pursuit of intellectual goals is incompatible with a love of intellectual excellence. One who loves intellectual excellence should also love the *excellent* pursuit of intellectual goods. The way in which these goods are pursued by the reckless is anything but excellent.

4.1.3 Summary

In this section, we have offered a portrait of the motivational virtue at the center of the life of the intellectually virtuous inquirer—the virtue of loving intellectual excellence. We characterized this virtue by explaining and illustrating four imperatives that its practitioner follows and by contrasting this virtue with those vices that oppose it. The one who loves intellectual excellence, we stated, loves the truth sacrificially, takes an interest in that which is worthy of inquiry and that which is explanatorily fundamental, and is careful to ensure that her beliefs and those of her community are supported adequately. The one who loves intellectual excellence stands opposed to the vices of being inadequately concerned for the truth, being complacent in the pursuit of intellectual accomplishments, valuing intellectual accomplishments only for their ties to other, extrinsic goods, and pursuing intellectual goods recklessly rather than excellently.

Key Ideas for Review

The **love of intellectual excellence** is a disposition to conduct inquiries in a way that displays a deep motivation for achieving intellectual goods responsibly. Intellectual goods include true belief, knowledge, understanding, and attitudes that are adequately supported.

The person who loves intellectual excellence follows four imperatives: sacrificing for intellectual goods, taking an interest in that which is worthy of investigation, taking an interest in that which is explanatorily fundamental, and ensuring that one's attitudes are adequately supported.

Four vices are contrary to the love of intellectual excellence: inadequate concern for the truth, inadequate concern for intellectual accomplishments, misdirected concern for intellectual accomplishments, and reckless concern for intellectual accomplishments.

Exercise 4.1

A. Applying the Imperatives of Love. For each of the following scenarios, explain why the character or characters involved do or do not succeed in following the four imperatives of loving intellectual excellence. For each scenario, discuss at least one of the imperatives.

1. John, a freshman in college, is taking his first philosophy class. The instructor has attempted to do justice to each side of the debate about global skepticism—the view that there is no knowledge. John writes in one of his weekly assignments for this course, "It seems like philosophers just go round and round. The debate never stops. They never come to know anything through all their arguing. If I've learned anything in this class, it's that I'm not a philosophical thinker. I just don't have the patience for all of this."

2. Sally and Mariah are debating whether there is good reason to think that Jesus's resurrection is a historical event. Mariah makes the point, "To determine whether there is good reason to believe that Jesus's resurrection is a historical event, we should probably consider when, more generally, there is good reason to believe that an event is historical. That is, we should start by considering the criteria that historians use to determine whether events actually happened."

3. After reading Nietzsche, Alex complains, "Wow. This guy really had some weird ideas. He thought that being humble and refraining from harming others were just signs of weakness. I wouldn't want to believe what he does. That's certainly not what my friends think. I disagree."

4. "Why do you like the Lord of the Rings movies, Thomas?" Emanuel asks. Thomas replies, "Because the effects are really dynamic. The scenery is nice too."

5. Eric tells his friends, "I've never really thought about whether there were any good arguments for believing in God. I guess I just thought he probably didn't exist. Lots of wars are fought over religion too. I thought it would be best to stay away from that stuff."

B. Identifying Virtue and Vice. In each of the scenarios below, identify whether the inquirer displays the virtue of loving intellectual excellence or exemplifies one of its contrary vices. Defend your answer by citing relevant material from the text of section 4.1.

1. Jasmine's assignment requires that she use three outside sources for her research paper. The topic of the paper is the early church's view of the

Trinity. She uses the Bible, Wikipedia, and the first website listed in the Google search results for "early church and the Trinity" as her sources. In her paper, she defends a thesis about the early church's view of the Trinity that she heard about in class, working these sources in where she can.

2. A psychologist discovers that the results of her study seem to conflict with the majority view in the contemporary establishment. She concludes that her study must have been improperly performed and decides to move on to a different topic, reasoning that the results might have gotten her in trouble if they had been published.

3. A candidate for an open pastoral position is interviewed by a church. In the interview process, the search committee asks if he has or thinks he will have reservations about the church's view that same-sex relationships are not morally acceptable. The candidate thinks to himself, *I don't have a decided view on this matter. Maybe if I thought about it, I'd disagree with the church. I'll simply ignore the issue while I serve here so that I won't entertain reservations about it. I can put up with their view while I'm here.*

4. A department chair breaks into the office of her colleague to discover whether he has been communicating with any other schools about job offers.

5. Knowing that if he were to fudge just slightly on the data of his experiment he would get a handsome reward by the company funding his research, a scientist massages the numbers until he gets the results he needs. *The results needed aren't very far off from what I've currently got, anyway*, he supposes.

4.2 Intellectual Courage and Caution

Generally speaking, the complementary virtues of courage and caution are concerned with enabling people to better navigate threats or obstacles to their goals. *Intellectual* courage and *intellectual* caution are virtues that equip people to navigate threats or obstacles to their pursuit of intellectual goods of the kind surveyed in the previous section—goods such as true beliefs, knowledge, and understanding. But intellectual courage and intellectual caution enable a person to navigate these obstacles well in different ways. **Intellectual courage** is *a tendency not to be overcome by obstacles to inquiry—a tendency to continue inquiry despite these obstacles.* **Intellectual caution** is *a tendency to sensitively regulate one's inquiries in light of known obstacles facing this inquiry.* A person can display both intellectual courage and intellectual caution in pursuit of the same inquiry and, indeed, is often better off for doing so.

To help us better understand what these virtues of inquiry involve, this section highlights some of the key obstacles often encountered in the process of inquiry, identifies how courage and caution distinctively equip their possessor to navigate these obstacles well, and contrasts courage and caution with their opposing vices.

4.2.1 *Navigating Obstacles to Inquiry*

Our focus here will be on two distinct kinds of obstacles to a successful inquiry. The first obstacle threatens the ability of an inquirer to successfully carry out an inquiry. It often comes in the form of an argument that the inquirer simply does not have what it takes to complete the inquiry successfully. The argument may highlight a deficiency peculiar to the inquirer or a deficiency of human inquirers more generally.

Certain forms of skepticism, for instance, present obstacles to successful inquiry. Consider the following example, which argues for a view called "global skepticism"—the view that no person can know anything:

1. For any person S to know any claim p, S must have evidence that rules out not-p. But for no claim p does any person S have evidence that rules out not-p. So no person S knows any claim p.

The idea behind this argument for global skepticism is that since none of us has adequate evidence to rule out the opposite of what we take our evidence to support, we cannot know the claims we take our evidence to support. For example, I might think that I ate oatmeal for breakfast because I seem to remember having eaten oatmeal for breakfast. But the skeptic will point out that my seeming to remember having eaten oatmeal for breakfast doesn't *rule out* my having *not* eaten oatmeal for breakfast. I might be misremembering what happened, confusing today's breakfast with yesterday's, or confusing today's breakfast with today's late-morning snack. The same goes for all other claims we might believe, according to the skeptic. Whatever evidence we might cite in their favor isn't enough to rule out that these claims are false.

Skepticism of this kind can present an obstacle to successful inquiry. It can thwart the inquirer's motivation from the start. If she doesn't have the abilities to achieve the intellectual goods at which her inquiry aims—goods such as knowledge—then it may seem that there's no point carrying out the inquiry and that she might as well give up.

The person with intellectual courage has a tendency not to be overcome by such obstacles. She has a tendency to persevere in pursuit of inquiry in spite of them. She remains undaunted in the face of uncertainty. Indeed, by considering why a person with intellectual courage will not be moved by the skeptic's objection to give up on inquiry in general, we can learn something revealing about the foundations of intellectual courage.

For the skeptic's argument to be persuasive, it turns out that certain intellectual goods must be attainable. More specifically, in order for the skeptic to make a positive case for his view about the impossibility of knowledge, humans must be able to have better reason for believing some claims than for believing others. In particular, we must be able to have better reason for believing the premises of the skeptic's argument than for believing their negations. But this possibility—to acquire better reason for believing something than for believing its negation—is itself an intellectual achievement; it is itself an advance in inquiry. Even if it were all we could achieve—if all we could do was determine which claims we ultimately have more reason to believe than to not believe—this would still be a worthwhile intellectual pursuit. And so the intellectually courageous person will not be moved by arguments such as the skeptic's that attempt to pose an obstacle to the ability of the inquirer to fulfill inquiry successfully since such arguments presume that inquirers can fulfill at least some inquiries with some measure of success.

Even more can be said about the foundations of intellectual courage on the basis of the present example. Suppose, as the intellectually courageous person will assume, that at least some measure of success in inquiry is attainable. It will follow that there must be some method or methods of inquiry whereby we can have some success in inquiry. There must be, for example, some method or methods of inquiry whereby we can come to have better reason for believing the premises of example 1 than for believing their negations (or vice versa). These methods will be those we employ when we are doing our best to believe the truth. For starters, we can use those methods wherein we gather evidence by using our properly working senses of vision, touch, taste, hearing, and smell as well as our properly working rational faculties. These foundational methods can be expanded through the use of patterns of argument such as those introduced in part 1.

In light of the foregoing, we can see that the foundation of intellectual courage is trust in those methods of inquiry that humans generally employ when they are doing their best to achieve intellectual goods. The foundation of intellectual courage is trust in one's properly working sensory and rational faculties and in one's competent use of argument structures that expand on these foundational faculties. Understanding that there can be no reason to think that successful inquiry is unachievable unless these methods can be employed to acquire better reason for some claims than for their negations, the person of intellectual courage chooses to place trust in the use of these methods. In using them she attempts to do her best to achieve intellectual goods, and she trusts that by using them she acquires more reason for believing some claims than others. For example, when she seems to see a cat as a result of her properly working vision, she trusts that in the absence of some further reason for thinking otherwise, she has more reason for thinking that there is a cat than that there is not. If it seems to her on the basis of her properly working rational faculties that the result of adding two and two is four, then in the absence of reason to think otherwise, she will trust that she has more reason to think this is so than to think it is not so. In this way, the foundation of intellectual courage is a certain kind of self-confidence—giving the benefit of the doubt to the outputs of those methods of inquiry one employs when one is doing one's best to achieve intellectual goods.[4]

This kind of self-confidence makes particularly good sense in light of a Christian, or more broadly theistic, worldview. On such a worldview, it is plausible that God has designed the world in such a way that we humans who bear God's image are capable of achieving intellectual goods through the use of those methods of inquiry we employ when doing our best to achieve intellectual goods. The ability to employ these methods has been given to us by God specifically with this purpose in mind—that we might come to hold true beliefs, gain knowledge, and achieve understanding of the world, ourselves, and God.

The self-confidence that forms the foundation of courage should not be confused with inflated hubris. This is precisely where the complementary virtue of caution comes in. Whereas the intellectually courageous person will be undaunted in the face of obstacles to successful inquiry, such as the obstacle raised by the specter of global skepticism, the intellectually cautious person will sensitively regulate his inquiries in light of an appreciation of such obstacles. Caution helps us to attend to what we should learn from the obstacles that courage motivates us to overcome.

In the face of the obstacle presented by global skepticism, for example, the cautious person will attend to the fact that the skeptic has correctly pointed out that for nearly any belief we might have, we cannot have evidence that rules out that belief being false. In other words, the skeptic is correct that the quality of our evidence is not so good that we can be infallible. There's always a possibility that what our evidence supplies us with is not in fact correct. The courageous person responds to this fact by not allowing it to overcome her and prevent her continued pursuit of inquiry. The cautious person responds to this fact by carefully regulating any future inquiries in such a way that he respects that such inquiries will almost never supply him with infallible evidence. He will not, as a result, generally seek or claim to have achieved infallible belief, and he will remain open to revising his beliefs, recognizing that it is possible that future evidence will render them no longer better supported than their negations. He appreciates and even owns the limitation highlighted by the obstacle to inquiry introduced by the skeptic.

Challenges to one's ability to complete inquiry successfully are not the only kinds of obstacles to inquiry. In addition, there are threats that certain bad things will come to those who pursue inquiry. These obstacles needn't directly challenge the ability of an inquirer to complete an inquiry successfully. Rather, they threaten those who would dare to pursue inquiry (whether they will be successful or not) with a kind of punishment for doing so—a price to pay for successfully completing inquiry or for trying to do so.

Consider the many and varied social pressures that exert an influence on what a person might select as a topic for inquiry or on how a person might go about pursuing a chosen topic of inquiry. In some social circles, merely pursuing inquiry into some topics is considered out of bounds. "We don't ask questions about that—we just believe it," you might be told. With this kind of attitude, there comes a social price to pay for pursuing the banned inquiry. And this presents an obstacle to pursuing inquiry quite different from the kind of obstacle highlighted above.

Arguments may even be offered on the basis of such social pressure. One might argue that for some treasured claim P, if you don't just accept P, you cannot go on being on good terms with a given group—so P. Such arguments are sometimes said to commit an *ad baculum* fallacy (or the fallacy of an appeal to force). They appeal to force in order to justify a conclusion. In the face of this kind of obstacle, a person of intellectual courage will have a tendency not to be overcome and to relinquish the pursuit of relevant intellectual goods. She will display a willingness to pay the price, if she must, in order to pursue inquiry concerning an important topic in a way that conforms to her best practices in trying to get to the truth.

A similar pressure can be exerted by oneself. A person can become so terrified of embarrassing himself, of revealing himself to not be as competent as his peers, that he is tempted to misrepresent the views of those who disagree with him in order to stack the deck unfairly in his favor when defending his views. Here the obstacle to pursuing inquiry comes in the form of a threat of experiencing embarrassment if inquiry is not pursued in a particular, dishonest way. The intellectually courageous person will display a tendency not to be overcome by such obstacles. He will have a tendency to boldly confront the best available objections to his views, even if this puts him in a position where he might come across to others as not as competent as his peers. He will do this out of a concern to pursue inquiry by using those methods that provide him with the best opportunity to achieve intellectual goods.

A tendency to persevere in the face of such obstacles does not imply an indifference to the importance of the threats they present. Again, this is where the complementary virtue of caution comes to the fore. The cautious person sensitively regulates her inquiries in light of limitations highlighted by obstacles facing her inquiries. For example, in some cases where there is social pressure not to pursue inquiry into a topic, this pressure is based on a concern that pursuing open, public inquiry into the topic could result in serious harm to members of the community. The cautious person may in such cases seek a way to pursue inquiry that is not open and public or, depending on the severity of the potential harm involved, may even be willing to refrain from inquiry altogether, at least temporarily.

The intellectually courageous person is someone who does not easily back down from inquiry in the face of an obstacle. Yet, if he is also cautious, then the manner in which he continues inquiry in the face of an obstacle may be narrowly tailored to respect the obstacle. In some cases he may even demur from pursuing inquiry altogether if the pursuit of such inquiry would bring about serious, unavoidable harm not outweighed by the potential intellectual goods to be attained through inquiry. In this way, the virtues of courage and caution can often complement one another. Courage motivates continued inquiry, and caution modifies the manner in which this inquiry is pursued. Yet in some cases courage and caution can pull a person in opposite directions. Courage motivates continued inquiry for the sake of achieving intellectual goods, but caution motivates pursuing inquiry in such a way that significant harm is avoided. Where the harm is bad enough and can't be avoided without suspending inquiry, caution can motivate suspending inquiry, while courage motivates continuing it.

4.2.2 Courage, Caution, and Opposing Vices

Intellectual courage and caution can be further illuminated by contrasting them with the opposing intellectual vices of cowardice, pedantry, and recklessness.

The cowardly person is one who tends to back down from the pursuit of inquiry at the first sign of an obstacle. Unlike the courageous person whose first instinct is to persevere in the face of such obstacles, the first instinct of the coward is to avoid the potential threats presented by obstacles to inquiry by abandoning inquiry altogether. Or if the threat is to a particular way of carrying out inquiry, the coward may avoid the threat by pursuing inquiry in another way.

This is so for both kinds of obstacles to inquiry identified in the previous subsection. At the first sign that pursuing inquiry into some topic will not result in intellectual goods such as knowledge or understanding, the coward's instinct is to relinquish the pursuit. If social ostracism looms as a punishment for pursuing inquiry, inquiring isn't worth the price for the coward. If pursuing inquiry in a way that utilizes the best methods one can for achieving intellectual goods will land one in an embarrassing situation, then the coward will seek alternative methods—methods aimed not at putting him in the best position to achieve intellectual goods but in the best position to avoid embarrassment.

Standing in contrast to the virtue of caution are two vices: pedantry and recklessness. Unlike the cautious person, the intellectually reckless person displays inadequate concern for the harm that can result from pursuing inquiry. She is so strongly motivated to acquire intellectual goods that she will attempt to gain them even at the expense of very serious, outweighing harm. She is too strongly disposed to take risks for the sake of achieving intellectual goods.

Imagine that you're a detective on the scene of an apparent homicide. You've completed four steps out of your eight-step investigative procedure, and at this point in your investigation, using methods that put you in the best position to achieve intellectual goods, you have more reason for thinking that a particular suspect, Tom, committed the murder than that anyone else did. Nonetheless, you recognize that in a considerable number of previous cases where you employed this same investigative procedure, things took a dramatic swing after step four. You had a suspect at step four that was your leading suspect, but during the later steps you ended up replacing him with another leading suspect, or the first at least ended up being exonerated. In such a case, even if you have reason to believe at this time in your inquiry that Tom committed the murder, committing to this conclusion would involve a very serious risk. That you could very well be wrong here is important in light of how much is riding on your decision. An intellectually reckless person may go ahead and commit to Tom's guilt because this is better supported by the present evidence than any other conclusion. But an appropriately cautious person will not do this. She will sensitively regulate her inquiries in light of an appreciation of the potential harm that can come about as a result of her pursuit of intellectual goods. Here, the cautious person will require stronger support than she might require in other cases before she will commit to a conclusion. Even though at the present time she has more reason to think Tom is guilty than to think he's innocent, this won't be enough for her to commit to his guilt.

Intellectual recklessness can sometimes even be exercised at the expense of *intellectual* goods. This can occur, for example, in a case where a person is so concerned to achieve some particular intellectual good that he ends up sacrificing other equally or more important intellectual goods. The goods sacrificed may be goods of his own or goods of others. A professional philosopher who obsessively attempts to resurrect a long-dismissed philosophical view may be guilty of such recklessness, sacrificing in this pursuit his own ability to pursue a more worthy project, or sacrificing the quality of his teaching.

Also standing opposed to intellectual caution is a kind of intellectual pedantry. Where the cautious person displays sensitivity to obstacles facing inquiry, the intellectual pedant is hypersensitive. Where the cautious person appreciates the limitations highlighted by obstacles, the pedant overestimates them. She has a tendency to overqualify, understate, or so carefully insulate her inquiries from risks that she can end up making little progress at all. Any conclusion she tentatively reaches dies the death of a thousand qualifications.

The intellectual pedant is so consumed with the limitations of inquiry that he has difficulty beginning or completing inquiries. He can't begin them because some assumption or other must always be taken on board for an inquiry to begin, and he can't cope with leaving such assumptions unexamined for the purpose of inquiring into what follows from them. He can't conclude an inquiry because any conclusion always depends on something or other being the case, and again he can't leave unexamined whether this latter thing is or is not the case for the purpose of completing the inquiry.

The cautious person, by contrast, recognizes that not every limitation needs to be identified as such in every context of inquiry. To get started on a project of identifying the best way to exercise responsible stewardship over the environment, the first step is *not* to search for a satisfying response to worries about global skepticism. The first step is *not* to attempt to establish the existence of physical objects. Nor do conclusions reached as the result of such an inquiry need to explicitly identify as limitations their reliance on these assumptions. The cautious person appreciates these limitations, but this appreciation need not lead her to overstress their importance. In contexts such as an inquiry into the best way forward for exercising stewardship over the environment, nearly any discussion of these limitations overstresses their importance.

Unlike the pedant, the cautious person recognizes that in some cases a commitment must be made even though not all loose ends have been tied up. Imagine the difficulty an intellectual pedant might have with coming to a conclusion about whom to vote for in a general election. There is always another issue to investigate, another story breaking in the news media. Given the pedant's overinflated concern with obstacles facing inquiry, he may never be able to settle on a conclusion and cast a vote. Caution does not demand this. In appropriately appreciating obstacles to inquiry, one appreciates as well the value of coming to conclusions in light of those obstacles and living with a degree of uncertainty.

The courageous person is the opposite of the coward. His first instinct is to persist in inquiry despite obstacles rather than to shrink in the face of

---

Key Ideas for Review

Intellectual courage is a tendency not to be overcome by obstacles to inquiry—a tendency to continue inquiry despite these obstacles.

Intellectual caution is a tendency to sensitively regulate one's inquiries in light of known obstacles facing this inquiry.

Some obstacles facing inquiry threaten to show that successful inquiry is impossible or unlikely. Others threaten to show that if inquiry is completed successfully, or completed via those methods one uses when doing one's best to achieve intellectual goods, then some bad will come about.

The foundation for intellectual courage is trust in those methods of inquiry one uses when doing one's best to achieve intellectual goods.

While intellectual courage is opposed to intellectual cowardice, intellectual caution is opposed to intellectual recklessness and pedantry.

---

them and surrender inquiry. The cautious person is the opposite of the reckless person and the pedant. He sensitively regulates his inquiries in light of an appreciation of the harm that can come about through his inquiry. He doesn't push ahead in the pursuit of inquiry regardless of what harm may come from the pursuit, like the reckless person. Nor does he overestimate or overstress the importance of limitations identified by obstacles facing inquiry. He knows how to begin and end finite chunks of inquiry, recognizing which limitations are necessary to identify and highlight in the process and which limitations can be safely set aside or tolerated for the purposes of completing the inquiry.

4.2.3 Summary

This section introduced the complementary virtues of intellectual courage and intellectual caution. Intellectual courage is a tendency to not be overcome by obstacles to inquiry, such as challenges that threaten to show that successfully completing inquiry is impossible or that it can come only at a price. The foundation of such courage is trust in one's God-given abilities to do the best one can in pursuing intellectual goods. Caution complements courage by sensitively regulating inquiry in light of an appreciation of the limitations highlighted by obstacles facing it. The courageous person is the opposite of the coward, while the cautious person is the opposite of the reckless person and the pedant.

Exercise 4.2

A. Identifying Intellectual Courage and Caution. For each of the following examples, make a case for why the character or characters do or do not display intellectual courage or intellectual caution. Cite relevant material from the text in section 4.2 in defense of your view.

1. The professor has tried to explain a new theory and appears ready to move on to another topic. Susan can't seem to make sense of the new theory. There's a question she has about the theory that she just can't see how to answer. But she worries that if she asks, others will become irritated with her for slowing up the class. So she keeps quiet.

2. Mark has been stuck on the same true-or-false exam question for ten minutes. He keeps second-guessing himself. Just before time runs out, he turns in the exam with the question left blank.

3. Kayla finds herself struggling to use the new software at work. But she's determined to learn. She signs up for an evening class to help her acquire the skills she needs to master it.

4. Mary has just learned about a scientific result that seems to conflict with common sense. Minimally, it conflicts with what she had previously thought on the basis of the methods of inquiry she generally uses when trying her best to get to the truth. As a result, she starts to doubt that she's any good at figuring out anything.

5. Jason's wife, Elizabeth, is meeting with a male friend she hasn't seen in years. Jason just can't squelch his curiosity concerning what Elizabeth will be like around this friend and what the friend is like. So he hires a private investigator to follow the two, without letting either of them know.

6. Senator McIntosh concludes his on-air comments by stating, "Nothing could be clearer than that the correct decision is to go to war."

7. Samantha is a job candidate with excellent credentials. Those on the hiring committee are so impressed with her credentials that they worry that she will outshine them if she is hired. Not wanting to be made to look inferior, they vote to deny her the position.

8. Edward just received feedback on a rough draft of his term paper from Professor Zed. One of Zed's comments said, "If you are going to make this claim here, you need to explain why you think the objection we discussed in the lecture is not persuasive." Rather than investigate the matter, Edward cuts the entire section from his paper.

9. Robert has worked hard on his analysis of recent trends in spending in the southeastern United States. He really wants to be able to draw conclusions from the work about the whole of the Southeast in order to impress his boss, but he recognizes that aspects of his research have been focused only on more local areas. When he composes the final

report, he carefully qualifies his conclusions, noting which conclusions may be representative of only more local areas and which may more likely represent the whole of the Southeast.

10. Alyson has been tasked by her employer with producing a brief document outlining the nature of the company's intended market base. A week after the deadline, she turns in a tome that begins with a fifteen-page section titled "Reasons to Be Hesitant about the Conclusions Stated Below."

4.3 Introspective Vigilance

This final section on internal virtues is concerned with the trait of introspective vigilance. This trait is concerned with bad patterns of inquiry to which many of us are prone—even by natural cognitive motivations. **Introspective vigilance** is *a tendency to attend carefully to one's own patterns of inquiry, and to root out, correct for, and prevent bad ones to the best of one's ability*. The introspectively vigilant person is someone who takes care to tend to her intellectual house. She is on alert for bad patterns of inquiry in herself, knowing herself and which patterns most tempt her, and she is careful to revise her beliefs and adjust her inquiries appropriately when she discovers that they have been reached, sustained, or carried out in a problematic way.

To better illuminate the nature of introspective vigilance, this section will discuss several common examples of bad patterns of inquiry for which the introspectively vigilant person will be on alert. It will also identify appropriate responses the vigilant person will display when he discovers that he has employed these patterns. The section will also identify two vices that are opposed to introspective vigilance: introspective aloofness and introspective arrogance.

4.3.1 Bad Patterns of Inquiry and Their Remedies

This subsection examines two pairs of closely related, problematic patterns of inquiry and identifies ways that an introspectively vigilant person may attempt to correct for them. We start with two problematic patterns of inquiry, each of which is a way of treating evidence in a biased or unfair manner. To see how these patterns operate, we can begin by thinking about the total body of evidence bearing on the truth or falsity of some claim P. This total body of evidence includes evidence in favor of P and evidence against P. The total body of evidence can be divided into smaller sub-bodies of evidence. In the absence of information to the contrary, there won't be any reason to think that any particular sub-body of this evidence is more important or weighty than another—that what one should conclude regarding P should be determined more by one sub-body of this evidence than by another sub-body. Likewise, in the absence of information to the contrary, there's no reason to think that the sub-body of the evidence concerning P that favors P is more important or weighty than the evidence that disfavors P. Yet two common problematic patterns of inquiry operate in opposition to these observations.

The first problematic pattern of inquiry is often called **confirmation bias**, which is *a pattern of inquiry in which inquirers disproportionately investigate evidence they have reason to think favors their own view.*[5] Imagine that William is considering whether to vote in favor of the new tax to fund the public streetcar link to the beach. Not having yet investigated many of the reasons offered in favor or against the tax, his initial inclination is to favor the tax. Because he favors the tax, he seeks out evidence that favors this view, and he forms his decision to vote for the tax on the basis of this evidence.

Confirmation bias of this kind is a common phenomenon, and it can be quite problematic. Since in the case of many real-world, complex matters there is bound to be evidence both in favor of and against a view, an investigation that systematically biases evidence that favors one view or the other frequently distorts an investigation. Conclusions drawn on the basis of such an inquiry can be irrationally one-sided.

This isn't to say that a sustained investigation focused exclusively on evidence that favors one view is never valuable. Such investigation *can* make a valuable contribution to a concerted, collective effort to thoroughly investigate a complex topic. It can be valuable, for example, to have some teams of researchers devote their energy to identifying the best reasons that can be marshaled in favor of one view, while other teams of researchers devote their energy exclusively to identifying the best reasons that can be marshaled for an opposing view—so long as when all-things-considered judgments are formed about the merits of the views, all the evidence is taken into account. Confirmation bias becomes problematic when the biased treatment of evidence is the only treatment of the evidence.

A second common way of treating evidence with bias involves treating certain sub-bodies of evidence as more important than others because of the way in which the sub-bodies are presented. For example, studies have found that the order in which sub-bodies of evidence are presented has a significant influence on how they are evaluated. Sub-bodies presented earlier are given greater weight than sub-bodies presented later.[6] A similar but less obvious effect has been identified in cases where subjects are aware of a total body of evidence, but only part of that evidence is explicitly presented to them. Despite their awareness of the unpresented evidence, people tend to weigh more heavily the evidence that is explicitly presented.[7]

There may be natural cognitive motivations that help to explain these common behaviors. For example, if we tend to assume that those who are presenting us with information are likely to present what is most important first and to make explicit what is most important while leaving implicit what is less important, this may help to explain these effects. To the extent that we are justified in making these assumptions, these patterns of inquiry are not particularly pernicious. But if not monitored closely, the patterns can become problematic.

For example, the presumption that people presenting us with information are likely to present that information in order of importance does not justify the more general claim that evidence acquired earlier is likely to be more important than evidence acquired later for the simple reason that not all evidence is acquired from other people. Moreover, there are often cases in which it is questionable whether we are warranted in expecting those presenting us with information to state explicitly what is most important and to present evidence in order of importance. Indeed, the prevalence of confirmation bias itself suggests one reason for questioning such an assumption. People may present the information they do because they have been biasedly focusing on that information since they had reason to think it confirmed their views. In light of such concerns, we should take care not to quickly conclude that the order in which evidence is encountered is indicative of its weight.

Introspectively vigilant people will be on alert for these kinds of biased treatments of evidence in themselves. They will attend to the way in which they have carried out their inquiries, asking whether they have investigated evidence selectively, or assigned greater weight to some sub-bodies of evidence than others without sufficient reason. To the extent that they are worried about their own tendencies to succumb to these biased treatments of evidence, they may even institute policies of inquiry designed to prevent them in the first place. They may, for example, adopt a policy of alternating investigation of evidence that favors a view and then that disfavors it, or a policy of explicitly stating for themselves all the evidence they are aware of rather than leaving some of it implicit.

Two additional examples of problematic patterns of inquiry each can be seen as consequences of an overactive tendency of persons to construct coherent narratives. An important part of our basic cognitive functioning is that we attempt to piece together new information with old, constructing a coherent narrative of how all the information we have fits together. Without such a tendency, our cognitive lives would be impoverished, and we would be able to make little progress building on stored information. Yet this tendency to construct coherent narratives can become overactive and lead to significant cognitive mistakes. It can lead us to make illusory connections.

For example, a commonly noted informal fallacy is the *post hoc* (or *post hoc, ergo propter hoc*) fallacy. The **post hoc fallacy** is *an informal fallacy in which one too quickly concludes that because one thing occurred after another, it occurred because of the other—it was caused by the other*. To illustrate this fallacy, imagine you start feeling sick to your stomach on a Friday evening. Like many of us would, you instinctively start wondering what could have brought this on. In many such cases, there will be a wide range of potential causes. Yet we sometimes fixate on a narrow range of these, such as what we ate for breakfast or lunch, and conclude that because the illness came about after we ate what we did, it came about because we ate what we did. Constructing a narrative in this way too quickly can involve making an illusory connection. As we observed, there are many other potential causes of the sick feeling. You might have come down with a virus instead. Nonetheless, it isn't uncommon to make such connections and, once making such connections, to persist in our thinking. You might go on for some time feeling unease about the kind of food you had eaten, even if it wasn't the culprit.

A similar error occurs when we string together a number of connections that are tenuous at best. This error is often called the **slippery slope fallacy**, which is *an informal fallacy in which one reasons in accordance with a chain of conditional ("if . . . then") statements where the connection between the conditionals' antecedents and their consequents is tenuous*. For example, a person may reason: if P, then Q; and if Q, then R; and if R, then S; so if P, then S, even though P provides at most weak support for Q, Q at most weak support for R, and R at most weak support for S. Of course, there is nothing problematic about reasoning in accordance with conditionals if each of the conditional claims is a claim we have good reason to be confident about. But in cases where the conditional claims are ones we should be only slightly confident about (at best), the connection between what we start with and what we end with becomes illusory. The problem here is much like the problem of dwindling probabilities identified in chapter 3.

Imagine that Francis is thinking about whether to vote for a particular political candidate, Ms. Archer. He reasons that if Ms. Archer is elected, then gender inequality will become a priority of her office. And if gender inequality becomes a priority of her office, her office will institute policies that overcorrect for this inequality, making it very difficult for men to get jobs. And if these policies are instituted, then Francis's own job security will be threatened. So if Ms. Archer is elected, his job security will be threatened. Such a line of reasoning is bound to contain tenuous connections and so illustrates well the slippery slope fallacy.

Again, the introspectively vigilant person will be on guard against making these kinds of mistakes in inquiries. While recognizing the value of attempting to construct a coherent narrative that unites together all available information, the introspectively vigilant person is wary of too quickly making spurious connections and might therefore institute corrective policies. Such policies might include always searching for additional potential causes in order to correct for a temptation to commit *post hoc* fallacies or flagging any instances of lengthy chains of reasoning used to reach conclusions and investigating how strongly the chain supports the conclusion when assigning specific confidence levels to each link in the chain. By instituting practices such as these, the introspectively vigilant person can help to mitigate the effects of bad patterns of inquiry to which many of us are prone.

4.3.2 Vigilance, Aloofness, and Arrogance

The virtue of introspective vigilance stands opposed to two vicious dispositions people can have toward their own bad patterns of inquiry. One of these vices is introspective aloofness. Aloof people tend to be unaware, unconcerned, and uninterested in their own patterns of inquiry. They may very well engage in inquiry, but they don't turn an introspective eye toward *how* they pursue inquiry. Their tendency is to go on pursuing intellectual goods in the manner they always have, unconcerned with identifying any ways to monitor or improve their methods of pursuit. (They are certainly not the kind of people to freely enroll in a logic class!)

Introspectively vigilant people are very different. They are in the first instance introspective. They regularly turn a critical eye toward their own processes of inquiry. They may even turn a critical eye toward their own vigilant governance of their inquiries. If they do, however, their inward turn won't amount to frivolous navel-gazing. Rather, it is motivated by a concern to avoid common bad patterns of inquiry to which they are susceptible. It isn't a tendency to look inward for its own sake.

Introspective vigilance likewise stands opposed to introspective arrogance. The introspectively arrogant tend to presume that they are less vulnerable to bad patterns of inquiry than the masses. They may be happy to look at their own patterns of inquiry, but they do so more in an effort to identify exemplary reasoning than in an effort to subject their own practices to critical scrutiny.

The temptation to this kind of arrogance may, unfortunately, be more common than we recognize. It has been shown repeatedly that people have a tendency toward self-enhancement: they tend to view themselves in a more positive light than they view others. People are far quicker to attribute some bad patterns of reasoning, such as certain biases, to others than to themselves.[8] Introspective arrogance, then, may be quite a temptation for many of us.

Key Ideas for Review

Introspective vigilance is a tendency to attend carefully to one's own patterns of inquiry, and to root out, correct for, and prevent bad ones to the best of one's ability.

Confirmation bias is a pattern of inquiry in which inquirers disproportionately investigate evidence they have reason to think favors their own view.

The ***post hoc* fallacy** is an informal fallacy in which one too quickly concludes that because one thing occurred after another, it occurred because of the other—it was caused by the other.

The **slippery slope fallacy** is an informal fallacy in which one reasons in accordance with a chain of conditional ("if . . . then") statements where the connection between the conditionals' antecedents and their consequents is tenuous.

Introspectively vigilant people stand opposed to such arrogance, which constitutes an additional bad pattern of inquiry for which introspectively vigilant people must be on guard. Understanding the tendency many of us have toward self-enhancement, they intentionally cultivate a practice of looking carefully and thoroughly for bad patterns of inquiry in themselves. They do what they can to learn about what these patterns are, how to identify them, and how to protect against them. They oppose an arrogance that would set them apart from the rest of humanity in this regard.

4.3.3 Summary

This section introduced the virtue of introspective vigilance. Introspectively vigilant people have a tendency to be on guard against bad patterns of inquiry in themselves, identifying, correcting for, and preventing these patterns as best they can. Two kinds of examples of bad patterns of inquiry were identified for illustrative purposes: patterns of inquiry that involve biased treatment of evidence and patterns of inquiry that involve identifying illusory connections. By standing on guard and opposing these bad patterns of inquiry in themselves, introspectively vigilant people stand opposed to the introspectively aloof and the introspectively arrogant.

Exercise 4.3

A. Identifying Introspective Vigilance. For each of the following examples, make a case for why the character or characters do or do not display introspective vigilance. Cite relevant material from the text in section 4.3 in defense of your view.

1. Eleanor has recently learned that people of her demographic have a tendency to disregard out of hand the views of people in another demographic. Eleanor doesn't want this tendency to distort her own inquiries, and so she strives to identify a way whereby she can ensure that she doesn't treat the views of people in this demographic any differently than she treats the views of people in other demographics, including her own.

2. Ever since he was sixteen, Elliot has thought that the early Christians invented the resurrection story about Jesus. Now a tenured professor, he has spent much of his life investigating the reasons for thinking that the early Christians might have pulled off this hoax.

3. Tim was recently amused to read that when asked to solve certain simple mathematical equations, a large percentage of college students go for a quick but wrong solution rather than doing the work to try to make sure they get the correct solution. *So much the worse for them*, he thinks. *Glad I'm not like that!*

4. Alexis wants to fit in with her peer group. She knows what their favorite brand of clothing is. So she tries to find reasons for thinking that this brand is good.

5. Priscilla is a member of a jury. She's convinced when she hears the case of the prosecution—so much so that when it is the defense's turn, she concentrates on what might be wrong with their presentation and on how what they've said might be accounted for by the prosecution. She reaches a guilty verdict.

6. Ray the reporter learns from a source that the president announced his decision to veto the bill after meeting with his secretary of state. Ray prints the headline, "President vetoes bill in light of advice from secretary of state."

7. After hearing a new objection to his views about the morality of recreational drug use, Philip returns to his dorm to search the internet for defenses of his favored position in order to restore his confidence.

8. Matt reasons as follows: "Everybody is a little biased, and so am I. It's just a fact of life. There's nothing we can do about it."

9. Susan complains, "I hate it when people exaggerate. Everybody does it so horribly all the time!"

10. During the campaign season, Erika, an undecided voter, intentionally decides to randomize the order in which she watches parts of the debates between the two candidates. Sometimes she watches one candidate's statements first and the other's next, and other times she reverses the order.

5

▶ ▶ ▶ ▶ ▶ ▶

Virtues of Intellectual Dependence

In part 2 we are concerned with learning about some of those key virtues of inquiry that enable success in achieving intellectual goods, such as true belief, knowledge, and understanding. Chapter 4 identified four virtues that we called "internal virtues" because they can be exhibited in a person's own private pursuit of intellectual goods. While they can also be exhibited as part of a collective pursuit of intellectual goods, a collective context for inquiry isn't necessary for them. By contrast, the virtues of inquiry that will be discussed in this chapter and the next demand a social context for inquiry. They are virtues that can be exhibited only as part of a collective pursuit of intellectual goods.

This chapter focuses on three virtues exhibited by inquirers who are in the position of depending on other inquirers in their pursuit of intellectual goods. The paradigm case of such dependence on others is when we depend on others as sources of information—in particular, when we depend on them to testify to us about something that they have better access to than we do. But there are other ways to depend on others as well. We can depend on them not simply as sources of views but also as sources of arguments. And we can depend on them as instructors in inquiry. Others can even be involved in aiding us in developing the virtues of inquiry. In all of these ways of depending on others, our success in inquiry will be better enabled by possessing and exercising the virtues identified in this chapter.

5.1 Trust

The most foundational virtue of the dependent inquirer is trust in others. Without trust in others, inquirers don't depend on others at all; they refuse to depend on them. Not trusting others stifles collective inquiry much in the same way that not trusting one's own best methods of inquiring for oneself stifles individual inquiry. The absence of trust cuts off the possibility of an inquiry in which one depends on others at the start.

But what exactly is it to trust someone else? And what kind of defense can be given of the value of such trust? We turn to these topics in the next subsection and then identify three vices that are contrary to trust in subsection 5.1.2.

5.1.1 The Nature and Value of Trust

Trusting others has much in common with trusting our own best methods of inquiring for ourselves. As we define it, **trust** is *a tendency to treat others' best methods of inquiry the same way as one's own in the absence of reason for doing otherwise*. Dependent inquirers who trust those on whom they are dependent have a tendency, in the absence of reason to think otherwise, to treat the best methods of inquiry of others the same way they treat their own best methods of inquiry—as enabling success in achieving intellectual goods. They treat the best methods of inquiry of others as means to achieve true belief, knowledge, and understanding.

Imagine that I've been waiting for an important package to arrive at the house. For the last few hours I've had to be away from the house at the office, but my wife has been at the house. I want to know if the package has arrived, so I call to ask my wife if anyone has come by with a package. She tells me that nobody has been by.

In this scenario, I am a dependent inquirer—in particular, dependent on my wife. If I exhibit the virtue of trust, then I will treat her best methods of inquiry the same way I would treat my own—as enabling success in achieving intellectual goods. If I trust her, then I will treat those methods whereby she came to believe that nobody had been by the house with a package the way I would treat my own methods for coming to that conclusion. If I had been at the house the last few hours, used my best methods of inquiry to determine if someone had been by the house with a package, and had thereby come to think that nobody had come by, I would trust myself to know that nobody had come by with a package. Thus if I trust my wife in this scenario, I should likewise take myself to know that nobody has come by with a package.

Sometimes, as in this case of the package, our trust in others involves trusting the same (or roughly the same) methods of inquiry in them that we must trust in ourselves. Presumably my wife's methods of inquiring into whether anyone has been by with a package are roughly the same as the methods I would have used had I been home. She likely used her hearing to detect whether anyone had knocked on the door and her vision to determine if a package had been placed outside. I trust these same methods in myself, and so I trust them in her.

In other cases, trusting someone else may demand trusting a method in them that is different from those we already trust in ourselves. This is especially common where we depend on a person with specialized training, because in such cases the person on whom we are dependent may have access to a method of inquiry to which we do not have access. For example, I might depend on a lawyer to defend my case in court. In doing so, I might trust her to employ methods of inquiry into my case that enable the achievement of intellectual goods regarding the best way to defend me. These methods may not be available to me—indeed, that's part of the explanation for why I hire a lawyer in the first place. Nonetheless, because I trust others in the sense of tending to treat their best methods of inquiry the same way I would treat my own, I treat my lawyer's methods as enabling successful inquiry so long as I don't have reason to think otherwise.

Such is the nature of trust. But on what grounds can it be defended? One powerful way to defend the value of trusting others is by appealing to the principle that one should treat *like cases alike*.[1] What I trust in myself is my conscientious use of those methods I employ when trying my best to achieve intellectual goods. As we saw in section 4.2, such trust can be defended on the grounds that there couldn't be any reason against it. By virtue of employing such methods, we will all converge on the idea that we should treat like cases alike. Treating like cases alike, in other words, is a method we will all come to trust in ourselves. When we apply this method to how we conduct inquiries when we depend on others, it implies that we should trust them as well. We should treat those methods they employ when doing their best to achieve intellectual goods the same way we should treat the methods we employ when doing our best to achieve intellectual goods. This is because the methods, and their users, are alike. In the absence of reason to think otherwise, I should grant that others are like me—they have roughly the same abilities for inquiry that I do. And in the absence of reason to think otherwise, I should grant that their best methods for inquiry are as trustworthy as my own. By following the principle of treating like cases alike, a person who trusts her own best methods for inquiry should come to trust others.

When we trust others, we treat them with the respect that the image of God in them deserves. In light of humanity's common origin and design in God, we can affirm the basic likeness of all humans. In the absence of reason to think otherwise, we will indeed be inclined to grant that to the extent that any of us is trustworthy, all of us are. By trusting others, we uphold their dignity as agents created in God's image, and we honor God's handiwork in designing humans with capacities necessary for knowing and loving him.

5.1.2 Credulity, Condescension, and Injustice

Three vices stand opposed to trusting others. By identifying them, we will better understand what trusting others does and does not demand. The first is the vice of credulity. **Credulity** is *an insensitivity to reasons for treating others' methods of inquiry differently from one's own*. Credulous people are too quick and careless in treating the methods of inquiry of others the same way they treat their own. In particular, they are insensitive to two kinds of reasons for treating the methods of inquiry of others differently from how they treat their own methods. This marks a difference between credulous people and trusting people, because trusting people need not be insensitive to these reasons, of which we can mention two.

The first reason for treating the methods of inquiry of others differently from the way one treats one's own methods is that the other may not be as good at employing methods of inquiry as oneself. While we must be very careful in identifying evidence for this reason, given our temptation to view ourselves more positively than we view others (see section 4.3), this does not imply that no such evidence is ever available. For example, you may have evidence that the person on whom you might depend does not have the same kind of specialized training in a given discipline that you have. Imagine that you are a senior expert in identifying different kinds of trees, and you want to know whether any trees of a particular kind are present in a location you haven't visited. Your research indicates that, despite popular belief, some such trees may be scattered throughout the area. You meet a junior researcher at a conference who has recently visited this location but who doesn't have your same level of training in identifying tree types. He tells you there are no trees of this type in the location, and rather than taking his testimony with a grain of salt in light of your superior experience in the field, you conclude straightway that the indications of your research must be flawed.

The second reason for treating others' methods of inquiry differently from your own is that you doubt their *methods*. Here you have evidence that the other inquirer's best methods of inquiry are not as good as your own or are simply not reliable. Suppose you have come across some research about a hot-button social issue that you find very interesting and compelling. You then learn about a flaw in the methods used as part of the research. You understand the flaw, and you understand how the flaw could affect the outcomes of the research. Nonetheless, you continue to allow the results of the research to exercise just as strong an influence over your own thinking on the matter as you did prior to learning about the flaw.

Each of these cases involves an exhibition of the vice of credulity. The characters in the example exhibit an insensitivity to reasons for not treating others' methods of inquiry the same way one treats one's own best methods. Such insensitivity doesn't mark people of trust. Their tendency is only a *tendency*—in the absence of reason for doing otherwise—to treat others' best methods of inquiry the same way they treat their own best methods.

The second and third vices oppose trusting others from the other side. They both involve failures to treat others' methods of inquiry the same way one treats one's own best methods, where one lacks sufficient reason for doing so. The second vice, then, is condescension. **Condescension** *is a tendency to not treat anyone else's best methods of inquiry the same as your own simply because they are not you.* Condescending people generally treat *all* other persons differently than they treat themselves. They put themselves on a pedestal, acting as if others' best methods of inquiry are inferior to their own *just because they are others'* methods. They are what we might call "intellectual egoists"—valuing their own methods of inquiry more than others' just because the methods are theirs. Such people fail to recognize and appropriately employ the principle of treating like cases alike and thus severely hamper their own ability to inquire successfully. They can attain only those intellectual goods they can achieve on their own. And this leaves their intellectual lives significantly impoverished.

Of course, there can be legitimate reasons to forego depending on someone else in the process of inquiry. When you are trying to figure something out for yourself, it makes perfect sense to tell someone else who already knows, "Wait, don't tell me!" Sometimes there is something valuable to gain in figuring something out for yourself, even if you could more easily learn it from someone else. This kind of foregoing of dependence on another is not incompatible with trusting the other. Indeed, to the extent that you really do think that you could get to the truth more easily by relying on the other, you *exhibit* trust in the other. In contrast, condescending people don't trust others simply because they are *others*.

The third and related vice is intellectual injustice. **Intellectual injustice** is *a tendency to treat others' best methods of inquiry differently from one's own on the basis of reasons that are irrelevant to whether others' methods or abilities are as good as one's own.* Unjust people don't treat others' best methods of inquiry differently from their own just because they are others. Instead of treating *all* others' best methods differently from their own, they treats *some* others' best methods the same as their own and *other* others' best methods of inquiry differently. And they do this in the absence of sufficient

185

reason to think that the others' best methods they treat differently from their own are indeed inferior to their own.

Probably the most pernicious example of this kind of injustice involves treating the best methods of inquiry of some others differently from one's own simply because of the gender, race, or class of those others.[2] Imagine if I treated my wife's inquiry about the package delivery differently from my own just because she is a woman. It's hard to believe that I would remain married very long acting like this! Yet there is some evidence that such unjust treatment on the basis of gender is more widespread than we might at first think. For example, it has commonly been reported that men outperform women on student evaluations. One explanation for this is that students tend to act differently when in a position of intellectual dependence on a woman than when in a position of intellectual dependence on a man. To do so is a violation of the demands of intellectual trust. Similarly, a reporter who treats the testimony of members of one racial group differently from the testimony of members of other racial groups on the basis of race alone exhibits the vice of intellectual injustice and thus violates the demands of trust.

Those who exhibit the vice of intellectual injustice commit a kind of *ad hominem* fallacy against those they fail to trust. An **ad hominem fallacy** is *a kind of informal fallacy that directs an argument against a person rather than against an argument*. The intellectually unjust make other *persons* their concern rather than those persons' abilities and methods as inquirers. On the basis of features of these others that do not provide reason to treat their methods of inquiry any differently from their own, unjust inquirers treat them differently. Their lack of trust is an attack against other inquirers—and an irrational attack at that.

When we conduct collective inquiry with condescension or injustice, we fail to adequately respect the dignity of our fellow humans. We may end up silencing or suppressing them. We may even end up stunting their further intellectual growth. People who trust others treat others' best methods of inquiry the same way they treat their own best methods, provided they don't have reason to do otherwise. By doing so they both enable their own success in inquiry and appreciate the image of God in their fellow inquirers.

5.1.3 Summary

This section introduced the virtue of trust in others, which is foundational for enabling successful inquiries for those who intellectually depend on others. People who trust others treat others' best methods of inquiry the same as their own, provided they don't have reason for doing otherwise.

> ## Key Ideas for Review
>
> **Trust** is a tendency to treat others' best methods of inquiry the same way as one's own in the absence of reason for doing otherwise.
>
> **Credulity** is an insensitivity to reasons for treating others' methods of inquiry differently from one's own.
>
> **Condescension** is a tendency to not treat anyone else's best methods of inquiry the same as your own simply because they are not you.
>
> **Intellectual injustice** is a tendency to treat others' best methods of inquiry differently from one's own on the basis of reasons that are irrelevant to whether others' methods or abilities are as good as one's own.
>
> An ***ad hominem* fallacy** is a kind of informal fallacy that directs an argument against a person rather than against an argument.

In doing so they treat like cases alike and respect the dignity of their fellow humans. Trust of this kind is opposed to credulity, condescension, and intellectual injustice.

Exercise 5.1

A. Evaluating Trust. For each of the following examples, make a case for why the character or characters do or do not display trust. If a character exhibits a vice that is contrary to trust, identify the vice. Cite relevant material from the text in section 5.1 in defense of your view.

1. After being given a confident "no" from his neighbor when he asked whether it was trash day, John proceeded to look it up online.
2. After being told about an objection Pedro has raised to the new school policy she favors, Helen responds, "Didn't he move here from South America? What does he know?"
3. Brent, an architect, is worried on the basis of his calculations that his kids' playhouse won't hold up long without repairs. He catches his kids in the playhouse and disciplines them for being there when they shouldn't. But when they protest that they were just up there—and even jumping—and it was fine, he decides to let them keep playing without making the repairs.
4. After her Alcoholics Anonymous meeting, Sheila is encouraged by another member of the group to try just a half pint of beer with her at the bar. "You'll be fine," the group member says. Since the other member is experienced, Sheila concludes that having the drink is probably safe.

5. When his cousin, a financial trader, tells Sid that he should make a change to his portfolio in the next quarter, Sid shrugs it off, thinking, *He would say that. He's rich.*

6. Francine has worked very hard on her paper, trying her best to ensure it doesn't have any flaws. As part of a class exercise, she receives feedback from two of her peers. While she doesn't think there are any errors in the paper, she eagerly looks through her peers' comments, open to the possibility that they may have caught something she missed.

7. Mike, who has always fancied himself a good leader, has been tasked with heading up a team to design a new drug. His team members keep noticing, though, that he's constantly looking over their shoulders and interrupting them to ask for explanations for why they are doing things the way they are doing them. He can't seem to let them do their part of the work.

8. Jenny is a member of the jury. "I just don't trust him," she says of the defendant during the deliberations. "Wearing clothes like that and unashamed of his unorthodox relationships. . . . What a weirdo!"

9. Scott's grade wasn't quite what he was hoping, and his paper came back with a good number of suggestions for future improvement from his professor. Rather than look through the suggestions, Scott concludes that what's really going on is that the professor doesn't like him.

10. Pamela's first book comes in for severe criticism by an experienced critic. She thinks to herself, *This critic is just getting old and senile.*

5.2 Interpretive Charity

Whenever we are in a position where we depend on others in our inquiries, we must interpret their communicative expressions in an effort to identify their views and the reasons they have offered for those views. The virtue that governs the virtuous inquirer's approach to these acts of interpretation is the virtue of interpretive charity. **Interpretive charity** is *a tendency to interpret others in as positive a light as possible, consistent with a respect for their communicative intentions.*

When we interpret others' communicative expressions, we must respect what we have reason to think they intended to communicate via these expressions. At the same time, we can do more or less to identify views and arguments that are both faithful to these intentions *and* have positive features. Interpretively charitable people do as much as they can to interpret others' views and arguments as having positive features, while not interpreting them in a way that violates their intentions. Below we will clarify in further detail what interpretive charity is and why it is valuable, and we will contrast it with the contrary vices of interpretive stinginess and interpretive face blindness.

5.2.1 The Nature and Value of Interpretive Charity

Interpretive charity kicks in when we attempt to evaluate the views or arguments of others. To evaluate these views or arguments, we must first identify what views or arguments we are trying to evaluate. And interpretive charity regulates how we identify the views or arguments of others for the purpose of evaluation.

We have described interpretive charity as a tendency to interpret another's communicative expressions in a way that is both consistent with their intentions and maximizes the chances that these expressions reveal views or arguments with positive features. The positive features with which charity is concerned are achievements of intellectual goods, such as true belief, knowledge, or understanding. Thus when charitable people interpret someone else's communicative expressions in order to evaluate this person's views or arguments, they do so in a way that (a) respects the other's intentions and (b) maximizes the chances that the expressions they are interpreting were intended to represent views or arguments whereby the other has achieved intellectual goods.

Which specific intellectual goods charitable people are concerned with will depend to some extent on whether they are interpreting a communicative expression of another that they have reason to believe expresses the other's views or an expression they have reason to believe expresses an argument the other endorses. When charitable people have reason to think that they are interpreting an expression of another's views, they will attempt to interpret this expression in such a way that it expresses a view that is true, as long as doing so is consistent with a respect for the other's communicative intentions. That is, as long as interpreting the other as expressing a true view doesn't conflict with what there is good reason to think she intended to communicate, the charitable person will endeavor to do so.

Imagine that Tayshaun has been looking for his keys all morning, and his roommate Zachary is aware of this and has been trying to help him find them. After searching for a while, Zachary gives up and moves on to something else. But later in the morning, Zachary suddenly yells at Tayshaun with excitement. "Hey, Tayshaun," he yells, making a jingling sound, "I found your wallet!"

As many of us would in similar circumstances, Tayshaun would likely respond by saying, "You mean my keys? Thanks!" Here Tayshaun is plausibly exercising interpretive charity in interpreting Zachary as holding the view that Zachary has just found Tayshaun's keys rather than his wallet. Given the background of the story, it does not conflict with what Tayshaun knows about Zachary's communicative intentions to interpret Zachary as having intended to have said "I found your keys" rather than "I found your wallet." And interpreting Zachary in this way maximizes the chances that the view Zachary has intended to express is a true view, since in light of the jingling, it is plausible that Zachary has found Tayshaun's keys rather than his wallet. By interpreting Zachary as having the view that he has just found Tayshaun's keys, Tayshaun puts Zachary's views in the best light possible, consistent with what he knows about Zachary's communicative intentions.

Examples like this one are commonplace. One reason for this is that, as fallible and sometimes clumsy humans, we don't always express ourselves very well. Commonly what comes out of our mouths doesn't match so well what we are thinking. Sometimes we struggle to try to put into words what we are thinking.

The problem isn't isolated to rather trivial examples. It also occurs in more serious contexts of inquiry. Scientists, philosophers, mathematicians— professional inquirers generally—sometimes misrepresent their own views. As it has sometimes been said, "There's the view, and then there's the statement of the view." Sometimes when inquirers try to *state* their view, they don't do it very well. They miss the view, misrepresent it, or don't put it as perspicuously as they could. Their statement of it is vulnerable to an objection, whereas if they had stated it better, their statement of it would not have been vulnerable to the objection.

Charitable interpreters are on guard in light of these possibilities. Since they are ultimately interested in achieving intellectual goods such as true belief, they will do their best to interpret others so that they learn something true from them. Surely it would be a mistake from the vantage point of trying to achieve intellectual goods if an inquirer interpreted someone else's poor statement of a view in a rigid way, identified how that statement of the view was false, and then proceeded to no longer consider views in its vicinity. Pursuing such an interpretive strategy could impede one's access to important truths that the other believed but simply didn't express well.

A similar point applies to interpreting the arguments of others. When they have reason to think that someone has intended to communicate an argument they endorse, charitable people will attempt to interpret this argument in such a way that it provides a source of knowledge or understanding. They will attempt to maximize the chances that the interpretation they offer is one whereby their conversation partner achieved such goods, as long as doing this does not conflict with this person's communicative intentions. Because arguments offer reasons for holding views, they, unlike mere views, are the kinds of tools that can provide knowledge or understanding. Charitable people are concerned about achieving such intellectual goods and so will do as much as they can, in their dependence on others in inquiry, to acquire such goods by depending on them.

One way to exhibit interpretive charity is to supply unstated premises for another's argument that is intentionally or unintentionally formulated as an enthymeme. An **enthymeme** is *a statement of an argument that leaves some premises or a conclusion unstated.* Often we can better represent a person's reasoning for purposes of evaluating it if we supply the unstated premises or conclusion.

Imagine that Catherine is wondering whether the party on Friday, which everyone knows Anna is hosting, will be any fun. So she asks Jerry, since he's an expert on party quality. Jerry says, "If Anna's putting it on, it will be a blast." Strictly speaking, Jerry has simply affirmed a conditional statement. However, in this context it would be charitable for Catherine to interpret Jerry as having expressed his endorsement of an argument—an argument he now offers to Catherine for thinking that the party will be fun. Catherine can reconstruct the argument by supplying its unstated premises or conclusion. If she does so with interpretive charity, she will aim to do so in such a way as to maximize Jerry's chances of having achieved knowledge or understanding via his endorsement of the argument. She might reconstruct Jerry's argument as follows: "Anna is putting on Friday's party. If Anna is putting on Friday's party, Friday's party will be fun. So Friday's party will be fun." Interpreting Jerry's statement as indicating his endorsement of this argument is consistent with what Catherine knows of Jerry's communicative intentions, and it gives him a good chance to have achieved knowledge or understanding via his endorsement of the argument. By endorsing the argument, he may very well know that the party will be fun.

Examples of this kind occur regularly for at least two reasons. First, given that we often share much background in common with those who depend on us in inquiry, and given that this background often serves as a necessary premise for arguments we give to others who share it, we often feel as if it is unnecessary to explicitly highlight the role this background plays because those who depend on us are already aware of it. They can, we might say, be relied upon to charitably identify it if necessary. Second, in light of our fallibility and clumsiness, sometimes we do not state arguments as carefully and thoroughly as we should. We might understand a claim on which our arguments depend to be obvious to others and so leave it unstated. But in doing so we might be making a mistake. The claim is precisely what is challengeable about the argument. Thus in light of how common it is to formulate our arguments as enthymemes, our approach to evaluating them is best made via the trait of interpretive charity. This maximizes our chances to acquire intellectual goods through our intellectual dependence on others.

5.2.2 Interpretive Stinginess and Interpretive Face Blindness

We will further illuminate interpretive charity by examining two vices that are contrary to it. The first is interpretive stinginess. **Interpretive stinginess** is *a tendency to resist interpreting what others have said in the most positive light*. Stingy interpreters resist interpreting others in a way that will maximize the chances of viewing them as having achieved intellectual goods.

A particularly strong and pernicious form that such stinginess can take is intentionally interpreting others in such a way as to put what they've expressed in a *bad* light. It is to interpret them in a way that *minimizes* their chances of having achieved intellectual goods. This approach to interpreting others is bad for others in that the interpreter is treating them unfairly—that is, in a way one wouldn't treat oneself. But it is also bad for interpreters since it will sometimes block them off from achieving the intellectual goods that they would be enabled to achieve through their dependence on others if they were not stingy in their interpretation.

Few people are stingy in this way toward everyone. But far too many of us are stingy toward at least some people in this way. Too commonly we are stingy specifically toward people who disagree with us. Consider, for example, contemporary political debates. Often debates between candidates involve horrible examples of interpretive stinginess. Since the candidates take it that their goal is to *win* a debate—and winning, from their vantage point, is a matter of coming across to viewers in a superior position to their opponent—candidates are often not primarily concerned with achieving intellectual goods. This kind of attitude encourages them to be stingy in their interpretations of their opponents. They are encouraged to interpret their opponents in a way that will make their opponents look bad. Often such stinginess is manifested in what is called a **straw man fallacy**, which is *the informal fallacy of representing one's interlocutor as having endorsed a position that the interlocutor did not endorse, attacking this position one has identified, and concluding that the interlocutor's view is false on this basis*. When we reason this way, we attack the logical equivalent of a "man of straw" rather than a real man.

Imagine that Dan is a candidate who supports a publicly funded safety net for families who suddenly lose their source of income. His rival, Marcia, attacks him, claiming, "Dan's view is that it's unimportant for people to work for a living. He thinks those who work for a living are doing nothing better than those who rely on public assistance. Clearly, anyone who supports this policy is out of his mind." This way of representing Dan's view is an expression of interpretive stinginess, and the argument offered against Dan's view commits a straw man fallacy. Whatever Dan's justification is for supporting the safety net, his support for it need not be understood as relying on these objectionable views. And, if it need not be interpreted this objectionable way, then there's a better way to interpret it that is consistent with faithfulness to Dan's communicative intentions. So a charitable interpretation of Dan's view will demand not interpreting Dan in this way.

Charitable people will resist the temptations to which the interpretively stingy succumb. Their concern is not primarily to win arguments or to come across to others as superior to their fellows. Rather, they are concerned with achieving intellectual goods. As such, they will put their interlocutor's views and arguments in as positive a light as possible, for only by doing so do they maximize their chances of learning something from them, which is what the charitable interpreter wants.

By far the most common way in which people fail to be charitable is by being stingy. There is also another, less common way to fail to be charitable, which is to exhibit what I will call "interpretive face blindness." Face blindness—a cognitive disorder known more technically as prosopagnosia—is a condition that inhibits one's ability to recognize faces. A person with face blindness may be able to tell perfectly well by sight that some human or other is in his general vicinity, but without some other nonvisual cues, he will struggle to identify which particular human he is looking at. He is not able to tell which human is which on the basis of visually recognizing faces.

In an analogous way, our interpretations of others can exhibit a kind of face blindness that is opposed to interpretive charity. We have emphasized throughout this section that there is an important qualification on just how far charitable interpreters will go in trying to interpret their interlocutor in the best possible way. Specifically, they will not interpret their interlocutor in a way that explicitly violates what they have best reason to think the interlocutor intended to communicate with her utterance. By contrast, **interpretive face blindness** is *a tendency not to interpret others in a way that is consistent with what one has best reason to think they intended to communicate.* What others intended is irrelevant to how one interprets them. By eliminating others' intentions from one's interpretive decisions, one eliminates *them*, as persons, from one's interpretive decisions. It is to be willfully blind to who others are as particular individuals.

Return to the earlier example involving Tayshaun and Zachary. Imagine that after Tayshaun says, "You mean my keys? Thanks!" Zachary replies, "No, I really mean your wallet." If Tayshaun were to go on interpreting Zachary as having the view that Zachary had found Tayshaun's keys rather than his wallet here, this would no longer be an exhibition of charity. Zachary has clarified for Tayshaun that, surprising as it might seem in the context, he really did intend to communicate that he had found Tayshaun's wallet. To continue interpreting Zachary otherwise is to disrespect Zachary's intentions.

Key Ideas for Review

Interpretive charity is a tendency to interpret others in as positive a light as possible, consistent with a respect for their communicative intentions.

An **enthymeme** is a statement of an argument that leaves some premises or the conclusion unstated.

Interpretive stinginess is a tendency to resist interpreting what others have said in the most positive light.

The **straw man fallacy** is the informal fallacy of representing one's interlocutor as having endorsed a position that the interlocutor did not endorse, attacking this position one has identified, and concluding that the interlocutor's view is false on this basis.

Interpretive face blindness is a tendency not to interpret others in a way that is consistent with what one has best reason to think they intended to communicate.

This kind of scenario tends to arise in cases that are in a certain way similar to the one just described—namely, where we have a hard time seeing how a person could really hold the view that they seem to have expressed. In such cases, we have a tendency (as we should, being charitable) to interpret them as holding a different view. However, when we have reason to think that they really did intend to express their views just as they did, we must resist this tendency. The best kind of evidence we can get for thinking that a person really did intend to express a view that we find difficult to make sense of is when they explicitly acknowledge this difficulty. They might say, "I know you may at first have difficulty understanding how I could think this, but . . ." Alternatively, they might repeat themselves, insisting that their expressed view is indeed their view, as in the case above. When a person does this, he is deliberately attempting to prevent us from making an interpretive mistake. Charitable people heed such attempts. They aren't blind to the intentions of others in the way the person with interpretive face blindness is. And because they exhibit concern for the intentions of others in this way, they leave open the possibility that they might learn something surprising from the other.

5.2.3 Summary

This section has introduced the virtue of interpretive charity and contrasted it with the vices of interpretive stinginess and interpretive face blindness. The charitable person tends to interpret others in a way that both is faithful to their communicative intentions and maximizes their chances of having achieved intellectual goods. By contrast, the stingy interpreters do not give others the interpretive benefit of the doubt, and people with interpretive face blindness do not adequately respect the intentions of others in their interpretations of them.

Exercise 5.2

A. Evaluating Charity. For each of the following examples, make a case for why the character or characters do or do not display interpretive charity. If a character exhibits a vice that is contrary to interpretive charity, identify the vice. Cite relevant material from the text in section 5.2 in defense of your view.

1. Miranda has just warned Philippa that second-hand smoke is dangerous for children. Philippa responds, "Miranda seems to think that every kid who encounters a smoker will end up all messed up. Well, that's crazy. My mother was a smoker, and I turned out just fine."

2. Henry reads an advertisement: "Zenga Juice—it takes you to paradise." *Those idiot advertisers*, he thinks. *Drinking something can't transport you anywhere.*

3. Rory begins his formal presentation saying, "I'm going to argue that the past can change. In fact, the past changes regularly. . . . Look—it happened again. The past just changed." In the audience, Stephen thinks to himself, "Surely Rory just means that our *views* about the past change."

4. Gemma offers the following argument to Dana: "You don't see anyone in the office, so Brandon isn't there." But Dana objects, "For that argument to work, it has to be that you think that necessarily, in any case in which anyone doesn't see something somewhere, the thing isn't there. But when I look out my window at the garden, I don't see any spiders in the garden. It doesn't follow that there aren't any spiders in the garden. So you're argument is no good."

5. Cecilia argues, "Most men over thirty cannot run a six-minute mile. So Ed probably can't run a six-minute mile." Bethany begins a response by claiming that Cecilia has just argued as follows: "Most men over thirty cannot run a six-minute mile. So no men over thirty can run a six-minute mile. Ed is a man over thirty. So Ed cannot run a six-minute mile."

6. Ryan asks Draymond whether he can read the sign on the other side of the road. Draymond replies, "I'm not wearing my glasses." Ryan understands Draymond to have expressed his endorsement of the following argument: "I'm not wearing my glasses. If I'm not wearing my glasses, then I can't read the sign on the other side of the road. So I can't read the sign on the other side of the road."

7. Said begins a talk by saying, "I'm going to argue that God, while remaining omniscient, does not know what human beings will do of their own free will in the future." Kelly understands Said to have expressed his commitment to the view that God is not omniscient.

8. Pastor Sam tells Kevin, "I don't know of a compelling biblical reason against doing genetic tests to determine whether your child will likely have a disease." Kevin later writes on his blog, "Pastor Sam thinks that we should all get our children screened to determine if they'll have diseases and that it's okay to abort children who will likely have a serious disease."

9. William has just defended the argument that because Jesus's resurrection from the dead is the best explanation we know of for the facts we know about the empty tomb and transformation of the disciples, Jesus in fact rose from the dead. Gena thinks to herself, *William was probably intending to claim not only that Jesus's resurrection the* best *explanation we know of but that it is a* good *explanation as well.*

10. Harriet has just learned that some philosophers have argued that the fact that God seems to be hidden from at least some human beings provides reason to think that God doesn't exist. *That's silly,* she thinks. *Nothing can be "hidden" unless it exists. So God's hiddenness can't provide reason for thinking that God doesn't exist.*

5.3 Intellectual Empathy

The virtuous inquirer will recognize that the views and arguments of others are not held in isolation. They are typically part of a complex, interlocking web of beliefs, experiences, feelings, and character traits. A person's views may be held for reasons that are themselves based on further experiences, and these views may be arrived on through the exercise of character traits, whether virtuous or vicious. Furthermore, it may be that in order to adopt certain views, a person must give up or modify certain other views or may need to interpret certain aspects of her experiences differently than she otherwise would. In this way, a view or argument both is a ramification of a person's complex psychological web and has ramifications for that web.

Given this way in which the views and arguments of others are situated in their own complex psychological webs, the most careful and thorough assessment of them must take their position in these webs into account. To fully understand these views and arguments in the first place, much less evaluate them, dependent inquirers must attempt so far as is possible to see these views and arguments from within the psychological web of the other—or within a comparable, even more favorable web. They must attempt to see views and arguments in relation to those other commitments and experiences to which they may be related. The chief virtue of inquiry that enables such seeing is what we will call "intellectual empathy." In this section, we will explain what intellectual empathy is, illustrate its function, and highlight several obstacles to its proper exercise, including vices that oppose it.

5.3.1 The Nature of Intellectual Empathy

The term "empathy" was introduced into the English language in a 1909 translation of the German word *Einfühlung* by Edward Bradford Titchner.[3] The German term itself may more literally be translated "feeling into" or "feeling one's way into." Typically when we discuss empathy today we have in mind the ability to feel one's way into the experiences, emotions, or concerns of another. We are empathetic when we put ourselves in others' shoes, endeavoring to understand what it is like to have these experiences, emotions, or concerns.

Our focus in this section is on a particular kind of empathy—intellectual empathy. **Intellectual empathy** is *a tendency to imaginatively reconstruct the position occupied by the views and arguments of others within a psychological web in which they make best sense.* As with all forms of empathy, it involves feeling one's way into the shoes of the other. However, what marks it off specifically as *intellectual* empathy is that it involves feeling one's way into the views and arguments of the other. Intellectually empathetic people attempt to imagine what might lead others to adopt the views they possess and what ramifications these views might or should have for their other views. They attempt to imagine what would be required for the arguments endorsed by others to be motivating and what other views these arguments might or should lead them to endorse. They attempt to imagine what traits of personal character might lead to the adoption of these views and arguments, and they attempt to imagine what kinds of experiences might support or be encouraged by adopting them. They attempt above all to understand what it would be like to hold these views or arguments within the best possible overall psychological web.

Understood in this way, intellectual empathy has clear benefits for inquiry. Indeed, the most thorough evaluation of a view arguably *demands* practicing intellectual empathy. By virtue of exercising intellectual empathy, we put ourselves in the best position we can to identify the best overall case for a view. We attempt to discern what the best possible way is for *us* as persons to adopt this view. The process of evaluating a view simply cannot ignore such an exercise if it really is to be thorough. Evaluating a view while overlooking the best case for it—while overlooking what the best way would be for *you* to adopt it—necessitates an incomplete inquiry. And the same goes for evaluating an argument.

The more immediate benefit of exercising intellectual empathy is a step removed from evaluation. By virtue of exercising intellectual empathy, we gain greater understanding of views and arguments and their place in the human psyche. This understanding itself is an achievement and is worthy of pursuit for its own sake. Practicing intellectual empathy, then, both enables us to gain greater understanding of those views and arguments we aim to evaluate and improves our ability to thoroughly evaluate these views and arguments.

In more practical terms, we might say the following about intellectually empathetic people's approach to dependent inquiry. First, they look to the other as a fallible guide in their exercise of imaginative reconstruction. They are quick to listen, quick to ask questions, and slow to make judgments. They seek the other's counsel about how the other's views and arguments fit into an overall web. Rather than quickly judging that another's view has harsh consequences and rejecting the view on that basis, empathetic people will *ask* the other about the apparent bad consequences. They will seek to understand whether and how the other has adapted a psychological web in order to eliminate or minimize these consequences. The other's responses will guide them in their own attempt to identify the best way for these views and arguments to fit together in a complete psychological web.

Second, their imaginative reconstruction is itself regulated by interpretive charity. It is charitable in the sense that they attempt, while remaining faithful to the communicative intentions of the other, to identify elements within the psychological web they are constructing that have the best overall consequences for this web. These overall consequences include intellectual consequences, such as whether the other has achieved intellectual goods, and nonintellectual consequences as well.

To get some grip on intellectual empathy in action, consider the following actual example.[4] A primary school teacher in Michigan, who is a white, suburban, middle-class woman, asks her classroom full of primarily impoverished, inner-city black students, "What do squirrels eat?" With a perfectly sincere look on his face, one student answers, "Hamburgers!" Several of his classmates giggle.

In this situation, it may be tempting to think the student is just making a joke. One might be tempted to respond, "Of course squirrels don't eat hamburgers! How silly! You know better than that." However, people of intellectual empathy will resist this way of dismissing the student's statement—especially given his apparent sincerity. They will endeavor instead to attempt to understand how such a seemingly remarkable claim might make sense within a complex psychological web. As it turns out, in this case there was a relatively straightforward way of making sense of the child's view. He had seen squirrels eating hamburgers at the garbage dumps in parking lots at fast food restaurants in the city. Being scavengers, squirrels in an inner-city environment are likely to eat in this kind of way somewhat regularly. Given the child's exposure to the eating habits of squirrels in the environment in which he had encountered them, the view that they eat hamburgers, even as a regular component of their diet, was not nearly as absurd as one might initially have thought. Within the child's psychological web, it made rather good sense.

Intellectually empathetic people seek in this way to imaginatively reconstruct the views and arguments endorsed by others, positioning them within a complex psychological web in which they make most sense. By doing so they afford themselves a better path toward understanding the other, understanding the other's views and arguments, and evaluating those views and arguments.

This sort of empathy is especially important for views with wide-ranging consequences and on which a wide range of diverse evidence has a bearing, such as those about controversial philosophical matters, or even *worldviews* themselves. It may be tempting when evaluating views of these kinds to focus on isolated consequences they have or on isolated pieces of evidence bearing on them to the exclusion of other consequences or items of evidence. But to do this is a failure of thoroughness and carefulness. Instead, a commitment to achieving intellectual goods will urge us to inquire with intellectual empathy.

Engaging in the work of intellectual empathy is no mean task. Indeed, few of us even achieve the kind of understanding of our *own* views and arguments that intellectual empathy urges us to achieve with respect to *others*. The nature and value of intellectual empathy highlights the demanding nature of an intellectually well-lived life.

5.3.2 Obstacles to Intellectual Empathy

A battery of obstacles stands in the way of intellectual empathy, including some vices opposed to it. Some of the most salient obstacles to exercising intellectual empathy derive from *differences* between us and the other to whom we would otherwise show intellectual empathy. These differences may be of various kinds, and the extent to which they present obstacles to our engaging in intellectual empathy will depend on features of our character.

Some of us are afflicted by biases toward individuals belonging to particular social groups to which we ourselves do not belong. These might be gender-based, race-based, class-based, or even religion-based biases. Such biases can keep us from exercising intellectual empathy by preventing us from taking seriously the views and arguments of others. Instead of doing our best to understand how these views and arguments might best fit within an overall psychological web, we dismiss them out of hand on account of who it is that holds them and the difference between that person and us. Here we commit an *ad hominem* fallacy, much like that identified in section 5.1.

Another kind of difference that can stand in the way of intellectual empathy is *disagreement* with the other. We are often unwilling to exercise intellectual empathy toward those with whom we disagree. Because the view they hold conflicts with our own views, we refuse to try on their intellectual shoes for size. The refusal might be enacted out of fear that our own views may be challenged or out of arrogance regarding the unassailability of our views. Regardless of its source, the refusal is evidence of a vicious closed-mindedness whereby we forestall the thorough investigation of viewpoints that differ from our own.

Intellectually empathetic people resist these obstacles. Their empathy is practiced impartially; it is not based on similarities with the other. In particular, they do not allow differences in gender, race, class, or religion to prevent them from imaginatively reconstructing the psychological web of the other. Nor do they succumb to a closed-mindedness that prevents them from recognizing that the other holds views opposed to their own. Rather, they eagerly engage in empathetic practices toward such others in order to achieve a more diverse understanding and appreciation of the views of others. They take it that there is much to learn from others, even if their openness to learning does not ultimately change their views.

Another kind of obstacle to intellectual empathy is intellectual laziness. As was stressed in the previous subsection, the project of intellectual empathy is a demanding one. It can be tempting to engage in a piecemeal or facile reconstruction of another's position instead of engaging in a thorough and imaginative reconstruction of the position. It can be tempting to quickly identify apparently negative ramifications of a view and dismiss it on that basis without considering ways in which a total psychological web might make accommodations that reduce the severity of these ramifications. Some of us even train ourselves to evaluate views in this way, always on the lookout for a counterexample and ready to move on to evaluating a different view once any remotely plausible example has been identified. Arguably, philosophers are sometimes guilty of this when they too sternly assume that there must be just one correct account of something like a character trait. When offered a philosophical account of humility, for example, we might find a case where we think it is appropriate to say humility has been displayed but where the account does not suggest that it has been. When we find such a case, we dispense with the account and search for a new one. In the process, we overlook the possibility that what had been proposed successfully identified one version of humility among others. We miss out on understanding something valuable that the account had captured.[5]

Intellectually empathetic people do not give in to temptations toward intellectual laziness. Though their project is a demanding one, it is equally a worthwhile one. Because of their foundational concern for intellectual goods

---

Key Ideas for Review

Intellectual empathy is a tendency to imaginatively reconstruct the position occupied by the views and arguments of others within a psychological web in which they make best sense.

Obstacles to the exercise of intellectual empathy include biases toward others who are different from oneself, closed-mindedness, and intellectual laziness.

The *biased* person refuses to engage in intellectual empathy toward those who are different from her.

The *closed-minded* person refuses to engage in intellectual empathy toward those who hold views at odds with his own.

The *intellectually lazy* person tends to engage only in piecemeal or facile reconstruction of the position occupied by the views and arguments of others.

---

and the goods promised via the difficult road of intellectual empathy, they stay the course, searching out the best possible psychological web in which a view or argument can be positioned. By doing so they attain a deeper understanding of the view or argument in question and are better positioned to evaluate it.

5.3.3 Summary

This section has introduced and illustrated the virtue of intellectual empathy and has identified obstacles to its exercise, including vices that oppose it. Intellectual empathy is a tendency to imaginatively reconstruct the views and arguments of others in their position within the best possible complete psychological web. Such empathy is valuable because it enables better understanding of views and arguments, and it is required for the most thorough evaluation of them. Common obstacles of intellectual empathy include biases based on differences between oneself and others, closed-mindedness, and intellectual laziness.

Exercise 5.3

A. Evaluating Empathy. For each of the following examples, make a case for why the character or characters do or do not display intellectual empathy. If a character exhibits a vice that is contrary to intellectual empathy, identify the vice. Cite relevant material from the text in section 5.3 in defense of your view.

1. Howard has just expressed his view that nothing anyone ever does is ultimately up to him or her. Iliana quickly notices that this view appears

to imply that it is inappropriate to hold people responsible for what they do. Since she thinks it is appropriate to at least sometimes hold people responsible for what they do, she concludes that Howard's perspective is misguided and suspends further inquiry into it.

2. On the campaign trail in Georgia, mayoral candidate Shelly says about her opponent Jim, "He's an atheist. Do you really think we can trust him to make the right moral decisions as mayor?"

3. Liam has been learning about different ancient schools of thought—Epicureanism, Skepticism, Stoicism, and so on. He decides to take his studies one step beyond his assignments by trying to live out the views of these various schools of thought for one week each without violating his conscience.

4. Ian's friend Brian sends him an article purporting to explain why a militant Muslim group thinks the US government has been among the most destructive governments of the past century. *Those people are crazy* he thinks to himself before trashing the article.

5. Jamie is deciding what classes to take his first year in college. He's interested in biology, but he has heard that the instructor will present evidence for human evolution—a view he rejects. "I'm just not comfortable hearing ideas like that," he says as he signs up for a different class instead.

6. Kip has just learned about George Berkley's view that all that exists are minds and mental properties. He reasons, "That view implies that there aren't any trees. But surely there are trees. Berkley's view isn't for me."

7. Lucy writes on her midterm, "Christianity is so full of contradictions. Just consider the doctrine of the Trinity. God is both three and one. Nobody has ever been able to make any sense of this."

8. Peter and David have been engaged in debate about free will for years. Each came to know that the other held the opposite view to his own and for that very reason sought out the other's best account for the view he preferred. They published papers engaging back and forth with each other on these topics, clarifying for many interested outside readers the fundamental issues at stake and to what extent there was agreement between them. Ultimately, neither convinced the other to change his view.

9. Lily's cousin has just told Lily, the newlywed, with a straight face, "I wish you much happiness. But marriage—I don't condone it." Lily decides that, despite appearances, her cousin must be joking.

10. Lewis has decided that the Bible teaches that God predetermines who will be saved and who will not be saved. A visiting speaker is coming to campus, and the title of her presentation is "The Pitfalls of Divine Determinism." Lewis boycotts the event.

6

▶ ▶ ▶ ▶ ▶ ▶

Virtues of Intellectual Dependability

O ur concern in chapters 5 and 6 is with intellectual virtues that can be displayed only in the context of collective inquiry. In chapter 5 we surveyed three virtues that are characteristically displayed when one depends on someone else in one's inquiries. There we discussed trust in others, interpretive charity, and intellectual empathy. This chapter is concerned with the other side of the equation—intellectual virtues that are characteristically displayed when others depend on you in their inquiries.

When others depend on you in their pursuit of inquiry, they depend on you to improve their chances of acquiring intellectual goods such as true belief, knowledge, and understanding. Accordingly, the virtues of intellectual dependability—virtues that enable you to better serve as a dependable partner for others' inquiries—are virtues that better equip you to help others achieve these intellectual goods. We will focus here on three intellectual virtues: intellectual generosity, communicative clarity, and audience sensitivity.

6.1 Intellectual Generosity

We began our discussion of the virtues of inquiry by examining the love of intellectual excellence. This trait we defined as a disposition to conduct inquiries in a way that displays a deep motivation for achieving intellectual goods responsibly. Our primary focus since introducing this trait has been on the intellectual goods of the inquiring individual. We've been concerned with how a virtuous inquirer goes about pursuing true beliefs, knowledge, and understanding for herself. However, a fully virtuous intellectual life requires that the inquirer pursues not only her own intellectual goods but also those of others. The foundational virtue that orients a person toward the intellectual goods of others is intellectual generosity.

We might profitably think of intellectual generosity as very much like love of intellectual excellence, only directed toward others' intellectual goods. **Intellectual generosity**, then, is *a disposition to contribute to others' inquiries in a way that displays a deep motivation for promoting others' intellectual goods responsibly*. Intellectually generous people devote their time and talents for inquiry toward helping others attain true beliefs, knowledge, and understanding, and even toward acquiring those intellectual virtues that will make others better as inquirers. They give of themselves to promote the intellectual flourishing of others. In this section, we will further illuminate the nature and value of intellectual generosity by examining its foundations and key features and by contrasting it with two opposing vices.

6.1.1 The Foundations and Key Features of Intellectual Generosity

At the foundation of intellectual generosity is a rejection of intellectual egoism, especially in its more extreme forms. **Intellectual egoism** is *a tendency to think that one's own intellectual goods are more important than others' just because they are one's own*. The intellectual egoist declares, "*My* intellectual goods are more important than your intellectual goods *just because they are mine*." She treats the fact that a course of action will promote an intellectual good for herself as providing greater reason for promoting that good than the fact that a course of action would promote a comparable good for someone else.

Egoism can come in more and less extreme varieties. An extreme egoism insists that the only intellectual goods that matter at all are one's own intellectual goods. Slightly less extreme is a version that insists that, even if others' intellectual goods matter, one's own intellectual goods always matter *more*, regardless of any particular features of these goods. In other words, the extreme egoist believes he should always pursue his own intellectual goods rather than someone else's because his own intellectual goods matter more, just because they are his. On the other end of the spectrum, the least extreme version of egoism simply maintains that when one compares the intellectual goods of oneself to the intellectual goods of another, the former always get *some* boost in importance—perhaps only a minimal boost.

Egoism in both its more and less extreme varieties is widely thought to be a violation of fairness, and in some forms it is even incoherent. For example, suppose that I am an extreme egoist, thinking that my own goods are more valuable than yours simply because they are mine. This leads quickly to incoherence since it implies that my own goods are more valuable than yours because they are mine, and your goods are more valuable than mine just because they are yours. So this version of egoism implies that my goods are more valuable than yours *and* yours are more valuable than mine—which is incoherent.

If we modify egoism to avoid this incoherence, the view tends to lose its motivation. For example, the egoist might retreat to a position where he claims simply that his goods are more valuable because they are his but denies that anyone else's goods are more valuable because they are theirs. This view avoids the above worry about incoherence, but it is very difficult to see how the view could be motivated. Why should all of us think that some particular person's goods are more valuable than the goods of all the rest of us?[1]

The foundation of intellectual generosity is an eschewal of such egoism. The intellectually generous person recognizes that others can achieve intellectual goods that are just as good or better than her own, thus rejecting the most extreme versions of egoism. Sometimes, by investing her intellectual resources in helping others to achieve intellectual goods, she is able to help others achieve intellectual goods that are better than the intellectual goods that would have been achievable if she had invested her resources in pursuing her own intellectual goods instead. The intellectually generous person doesn't unfairly treat her own intellectual goods as more important than others'. She doesn't take herself to know that she's always better off promoting only her own goods just because they are hers. If anything, she does something approaching the opposite. Indeed, drawing on the New Testament, we will suggest below that the ideally intellectually generous person treats others' intellectual goods as *more* important than her own. Such an ideally intellectually generous person is the *complete* opposite of an intellectual egoist, centering her intellectual life on others rather than on herself.

Foundationally, then, the intellectually generous person rejects egoism, especially in its extreme varieties. This puts her in a position where she can—at least sometimes, if not always—treat others' intellectual goods as more important than her own and thus worthy of promoting. We can continue to illuminate the nature of intellectual generosity by considering some of its key features. In doing so, we will return to the imperatives of loving intellectual excellence, this time thinking about how they apply to the context in which others depend on us in their inquiries.

We proposed in section 4.1 four imperatives that will be followed by the person who loves intellectual excellence. The first was that he is willing to sacrifice for the achievement of intellectual goods. Applied now to the context in which others depend on us in their inquiries, following this imperative will require that the intellectually generous person is willing to sacrifice for the promotion of others' achievements of intellectual goods. The kind of sacrifice demanded can be very similar to the kind of sacrifice we surveyed in section 4.1. It may involve investments of time, resources, or attention in the other. Just as before, a person's concern to promote the intellectual goods of others may radically alter his career direction. An intellectually generous person may, for example, sense a calling to be a teacher.

In some cases, the sacrifice demanded for the sake of promoting someone else's intellectual goods will be a sacrifice of some of one's own intellectual goods. In other words, the intellectually generous person sometimes views it as appropriate to give up pursuing her own intellectual achievements for the sake of helping others to secure intellectual achievements for themselves. When exactly the intellectually generous person makes such a sacrifice depends to some extent on the values of the goods in question. She considers how valuable the intellectual goods the other would achieve are, and how valuable her own goods are, making a comparison between the two.

Noticing the importance of such a comparison brings us to the second and third imperatives of loving intellectual excellence: those who love intellectual excellence take an interest in those intellectual goods that are most valuable, including true beliefs about what is explanatorily most fundamental. Recall that in section 4.1 we discussed the idea that some intellectual goods are more valuable than others. This fact is quite important if any comparison of the kind we were just envisioning is to be carried out.

In section 4.1 we proposed that some true beliefs are more valuable than others because of the importance of their subject matter or the role they play in supporting other beliefs. We likewise proposed that knowledge of a claim or understanding of a subject matter are more valuable than mere true belief in that same claim or regarding that same subject matter. Because of their superior value, we said that those who love intellectual excellence will display greater concern for these goods than for others. Applying these principles to intellectual generosity, we can say that an intellectually generous person takes a special interest in promoting the most valuable intellectual goods of others. Indeed, we can expect that an intellectually generous person is prepared to sacrifice less valuable intellectual goods of his own for the sake of promoting more valuable intellectual goods of others.

We can add an important detail about the comparative values of intellectual goods here. An exceedingly valuable intellectual good is the possession of intellectual virtues themselves. This is because the possession and exercise of these intellectual virtues *enables* the attainment of the other intellectual goods. Indeed, without the possession of intellectual virtues, the most valuable kinds of other intellectual goods are likely to be unattainable. Some have even argued that no knowledge can be had at all without the possession of intellectual virtues.[2] But even if this is too strong, it remains plausible that knowledge achieved via intellectual virtue is more valuable than knowledge not achieved by it. Accordingly, fostering the intellectual virtues of others will be high on the list of priorities of the intellectually generous person. We may expect, then, that if presented with opportunities where they must choose between pursuing their own acquisition of true beliefs or knowledge or promoting the acquisition and maintenance of intellectual virtue for others, intellectually generous persons may frequently opt to pursue the latter. This is a common motivation for those who serve in teaching roles, whether they are formally recognized as teachers or not.

By considering how the first three imperatives of loving intellectual excellence apply to the context where others depend on us in their inquiries, we have clarified that the intellectually generous person is at least willing to sacrifice promoting less valuable intellectual goods of her own in order to promote more valuable intellectual goods of others. But based on the words of Scripture, we might take the demands of intellectual generosity a step further. Paul commands the Philippians, "Count others *more* significant than yourselves" (Philippians 2:3, my emphasis). It appears that Paul is here enjoining believers to act in accordance with the *complete opposite* of egoism—even of the least extreme variety. Rather than treating our own goods as if they are more important than the goods of others, he is suggesting that we treat the goods of others as if they are more important than our own *just because they are others'*.

If we are to follow Paul's injunction here, then the fact that a course of action will promote an intellectual good for someone else ought to give us *more* reason to promote that good than is provided by the fact that a course of action would promote a comparably valuable intellectual good for ourselves. The ideally intellectually generous person will not only be willing to sacrifice promoting his own less valuable intellectual goods in order to promote the more valuable intellectual goods of others, but he will also be willing to do this in cases where the values of the goods in question are equal. For example, faced with a decision about whether to invest himself in conducting his own experiments or aiding someone else to conduct hers, where the information to be gathered through the experiments is equally valuable, the intellectually generous person who satisfies Paul's more demanding requirement will tend toward helping the other conduct her experiments. In this way, we are to put others ahead of ourselves. And in so doing, we take on an attitude of Christ's that motivated his very incarnation (cf. Philippians 2:5).

Why is this sort of generosity valuable? One reason is that it uniquely promotes relationship with the other. By promoting the intellectual goods of someone else rather than your own intellectual goods, you not only promote these goods but also promote the goods of union with the other. You unite yourself with the other in some respect in aiding her to achieve the relevant goods. And this relational union itself is valuable. No comparable relationship is equally promoted when you instead promote your own goods rather than the other's goods.[3]

The intellectually generous person is willing to sacrifice in order to promote others' intellectual goods, and she takes a special interest in promoting the more valuable intellectual goods of others. She also follows the fourth imperative of loving intellectual excellence: she is concerned to ensure that the beliefs held by others are adequately supported. In chapters 4 and 5, we identified some ramifications of the application of this imperative to the context of individual inquiry. For example, a person committed to this imperative is introspectively vigilant, looking out for bad patterns of inquiry in himself, understanding that he may be tempted by certain biases. In a similar way, the application of this imperative to the context in which others depend on us in their inquiries leads us to contribute to their inquiries in ways that enable them to maintain better-supported beliefs.

One form this can take is when we serve as critical conversation partners or sounding boards for others. As they think through the reasons for and against views, we identify pertinent information they might have missed or weigh in with our opinions to give them an alternative perspective. We may even take on the role of defending a view we do not ourselves agree with for purposes of enabling the other to achieve the best possible understanding of the relevant subject matter.

In section 6.3 we discuss in further detail how this may play out as one regulates one's communications in light of a sensitivity to one's audience. We will observe that one feature of an audience to which the dependable inquirer must be sensitive is the audience's needs. Our observations here suggest that these needs can include the need for well-supported beliefs. Because they do, the intellectually generous person regulates her contributions to others' inquiries in such a way as to help others achieve beliefs that are adequately supported, given their subject matter.

Intellectually generous people apply the imperatives of loving intellectual excellence to the context where others depend on them in their inquiries. They are willing to sacrifice in order to promote others' intellectual achievements, they take a special interest in those intellectual goods of others that are most valuable, and they take care to ensure that others' intellectual goods are achieved with intellectual responsibility. In the following section we further illuminate intellectual generosity by contrasting it with two opposing vices.

6.1.2 Vices Opposed to Intellectual Generosity

Two vices oppose intellectual generosity. The first is intellectual selfishness. **Intellectual selfishness** is *a tendency to act as if one is an intellectual egoist.* The selfish person to some extent succumbs to intellectual egoism. At the very least, he acts in accordance with it, even if he would not explicitly embrace it or express his commitment to it publicly. Like egoism itself, intellectual selfishness comes in more and less extreme versions. The selfish person treats his own intellectual goods as more important than the intellectual goods of others just because they are his. The extremely selfish treat their own intellectual goods as if they are the only goods that matter at all; the minimally selfish treat their goods as if they are at least somewhat more important than others'.

Such selfishness can manifest itself in at least two ways. One way is when the selfish person refuses to allow others to depend on her for intellectual goods. She refuses to share her true beliefs, knowledge, or understanding with others. She wants exclusive rights to these goods. This kind of intellectual selfishness can be motivated by an aim to achieve a competitive advantage.

Imagine that you are part of a group of students all being trained for the same career. You're all in your final year of study, and it's time to apply for jobs. You learn about a job that hasn't been widely advertised. You are tempted to keep this information to yourself and to refuse to share it with your student cohort, even if they ask you to share such information. By doing so you might secure for yourself a competitive advantage by limiting the applicant pool for the job, but doing so would be intellectually selfish.

A second way that intellectual selfishness can manifest itself is when the selfish person allows others to depend on him in their inquiries but only in such a way as to *perpetuate* this dependence. He will share his true beliefs, knowledge, or understanding with others, but only if in doing so he can keep them dependent on him. What he wants to avoid is others attaining a status as inquirers that is equal to his own. He wants to ensure his own pride of place in the social dynamic of inquiry.

This kind of selfishness can be exhibited through the selective sharing of information, where further information is always necessary but those who need it can acquire it only via dependence on the selfish person. It can also be exhibited through a refusal to share with others the tools of a trade—tools that would equip the other to acquire necessary intellectual goods for herself. In both these forms of selfishness, the selfish person succumbs to intellectual egoism and thereby stands opposed to intellectual generosity.

A second vice opposed to intellectual generosity is intellectual patronization. **Intellectual patronization** is *a tendency to promote another's intellectual goods in such a way that one inhibits the other from acquiring or utilizing intellectual virtues*. This vice can be somewhat more subtle than intellectual selfishness, at least from the perspective of those who exhibit it. They may be quite well-meaning in their attempt to promote the intellectual goods of others. Yet they have a tendency, in the way in which they promote others' intellectual goods, to prevent others from exercising their own intellectual capacities in attaining intellectual goods. They do too much to help others attain true beliefs, knowledge, or understanding. They intervene to offer aid where it isn't called for, thereby preventing people from exercising self-reliance in their inquiries and bettering themselves as inquirers.

While intellectually generous people are also self-giving in the promotion of others' intellectual goods, they recognize that there are various intellectual goods of different values. Among them are the goods of possessing and exercising intellectual virtues and acquiring other intellectual goods for oneself by means of using these virtues. Intellectually generous people are attuned to these intellectual goods and will not promote others' acquisition of true beliefs, knowledge, or understanding in a way that hinders their development and exercise of intellectual virtues. Doing so would involve a failure to appreciate the relative value of intellectual goods—something that is foundational to properly attuned intellectual generosity.

Intellectually generous people are opposed both to selfishness and to patronization. Unlike the selfish, they put the goods of others ahead of their own. At the same time, in putting the goods of others ahead of their own, they are sensitive to the total overall goods of others; in particular, they do not patronize others by limiting their development of the very capacities necessary for their greatest intellectual flourishing.

6.1.3 Summary

This section has introduced the virtue of intellectual generosity, the first virtue of intellectual dependability. Intellectually generous people have a tendency to contribute to others' inquiries in a way that displays a deep motivation for promoting others' intellectual goods responsibly. The intellectually generous apply the imperatives of loving intellectual excellence to the context in which others depend on them in their inquiries. Ideally intellectually generous people go so far as to put the intellectual lives of others ahead of their own. Standing opposed to intellectual generosity are the vices of intellectual selfishness and intellectual patronization. The selfish succumb to intellectual egoism, treating their own intellectual goods as more important than others' goods.

Key Ideas for Review

Intellectual generosity is a disposition to contribute to others' inquiries in a way that displays a deep motivation for promoting others' intellectual goods responsibly.

Intellectual egoism is a tendency to think that one's own intellectual goods are more important than others' just because they are one's own.

Intellectual selfishness is a tendency to act as if one is an intellectual egoist.

Intellectual patronization is a tendency to promote another's intellectual goods in such a way that one inhibits the other from acquiring or utilizing intellectual virtues.

Patronizers promote the goods of others only in such a way as to inhibit their development or exercise of intellectual virtues.

Exercise 6.1

A. Evaluating Generosity. For each of the following examples, make a case for why the character or characters do or do not display intellectual generosity. If a character exhibits a vice that is contrary to intellectual generosity, identify the vice. Cite relevant material from the text in section 6.1 in defense of your view.

1. Kim and Ken are coworkers, and Ken has been tasked with training Kim on how to use the new company software. Rather than teach her how to use it, he simply says, "It's pretty intuitive. If you're not sure how to do something, just come ask me."

2. Nathan is working on his philosophy essay. He has decided he wants to argue against a view called "utilitarianism," but he's not sure how to object to it. So he goes to his instructor, Norris, and asks him how to object to it. Norris refuses to identify objections to utilitarianism but instead asks Nathan a series of carefully crafted questions to try to help Nathan discover for himself why he thinks the view is wrong.

3. Michael asks his mother, Minna, if she can help him to understand why he's getting some of his math homework problems wrong. Minna refuses, saying she's busy watching her favorite reality TV show.

4. Michelle is part of a study group preparing together for an exam. At the start of the study group, she declares that she has done all the practice problems, and she distributes a list of answers to all the members of the group. She says "good luck" and leaves.

5. Miriam and Maggie each have proposals about how best to solve their community's water shortage crisis, but their ideas need testing in order

to be confirmed. Maggie doesn't have any reason for thinking her proposal is better than Miriam's, and she understands that Miriam really needs her help to test the proposal because Maggie is the best qualified person to help. So Maggie decides to put testing her own proposal on pause while helping Maggie to test hers.

6. Natalie and Natasha are taking a practice physics exam and are working on the same problem. Natalie finishes before Natasha, who's still working out her answer. But Natalie just can't hold back: she blurbs the answer out loud before Natasha can finish her work.

7. Opie is the president of a private, Christian university. At a university-wide chapel service, he declares, "Fellow faculty: There are some views that we cannot tolerate among our instructional faculty, even if they aren't forbidden by our university statement of faith." The faculty members become worried for their job security, as without further information they simply have no way of knowing what views Opie has in mind.

8. Maureen is tired of her husband, David, telling her that they don't have enough money to buy something every time she asks him about purchasing something for herself. She asks David if she can look at their family budget for herself to see if she can better understand how they can make some of these purchases possible. David responds, "Wouldn't you rather that I just handle this so that you don't have to worry about it?"

9. Oswald has just identified what seems to him to be a never-before-recognized argument for an important theological view. The argument has a direct bearing on a debate his students have been having in their theology club. But Oswald worries that if he shares the argument with others, they might steal it from him and claim that they discovered it. So he keeps quiet until he can write a book about it and claim the credit for himself.

10. While both Persephone and her husband, Preston, are trained archaeologists, Persephone now works as a banker, and Preston works as an archaeologist. Preston has a new theory about the life of an ethnic group in ancient Egypt, but in order to test it he needs the help of a trained archaeologist who will help him pro bono. He asks Persephone if she'll put her own projects on hold to help him. When she thinks about what she would be working on instead, it's not clear to her that what she would otherwise be doing would be any more or less important than discovering whether Preston's theory is true. So she agrees to help.

6.2 Communicative Clarity

When others depend on us in their inquiries, we must communicate with them. One of the greatest obstacles to successful communication is confusion. Sometimes our listeners will become confused about what we have said due to their own interpretive faults. But other times there is more that we could have done to prevent their confusion. Eliminating sources of confusion in one's communications to others is a valuable tool to help increase others' chances of achieving intellectual goods through their dependence on us. We call this tool the virtue of communicative clarity. **Communicative clarity** is *a tendency to eliminate sources of confusion from one's communications to others.*

In this section, we will identify some sources of confusion in our communications and identify ways they can be eliminated. We'll start with sources of confusion that derive from ambiguous terms and grammatical constructions.

6.2.1 Confusing Words and Grammar

At the level of individual words and phrases, the greatest source of confusion is ambiguity. An **ambiguous term** is *a word or phrase that can reasonably be understood in multiple distinct ways in the context, where the way it is understood makes a difference.* Suppose that Andrew, your friend, begins a story he wants to share with you by saying, "Let me tell you about Jerry. He was a rat." Without further details, the term "rat" here may be ambiguous. It could be understood to mean a rodent that eats cheese, or it could be understood to mean a person who "snitches" on his friends. Until Andrew clarifies the meaning of this ambiguous term, it can serve as a source of confusion for his audience.

A similar phenomenon can occur with larger phrases due to their grammatical structure. Imagine that Andrew continues his story: "I once saw Jerry in my pajamas." Here Andrew's claim is again ambiguous between two readings. On one reading, it is Andrew who was in his own pajamas, and he saw Jerry, who was not in pajamas. On another reading, it is Jerry who was in Andrew's pajamas. Without further information, it is unclear which way the phrase "in my pajamas" should be understood.

Ambiguities of individual terms and phrases of these kinds can lead your audience to draw inferences that you, as a communicator, would not want them to draw. Imagine that Andrew was intending to tell you a story about a rodent he once saw while he was wearing his own pajamas. However, when you heard Andrew's story told in the way it was told above, you reasoned as follows:

1. Andrew saw Jerry, a rat. And all rats have it coming to them. So somebody Andrew saw has it coming to him.

Or imagine you reasoned:

> 2. Andrew once saw Jerry wearing his pajamas. Andrew could have seen Jerry wearing his pajamas only if they were roughly the same size. So Jerry must be roughly the same size as Andrew.

In each case, due to the ambiguity of the words or phrases involved in Andrew's presentation of the story, you would be drawing a conclusion on the basis of the story Andrew had told that he would not have intended for you to draw.

Logicians have names for the fallacies exhibited in examples 1 and 2. Example 1 commits the fallacy of equivocation. The **fallacy of equivocation** is *an informal fallacy in which an argument employs a term with different meanings in different claims.* In the argument of example 1, if the two premises are both to be true given the setup of the case, then "rat" must be used with a different meaning in each. It must be used to refer to a rodent in one premise but used to refer to snitches in the other.

Example 2 commits the fallacy of amphiboly. The **fallacy of amphiboly** is *an informal fallacy in which a grammatically ambiguous phrase functions in one way in one claim and in a different way in another claim.* If the premises of example 2 are both true given the setup of the case, then the phrase "wearing his pajamas" must function in one way in one premise and in a different way in the other. In one it modifies Andrew: it is Andrew who was wearing the pajamas. In the other it modifies Jerry: it was Jerry who was wearing them.

While the foregoing examples may seems somewhat trivial—surely you wouldn't commit *those* kinds of mistakes!—the phenomenon they illustrate is quite widespread. Consider how badly *-isms* are abused in exactly this way. For nearly any -ism—socialism, libertarianism, realism, pragmatism, humanism, to name a few—there will be numerous distinct ways in which that term is commonly employed. This provides very strong incentive, given the foregoing observations, for people to clarify in what sense they are using these terms when they use them. Nonetheless, it is quite common for people to use such -isms without offering any clarification regarding their intended meaning of the term. Such ambiguity could provide a potentially dangerous source of confusion. At the very least, those who fail to clarify their intended meaning in this way put their audience in a poorer position with respect to achieving intellectual goods through depending on them.

People who exercise communicative clarity employ tools to avoid these sources of confusion. If they use a term or phrase that has a few distinct meanings known to their audience, they make it clear which of these meanings they have in mind. Andrew could easily have begun his story, "Let me tell you about Jerry. He was a rat—a rodent, not a snitch." Here Andrew isn't reinventing the wheel in explaining to his audience exactly what a rat (of the rodent kind) is. He is simply identifying for them which of two competing interpretations for his term "rat" is the one they should employ. Where there is danger of confusion on the basis of terminological ambiguity, this tool will prove useful to those who possess communicative clarity.

A comparably similar device can be employed in order to avoid ambiguities created by grammar. Here the trick is to modify one's grammar in such a way as to remove the ambiguity. Again, Andrew could have said, "While wearing my pajamas, I once saw Jerry." This simple grammatical modification removes the source of confusion in his original statement. Such grammatical modifications are nearly always available, even if using them sometimes leads one to employ more syntactically complex sentences. Those who exercise communicative clarity develop skills to eliminate such ambiguities.

Sometimes eliminating ambiguities can be achieved only by providing a definition of one's terms. For example, there are at least two major kinds of views called "libertarianism." One is a political view, and the other is a philosophical view about the nature of free will. Nonetheless, there is variety among political libertarians and variety among philosophical libertarians. It might be more appropriate to think of libertarianism of the political kind, as well as libertarianism of the philosophical kind, as a family of views. Within each family of views are significantly different members—just like in one's biological family. Sometimes which particular member of the family of libertarian views one has in mind makes a difference for what one wants to communicate. In such cases, it may not be sufficient to simply clarify one's meaning (for example, "I mean libertarianism of the political kind rather than the philosophical kind"). Instead, one may need to provide a precise definition of the particular political libertarian view in mind. Without such precision, one's communication may provide a source of unnecessary confusion.

Providing a definition for a view or term, while sometimes necessary, is often not a simple matter. In defining a term, we typically aim to offer, at a minimum, the necessary and sufficient conditions for the application of that term. **Necessary conditions** for the application of a term are *conditions that are such that, if the term is to be correctly applied, the conditions must be met.* **Sufficient conditions** for the application of a term are *conditions that are such that, if they are met, then it is appropriate to apply the term.*

Suppose that our context demands that we provide a definition of the term "rat"—of the snitching variety. We might need a definition because there's disagreement about whether some particular individual qualifies as a rat, and whether he qualifies makes a difference for how we will treat him. A promising sufficient condition for being a rat is that a person has willingly divulged incriminating information about his friends to the FBI. This is a sufficient condition in the sense that if anyone satisfies this condition, doing so *suffices* for the term "rat" to be appropriately applied to him. However, this condition is plausibly not a necessary condition for being a rat—a condition that something *must* satisfy if the term "rat" is to be properly applied to it. In order to be a rat, a person need not have divulged information *to the FBI*. Divulging information to some other body of law enforcement may be sufficient. On the basis of this observation, we might offer the following definition of a rat: a rat is someone who willingly divulges incriminating information about his friends to a body of law enforcement. For this to be the correct definition of a rat, it must provide both necessary and sufficient for being a rat, which arguably it does.

Our attempt to provide a definition of "rat" in the previous paragraph highlights four important lessons. First, defining key terms can be difficult. Even in cases where we use these terms quite commonly, if the context demands providing a more precise account for them, we can find ourselves at a loss to do so. Second, in such situations, progress can sometimes be made by focusing on sufficient or necessary conditions individually. When focusing on sufficient conditions, we try to answer what would *suffice* for it to be the case that the term in question is properly applied. When focusing on necessary conditions, we try to answer what *must* be the case for the term in question to be properly applied. Sometimes if we can answer either of these questions well, our answer will be enough to determine whether our term applies. If the person we were concerned with in the previous example was someone who had not divulged any incriminating information, and we agreed that it is a necessary condition for someone to be a rat that he has divulged incriminating information, then on the basis of this necessary condition alone we could resolve the issue of whether the person in question is a rat. In such cases, providing a complete definition may not be necessary.

Third, in addition to providing necessary and sufficient conditions for the correct application of a term, a definition should be *illuminating*. Imagine that, becoming frustrated with the difficulty of providing necessary and sufficient conditions for "rat" in the way we attempted to above, we simply proposed instead that a rat is a snitch and declared our problem solved. While this proposed definition may well have identified necessary and sufficient conditions for being a rat—it's both necessary and sufficient for someone to be a rat that he is a snitch—the definition is not *illuminating*. It could not help us to resolve our dispute about whether the individual person with whom we were concerned is a rat, because "rat" and "snitch" are simply synonyms. We get no closer to understanding the one term by defining it in terms of the other.

The same basic mistake can be made in cases where we define terms using variants of those terms themselves. It would not be illuminating to define a rat as "someone who rats." In order to provide an illuminating definition, we should highlight conditions that identify features that would help to explain *why* the term in question is appropriately applied. In our definition of "rat," the necessary condition of divulging incriminating information helps to illuminate why a particular individual would, or would not, qualify as a rat.

Fourth, sometimes when we define terms, the terms we use in our definition call for definition. Supposing that our proposed definition of the term "rat" is correct, there may be contexts in which the precise meaning of the term "willingly" needs to be clarified. If a person divulged information under duress, does he count as a rat? This will turn on how we understand the term "willingly" in our definition. Accordingly, it would be helpful in such a context to define the term "willingly" in order to clarify our definition of the term "rat." If identifying a definition of "willingly" proves elusive, we may at least attempt to identify illuminating necessary or sufficient conditions for a person to qualify as one who "willingly" divulges information.

6.2.2 Confusing Structures

In addition to confusing words or phrases, larger components of our communicative efforts can also provide sources of confusion. This tends to occur especially in contexts where our communication is aimed at providing reasons for a view. Our discussion in this section focuses on these contexts, highlighting three common sources of confusion in the structures communicators employ to offer reasons for views.

A first common structural source of confusion occurs when communicators don't adequately identify which conclusion they seek to defend in their communication. In an academic context, we commonly refer to this conclusion as the thesis, and there is a common expectation that any piece of academic writing that presents reasons for a view will have a clearly identifiable thesis statement. Many academic disciplines emphasize that a thesis statement should be identified early in one's presentation of material and that one's presentation of material should be organized around one's defense of that thesis. This kind of structure has proven helpful in academic contexts, and it can be transferred to nonacademic contexts as well.

A common way in which communicators fail to adequately identify the conclusion that they aim to defend is by merely indicating the general topic with which they are concerned without indicating what specifically they wish to affirm about the topic. For example, a student might write an introduction to a paper about free will and divine foreknowledge as follows:

3. Philosophers and theologians have spilled much ink about the topic of free will and divine foreknowledge. Are the two compatible? There have been views on both sides. This paper will start with an examination of Augustine's views on the matter and will then move on to Aquinas's.

While example 3 indicates the topic and sets out a structure for the student's essay, it does not identify a thesis statement. It does not state what specifically the student has to say about the matter. No conclusion is identified. Those who exercise communicative clarity will avoid this source of confusion in their communications to others.

A second common structural source of confusion occurs when the relationship between the reasons one offers for a view are left unclear. In the process of defending a view, a person might identify a wide range of reasons in support of it. Sometimes in doing so what is left unclear is how these distinct reasons are related to one another. Do some of the reasons offer support for the other reasons (which would make the latter reasons subconclusions in an overall argument)? Does the strength of the evidence provided by some of the reasons depend on the strength of the evidence provided by others (such that the arguments generated by some fail if the arguments generated by others succeed)? These important questions are sometimes overlooked, leading to structural ambiguity.

Consider the following passage:

4. Being religious has significant benefits. Religious people are happier. They have more meaningful relationships. And they are more generous.

While not immediately obvious, the first sentence of example 4 is plausibly a conclusion defended on the basis of the other sentences. But the precise relationship between the other sentences is unclear. Does each of the other sentences provide an independent source of support for the conclusion? Or might some of the other claims provide evidence for the others (making these others subconclusions)? In particular we might wonder whether part of the reason religious people are happier is that they have more meaningful relationships or that they are more generous. If this ambiguity were resolved by the author, the passage would exhibit greater communicative clarity. Supposing that the final two sentences do provide reason for affirming the second sentence, this ambiguity might be resolved as follows:

5. Being religious has significant benefits. One benefit is that religious people are happier. They are happier since they have more meaningful relationships and are more generous.

Finally, a third source of structural confusion arises when a communicator includes passages within his defense of a thesis that do not clearly play a unique role in any argument for that thesis. There are two ways this source of confusion can arise. In some cases, communicators simply include extraneous material in their defense of a thesis, where this material is not intended to contribute to an argument for the thesis. In terms of the project of defending the thesis, the material is irrelevant. The second way this source of confusion can arise is where the material is relevant for a defense of the thesis, but the work it does in contributing to the defense of the thesis is already fulfilled by another passage in the communication. In such cases, from the perspective of the project of defending the thesis, the material in question is redundant. Both kinds of cases are exacerbated when the communicator prefaces them with transition statements that give the false appearance that they do contribute something unique to the overall argument structure. Such misused transition statements include words such as "moreover," "however," and "in addition."

Including irrelevant or redundant material in one's defense of a thesis can lead to confusion because one's audience members are likely to try to identify a unique role for the material in question in defending the thesis. In the case of irrelevant material, a communicator can send his audience off on a wild goose chase, where finding the object of their inquiry is hopeless. In the case of including redundant material, a communicator can reduce his audience's confidence that they understand the other part of his communication, where appears to play the same role as the redundant material. *If it doesn't play the same role as this material*, they may think, *then surely I don't understand what it is doing.*

To avoid this last structural source of confusion, the person who effectively exercises communicative clarity can do the following. To the extent possible given the communicative medium, she can exercise oversight over what material she includes. Suppose the communicator has the opportunity to revise a written draft. One strategy she can employ to eliminate this last structural source of confusion is to comb through the draft, paragraph by paragraph, and identify the function that each paragraph plays with respect to defending her thesis. Does the paragraph contribute to an argument for the thesis? If not, perhaps she can eliminate it. Is the contribution it makes to an argument for the thesis already made by another paragraph? Again, perhaps she can eliminate it.

Some redundancy of information in a communication may be called for. It is often worthwhile to repeat a thesis statement, perhaps putting it into different but equivalent words. Likewise, it is often helpful in the conclusion of a communication to summarize how you have gone about defending a thesis.

But notice that in these instances of redundancy, what is repeated is information, not function. In other words, there are times that the same information can serve a different function within a communication. In a restatement of the thesis, the function of the restatement is to draw additional attention to the thesis, and perhaps to help readers who are more likely to understand one way of putting the thesis than the other. Much the same point applies to concluding summaries. What is problematic is not repetition of information but repetition of function.

Those who effectively exercise communicative clarity seek to root out all sources of confusion in their communications. To do so, they adopt a range of tools, such as those highlighted in this and the previous subsection. They attempt to remove any source of confusion in their terminology, their grammar, and the wider structure of their communications. In all of this, their aim is to put their audience in the best position to achieve intellectual goods from their communications.

6.2.3 Summary

This section has introduced the virtue of communicative clarity. People who possesses communicative clarity tend to eliminate sources of confusion in their communications to others. Sources of confusion can derive from ambiguous words or grammar and from structural flaws. To eliminate these sources of confusion, people who effectively exercise communicative clarity employ a range of tools. They may make use of necessary and sufficient conditions or

Key Ideas for Review

Communicative clarity is a tendency to eliminate sources of confusion from one's communications to others.

An **ambiguous term** is a word or phrase that can reasonably be understood in multiple distinct ways in the context, where the way it is understood makes a difference.

The **fallacy of equivocation** is an informal fallacy in which an argument employs a term with different meanings in different claims.

The **fallacy of amphiboly** is an informal fallacy in which a grammatically ambiguous phrase functions in one way in one claim and in a different way in another claim.

Structural sources of confusion include failure to adequately identify one's conclusion, failure to identify the relationship between reasons one offers for a conclusion, and inclusion of material that is irrelevant or redundant with regard to a defense of one's thesis.

Necessary conditions for the application of a term are conditions that are such that, if the term is to be correctly applied, the conditions must be met.

Sufficient conditions for the application of a term are conditions that are such that, if they are met, then it is appropriate to apply the term.

conclusion and premise indicators, and they may exercise oversight over what material is included in their defenses of theses.

Exercise 6.2

A. Identifying Sources of Confusion. In each of the following passages, a character offers a communication that could contain a source of confusion for the character's audience. Identify what the potential source of confusion is in light of your understanding of the material in section 6.2, and offer a way for the character to eliminate it.

1. Quentin includes the following paragraph in his paper defending his view about the morality of abortion: "It's been really difficult for me this semester in class. The arguments just go back and forth, and I find it overwhelming at times. I like subjects where things are more cut and dry."

2. Roddy begins his story: "It was blazing fast. The bat went whizzing by, and we all ducked."

3. Quinn begins her thesis paper: "Predestination is a complicated topic. There is a lot to say on both sides. This paper will look at Jonathan Edwards's view, and then Jacob Arminius's."

4. Olga, a political candidate, claims, "Extremism is the most dangerous challenge we currently face."

5. In preparation for the upcoming trip, Ruby tells her friends, "On the lake, you can often see deer grazing and go kayaking."

6. Jan is thinking about where he and his wife should go this afternoon. He says, "It was raining this morning. So there may be nobody at the bank."

7. Holding a straight stick, Rufus argues, "What you see when you look at this stick submerged in water is bent. What you see when you look at this stick submerged in water is this stick. So this stick, submerged in water, is bent."

8. Terence tries to convince his roommate to go with him to the movie: "It's awesome. There's action, stunts, fight scenes, chase scenes, and explosions."

9. Tanya attempts to exonerate herself: "It's not fair to blame me. I couldn't have done otherwise. Moreover, it wasn't possible for me to do any different."

10. "It wasn't really a lie," Uma says. "You have to think more carefully about his intentions."

6.3 Audience Sensitivity

If we want to help others who depend on us to achieve intellectual goods, we need to keep their unique intellectual features in mind. The way we communicate to some audiences will have to be different from the way we communicate to other audiences. It is perfectly reasonable that I would communicate a plan for our family's daily activities differently to my wife than to my toddler. Likewise, a professional scientist may reasonably communicate the results of his research differently to a panel of colleagues than he would in a lecture open to the public. Tailoring the way one communicates to a particular audience is an important virtue of a dependable inquirer. We call this virtue **audience sensitivity**, which is *a tendency to regulate communications in such a way that one best enables a particular audience—with its particular views, concerns, needs, and abilities—to achieve intellectual goods.*

In this section, we begin by exploring how four features of an audience can demand altering one's approach to communicating ideas to that audience. We then briefly discuss two vices that stand opposed to audience sensitivity: intellectual narcissism and intellectual snobbery.

6.3.1 Four Features of an Audience

This subsection explores four features of an audience that can require communicators to alter the way they present their ideas in order to serve the audience: the audience members' abilities, views, concerns, and needs.

First, audiences differ in their abilities for inquiry. Some are better able to engage independently in complex inquiries or to think abstractly than are others. Those who are sensitive to their audience will take these differences in abilities into account when communicating with them.

As we discussed in the section on intellectual generosity, one should avoid patronizing one's audience members—preventing them from employing their own abilities for inquiry where they can. Whether a communication can be seen as patronizing an audience will depend on the audience's abilities. Audience members who are able to work out an implication of a speaker's ideas for their own concerns may benefit from an opportunity to identify this implication for themselves and may be harmed by not being offered such an opportunity. Audience members who are not able to identify the implication would be harmed by not having the connection made for them by the person on whom they depend. Dependable inquirers must therefore be sensitive to the abilities of their audiences and tailor their communications accordingly.

Likewise, audience members differ with respect to their abilities to think abstractly. Some audience members have a greater need for illustrations of abstract ideas than others. These illustrations bring the abstract down to the concrete. They put flesh on the bones of abstract ideas, helping audience members to associate these ideas with phenomena with which they are more familiar. Such illustrations are very common, for example, in the philosophy classroom. The teacher might be interested in making a point about the general category of things called "doxastic attitudes." To explain what doxastic attitudes are, the teacher says that they include the attitudes of believing, disbelieving, and suspending judgment. The instructor might then illustrate what belief, disbelief, and suspension of judgment are like by pointing to examples of claims that the students in the class may themselves believe, disbelieve, or suspend judgment regarding. For other audiences, this kind of illustration of what a doxastic attitude is will be unnecessary. An audience's ability to think in purely abstract terms can in this way influence the way in which a dependable inquirer will communicate ideas.

Second, audiences differ in the views their members hold. There are at least two ways in which sensitivity to the views held by audience members can lead one to modify the presentation of ideas to that audience. Sometimes one will have ideas that can be defended in multiple, distinct ways. If one of these ways involves appealing to views widely held by audience members and the other involves appealing to views not widely held by audience members, then it can be valuable, for the sake of convincing an audience, to defend ideas in the way that appeals to the more widely held views. By employing this strategy, the communicator may help a greater percentage of an audience to achieve intellectual goods than otherwise would have.

A general strategy to maximize the appeal of views with an audience is to employ logically weaker claims in defense of one's views. Claim P is logically weaker than claim Q if Q implies P but P does not imply Q. For example, "Some animals are conscious" is logically weaker than "Some birds are conscious" since "Some birds are conscious" implies but is not implied by "Some animals are conscious." Employing logically weaker claims in defense of views allows the communicator to maximize the appeal of views with an audience because, other things being equal, it is more likely that an audience member will believe a logically weaker claim than a logically stronger claim. By committing to a logically weaker claim, one takes on a less demanding commitment than one takes on by committing to a logically stronger claim.

Imagine that you wanted to convince your audience that at least some animals deserve legal protections, and that you wanted to defend this conclusion on the basis of a claim about animals' possession of consciousness. If you defend your conclusion by appealing to the more general and logically weaker claim "Some animals are conscious," rather than the more specific and logically stronger claim "Some birds are conscious," you may be more likely to convince a greater portion of your audience since some audience members might think that some animals are conscious but not that some birds are conscious. By making a more general and logically weaker claim about animal consciousness, you are thereby more likely to persuade more audience members to adopt your thesis.

Another way in which sensitivity to the views of audience members can alter how one communicates views is by leading one to avoid discussing certain views. This avoidance will normally be motivated by realizing that at least some audience members reject the views in question. By not explicitly endorsing views an audience rejects—and even avoiding endorsing views audience members know imply views they reject—the communicator maximizes the appeal of ideas with the audience.

One especially interesting context in which avoiding views in this way makes a difference is when the communicator aims to convince an audience of a claim that they do not accept prior to hearing the communication. When one defends a view that an audience does not accept by appealing to views that the audience also rejects, one commits a rhetorical fallacy called **begging the question**, which is *a rhetorical fallacy in which one employs premises one knows are rejected by one's audience*. The most obvious kind of case in which this fallacy occurs is when one defends a view by appealing to the view itself or to a differently stated version of the view, though it is also possible to commit the fallacy in more subtle ways. Imagine that an attendee at a meeting of disgruntled employees contemplating collective resistance to the company president says, "You're not going to change the president's mind about the proposal. He's settled the matter." Here the claim that the president has "settled the matter" is just a different way of stating that he's not going to change his mind. More subtly, we might imagine the attendee saying, "You're not going to change the president's mind about the proposal. His office won't process any requests about the matter," in a context in which the other members present think that the president's office likely will process such requests. In each instance, the fallacy is a rhetorical fallacy because it's unlikely to convince the audience.

Begging the question is not always avoidable if you wish to defend your views. Sometimes the fact that your audience rejects the views necessary to defend your view is their own fault. However, where there is a way to defend your ideas that doesn't involve employing views your audience rejects, it is preferable to defend your ideas in this way, modifying your communication in light of a sensitivity to your audience's views.

Third, audiences differ in the concerns of their members. By speaking of the audience's concerns, we have in mind something distinct from the audience's views. The audience's concerns consist in the topics the audience members care about. Their concerns are what motivate them. And these concerns tend to come on a continuum: some concerns motivate an audience more strongly than others. Communicators who are sensitive to their audience's concerns attempt to engage with these concerns, identifying ways in which their ideas address and interact with them. In doing so they present their ideas in such a way as to make them relevant for their audience.

Imagine that a philosopher is working on new ideas he has about the nature and ethical rules concerning a controversial belief. He thinks what he has to say about the controversial belief applies to controversial beliefs in a variety of domains, including politics, ethics, religion, and so on. It would be a shame if he gave exactly the same presentation when presenting his views before the National Rifle Association as he did when presenting them to the Religious Liberty Commission. Even if we assume that these groups have roughly similar intellectual abilities to understand the content of the philosopher's views and roughly similar views about relevant topics, the concerns of the groups differ. And they differ in a way that the philosopher should display sensitivity toward in his presentation, perhaps focusing on controversial political beliefs before the National Rifle Association and controversial religious beliefs before the Religious Liberty Commission.

Fourth, audiences differ in the needs of their members. In particular, some audiences need a greater exposure to some information relevant to assessing their ideas than do other audiences. An audience that largely agrees with the case the communicator might make for a view may have greater need to learn about the evidence against the views and how one might respond to that evidence. An audience that largely disagrees with the communicator's views may have greater need of hearing the positive case to be made for the views.

For example, suppose a philosopher characterizes himself as overall sympathetic with the belief that God exists, though he is not very confident about this. He spends significant amounts of time around other philosophers who don't believe in God (atheists) as well as those who do (theists). The philosopher tends to think that the atheists are overall too dismissive of the reasons for believing in God, while many of the theists are overconfident in their estimation of the reasons for belief in God. Accordingly, around the atheists, the philosopher takes on the persona of a defender of theistic belief. He is even willing to be considered a representative of theism for the sake of conversations. Around the theists, he does the opposite, being willing to be considered a skeptic about God's existence for the sake of conversations.

The kind of skill this philosopher exhibits is what is sometimes called "playing the devil's advocate." When one does this, one attempts to provide the best possible defense of a view, even if one doesn't agree with this view. Doing this can often provide a very useful service to one's audience, addressing the members' needs to encounter evidence they might have overlooked or underestimated. When one has thoroughly investigated a view and come to the conclusion that it is correct, one is often among the best equipped persons to highlight its weaknesses. Sometimes highlighting the shortcomings of, objections to, or weaknesses in one's own views can better serve an audience's needs than providing a positive case for those views. In this way, an audience's needs can make a significant difference for how a view is presented to that audience.

Those who possess and exercise the virtue of audience sensitivity are aware of these four features of their audiences—their abilities, views, concerns, and needs. In displaying sensitivity to these features of their audience, they will tailor the communication of their ideas differently from one audience to another, sometimes modifying the manner of their communication of these ideas, and sometimes modifying the content of their communication.

6.3.2 Vices Opposed to Audience Sensitivity

Two vices stand opposed to audience sensitivity: intellectual narcissism and intellectual snobbery. While both vices stand in the way of audience sensitivity, each does so for unique reasons.

Intellectual narcissism is *a tendency to direct everyone's attention to one's own self-identified intellectual superiority over others.* The narcissist has come to the conclusion, whether justified or not, that he is intellectually superior to others, including his audience members. The narcissist *enjoys* perceiving himself in this way, and he seeks for others to perceive him in this way as well, thinking that this too will add to his enjoyment of his superiority. He does all he can to attract the attention of others to his perceived superior qualities so that others too might recognize his greatness.

Intellectual narcissism is opposed to audience sensitivity since the narcissist is too concerned with himself to be concerned with others. His concern for himself—in particular, his concern to be perceived as superior—is so strong that the only concern he displays toward others is motivated by furthering this perception of superiority. He might display a kind of concern for his audience's features, but the whole aim of his sensitivity to these features is to better produce in his audience a perception of his superiority.

This kind of sensitivity to one's audience differs markedly from the virtue of audience sensitivity discussed above. As we defined audience sensitivity, it is ultimately aimed at better enabling one's audience to achieve intellectual goods. Those who display the virtue of audience sensitivity attend to the unique abilities, views, concerns, and needs of their audiences so as to help those audiences achieve intellectual goods. To the extent that an intellectual narcissist attends to the unique features of an audience, it is only as a means to leading them to perceive the narcissist as an intellectual superior.

One way intellectual narcissism might be manifested is through communications of one's ideas intended to wow an audience rather than to help them achieve true beliefs, knowledge, or understanding. The narcissist won't be bothered if the concepts employed are beyond the repertoire of the audience or are communicated entirely in abstract form to an audience that needs illustrations. Likewise, the narcissist won't be bothered if the views, concerns, or needs of the audience are completely ignored.

A second vice opposed to audience sensitivity is **intellectual snobbery**, which is *a tendency to underestimate an audience's intellectual abilities and to forego an effortful presentation of one's ideas in a way that is narrowly tailored to the unique features of the audience, unless that audience is among a select group one regards as worthy of one's best efforts.* The snob's problem isn't so much that she looks up at herself (like the narcissist) but that she looks down at her audience. She isn't equally concerned to promote the intellectual goods of all audiences. She believes that most audiences aren't worthy of her ideas. Only a select few, elite audiences deserve her best efforts. As a result, she has a tendency to underestimate her audience's intellectual abilities and to forego an effortful presentation of her ideas narrowly tailored to the unique features of each of her audiences. For just the right audience, she might display audience sensitivity. But she doesn't possess this trait as a general feature. She's too discriminating about which audiences she makes an effort for.

The snob can't be depended on by most audiences. By definition, she can be depended on only by the select few she regards as worthy of her best efforts. Even if she really is intellectually impressive, most audiences are better off learning from someone else. Specifically, they are better off learning from those who are less discriminating in their practice of audience sensitivity. The

Key Ideas for Review

Audience sensitivity is a tendency to regulate communications in such a way that one best enables a particular audience—with its particular views, concerns, needs, and abilities—to achieve intellectual goods.

Begging the question is a rhetorical fallacy in which one employs premises one knows are rejected by one's audience.

Intellectual narcissism is a tendency to direct everyone's attention to one's own self-identified intellectual superiority over others.

Intellectual snobbery is a tendency to underestimate an audience's intellectual abilities and to forego an effortful presentation of one's ideas in a way that is narrowly tailored to the unique features of the audience, unless that audience is among a select group one regards as worthy of one's best efforts.

snob may not even deign to communicate with most audiences, but even if she does, she's unlikely to communicate in a way that enables them to achieve intellectual goods. The snob is therefore of little help to the community of inquirers.

6.3.3 Summary

This section has identified the intellectual virtue of audience sensitivity. Those who display the virtue of sensitivity to an audience tend to regulate their communications in such a way that they best enable the particular audience, with its particular views, concerns, needs, and abilities, to achieve intellectual goods. Standing opposed to audience sensitivity are the vices of intellectual narcissism and intellectual snobbery.

Exercise 6.3

A. Evaluating Audience Sensitivity. For each of the following examples, make a case for why the character or characters do or do not display audience sensitivity. If a character exhibits a vice that is contrary to audience sensitivity, identify the vice. Cite relevant material from the text in section 6.3 in defense of your view.

1. In an introductory philosophy of religion class, Professor Jones gives an abstract characterization of the nature of pragmatic arguments for religious theses. He then discusses an objection that targets all such pragmatic arguments. Never does he give a specific example of a pragmatic argument for a religious thesis.

2. Wanda has been offered an opportunity to defend her view that transgendered persons should be able to access bathrooms of the gender to which they have transitioned for an audience at the Social Conservatives Club. She begins her presentation by noting that her argument will not depend on views about whether it's really possible for people to "change" their gender. She acknowledges that she thinks this is possible, but she understands that her audience may not think it is, so she will defend her views without relying on the assumption that it is possible.

3. Abraham tells his audience, "The explanation for why this is the case is probably too complicated for you to understand."

4. After presenting an interpretation of a biblical passage, the Bible study leader, Jennifer, pauses and asks each of the members of the group to reflect privately for a few moments about how the interpretation might present a challenge or opportunity for his or her own life.

5. Yvon is giving a speech in front of her peers. In a tone they haven't heard her use before, she begins, "The polymorphism of cleverness is upon closer examination almost open-minded in its objectivity." The remainder of the speech sounds the same way.

6. Wesley is working on an argument he will present for the claim that no young child ever deserves corporal punishment. Wesley's own view is that punishments in general are not justified on the basis of being deserved, but only on some other basis. Yet in defending his argument, he instead decides to use the premise that punishments for young children in particular cannot be justified on the basis of being deserved.

7. Victor, a psychologist, has been asked by his church group to present his research findings about the value of giving to others. Victor does so without referencing any biblical or religious themes.

8. Valerie, a theologian, has been invited to share her ideas about environmental responsibility to the League of Atheist Environmentalists. She begins her presentation by emphasizing the way in which her ideas are rooted in a commitment to a particular view of God's orderly creation of the cosmos.

9. As part of a debate about the morality of same-sex couples rearing children, Vince argues as follows: "Child rearing by same-sex couples is morally problematic because it teaches the children that child rearing by such couples is morally acceptable."

10. Brianne, like most of the members of the Theology Club, thinks that divine determinism is false. She has argued against the view, but she thinks her fellow members don't give the view the credit it deserves. So when given the opportunity to discuss it, she works hard to present the best case in favor of it that she can.

Appendix

Argument Forms and Proof Rules

Famous Valid Argument Forms

Modus Ponens	*Modus Tollens*	Disjunctive Syllogism (options 1 and 2)	
If P, then Q.	If P, then Q.	Either P or Q.	Either P or Q.
P.	Not-Q.	Not-Q.	Not-P.
So Q.	So not-P.	So P.	So Q.

Constructive Dilemma (options 1 and 2)		Hypothetical Syllogism
Either P or Q.	Either P or Q.	If P, then Q.
If P, then R.	If P, then R.	If Q, then R.
If Q, then S.	If Q, then S.	So if P, then R.
So either R or S.	So either S or R.	

Famous Invalid Argument Forms

Denying the Antecedent	Affirming the Consequent	Affirming a Disjunct (options 1 and 2)	
If P, then Q.	If P, then Q.	Either P or Q.	Either P or Q.
Not P.	Q.	P.	Q.
So not-Q.	So P.	So not-Q.	So not-P.

Rules of Implication (Proof Method)

MP	MT	DS (options 1 and 2)		HS	CD (options 1 and 2)	
P → Q	P → Q	P v Q	P v Q	P → Q	P v Q	P v Q
P	~Q	~Q	~P	Q → R	P → R	P → Q
So Q	So ~P	So P	So Q	P → R	Q → S	R → S
					R v S	S v R

Simp (options 1 and 2)		Conj	Add (options 1 and 2)	
P · Q	P · Q	P	P	P
So P	So Q	Q	So P v Q	So Q v P
		So P · Q		

Rules of Equivalence (Proof Method)

DN

P :: ~~P

Comm

P v Q :: Q v P

P · Q :: Q · P

Re

P :: P v P

P :: P · P

Cont

P → Q :: ~Q → ~P

As

P v (Q v R) :: (P v Q) v R

P · (Q · R) :: (P · Q) · R

Ex

(P · Q) → R :: P → (Q → R)

MI

P → Q :: ~P v Q

Dist

P · (Q v R) :: (P · Q) v (P · R)

P v (Q · R) :: (P v Q) · (P v R)

DeM

~(P · Q) :: ~P v ~Q

~(P v Q) :: ~P · ~Q

ME

P ↔ Q :: (P → Q) · (Q → P)

P ↔ Q :: (P · Q) v (~P · ~Q)

Rules of Indirect Proof (Proof Method)

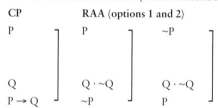

CP

P

Q

P → Q

RAA (options 1 and 2)

P

Q · ~Q

~P

~P

Q · ~Q

P

Rules of Implication
(Expanded Proof Method)

∀-elimination	∃-introduction
∀x(Px)	Pa
So Pa	So ∃x(Px)

Rules of Indirect Proof
(Expanded Proof Method)

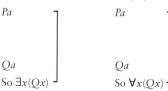

Indirect ∃-introduction

∃x(Px)

Pa

Qa

So ∃x(Qx)

Indirect ∀-introduction

∀x(Px)

Pa

Qa

So ∀x(Qx)

Rule of Quantifier Equivalence
(Expanded Proof Method)

$\forall xP :: \sim\exists x\sim P \quad \exists xP :: \sim\forall x\sim P$

$\forall x\sim P :: \sim\exists xP \quad \exists x\sim P :: \sim\forall xP$

Famous Strong Argument Forms

Statistical Syllogism

$x\%$ of A are B.

Y is an A.

So Y is a B.

Induction by Enumeration

$x\%$ of a sample of A are B.

So $x\%$ of A are B.

Argument from Authority

X asserts P.

So P.

Argument from Analogy

X is like Y in respects R_1–R_n.

Y has P.

So X has P.

Inference to the Best Explanation

H is the best available explanation for why D.

So H.

Notes

Part 1 The Skills of Reasoning

1. Zagzebski (1996), 106–16, lists several key differences.

Chapter 1 Introduction to Arguments

1. While the foregoing paragraphs are certainly written in a way sympathetic toward some version of foundationalism in epistemology, endorsing such a view is not required for appreciating the present point that at least some of our beliefs are believed on the basis of other beliefs. And it is this present point that is most important here.

2. While there is considerable debate about what precisely constitutes the image of God in human beings, it is widely thought that part of what this image entails involves our rational capacities. One can find this emphasis in nearly any systematic theology or theological dictionary that addresses the topic. Some texts emphasize the social dimension or the eschatological dimension of this image, but even here some assumptions are required about those rational capacities necessary for the social and eschatological functions in view. It is a widespread idea, then, that our rational faculties are at least an important part of what equips us to bear God's image.

3. Emotivism provides a good example of such a view about moral discourse, while logical positivism provides a good example of this kind of view about religious discourse.

Chapter 2 Deductive Logic

1. More exactly, the words or phrases must be used in such a way that the resulting statement has a truth-value that is determined by the truth-value of the simpler statements.

2. Another important difference is this: By making all logical vocabulary explicit when identifying an argument's form for the sake of using the Counterexample Method,

we sometimes identify a different form than we would have identified when using the Famous Forms Method. Consider again example 18 from the previous section:

18. If Ellie either paid her rent or bought a new television, then Ellie's bank account is now low. Ellie either paid her rent or bought a new television. So Ellie's bank account is now low.

If we make all the logical connectives in this argument explicit, then we will end up using three capital letters rather than two when we identify the argument's form. If we replace "Ellie paid her rent" with P, "Ellie bought a new television" with Q, and "Ellie's bank account is now low" with R, then we get the form identified in example 19:

19. If either P or Q, then R. P or Q. So R.

However, in the previous section we determined that when using the Famous Forms Method, which does not require making all of an argument's logical connectives explicit, we could use only two capital letters when identifying the form of this argument. We used P for "Either Ellie paid her rent or bought a new television" and Q for "Ellie's bank account is now low." This yielded:

20. If P, then Q. P. So Q.

3. Logicians describe this as treating universal statements as if they do not have existential import—as if they do not imply that there are members of their subject classes. By representing universal statements in this way—as if they do not have existential import—we are following the conventions of modern categorical logic as opposed to Aristotelian categorical logic.

4. If we think about moving from the statement on the right to the statement on the left in this rule, the name "exportation" may seem sensible, as we are exporting the Q from its place in the second statement and conjoining it to the P. Let's break this rule down by moving from left

to right. The first claims tells us that if P and Q are both true, then R is. Now, suppose the antecedent of the second claim, P, is true. It will then follow from the first claim that if Q is also true, then R is true—which is the consequent of the second claim. To see how the move from right to left is justified, imagine that we have both P and Q. If we do, we can just apply MP twice to the right-hand statement and get R. Thus the right-hand statement implies that if P and Q are both true, so is R.

5. To see why the move from left to right is justified, notice that P v ~P must be true. Either P is true or it isn't (hence, ~P). Now, if it is the case that ~P, then by Add it is the case that ~P v Q. Likewise, if it is the case that P, then it follows from P → Q and MP that Q. And it follows from Q and Add that ~P v Q. So as either P is true or ~P is true, it must be that ~P v Q is true given P → Q. Now try moving from right to left. Suppose that P is true. By DN, ~~P is also true. By DS, ~P v Q and ~~P implies Q. Thus, given ~P v Q, if P is true, then Q is true. Suppose instead that P is false. It follows immediately that P → Q, for the only way for P → Q not to be true is if P is true and Q is false. So whether P or ~P is true, ~P v Q implies P → Q.

6. In light of what we know about the meanings of the dot and the wedge, we should be able to work out why these inferences are justified in each direction.

7. While this rule appears complicated, we again should be able to work out why each movement is justified from what we know about the meanings of the tilde, dot, and wedge.

8. The first rule here should be intuitive. Arrows in each direction are equivalent to the double arrow. We can see why the second rule is justified when we note that the double arrow is a way to symbolize logical equivalence. It tells us that for logical purposes what is on the one side of the connective is equivalent to what is on the other side. Thus either what is on each side is true or what is on each side is false. Here, either both P and Q are true or both P and Q are false.

9. There is one interesting difference between indirect ∃-introduction and indirect ∀-introduction. The first step of indirect ∀-introduction is a perfectly legitimate step of argument independent of its use in indirect ∀-introduction. For example, claim 3 in example 35 could have been justified simply by ∀-elimination. We write the justification for it that we do in example 35 simply because of its role in the proof—namely, that it is used as the first step in indirect ∀-introduction. If it hadn't been, then our justification would simply have been "from 1 by ∀-elimination." By contrast, the first step in indirect ∃-introduction cannot be justified independently from its use in indirect ∃-introduction.

10. To be more precise, P is an expression that is such that, when following the expression that proceeds it in examples 36–39, it constitutes a statement of the Expanded Proof Method.

Chapter 3 Inductive Logic

1. This is not to say that example 6 couldn't be a strong argument. In section 3.3 we will learn about a way to employ the information provided in example 6 to construct an argument that is strong given certain restrictions. The present point is simply that example 6 does not exhibit the argument form of induction by enumeration.

2. One additional observation must be made here about examples 6 and 8. While we have spoken as if these arguments each employ a single argument from authority in order to defend their subconclusions, this is not entirely accurate. They actually employ a conjunction of arguments from authority. In arguing from the reports of 50 percent of smokers studied in a recent survey to the truth of what they reported, we are arguing that for *each* smoker, since he or she reported being a drinker, he or she is a drinker. In other words, we are iterating or multiplying uses of the argument from authority form. Exactly how many uses are involved depends on how many members are included in the population with which our premise is concerned. From the perspective of our present aims in evaluating them, arguments like examples 6 and 8 are best understood as employing the same number of instances of an argument from authority as the number of members in the sample to which they refer.

In light of this, a further kind of information can challenge the strength of these kinds of arguments. If we are to be in a position to conclude that these arguments are strong, we cannot know that the result of multiplying the probabilities that each of the members of the samples has reported the truth is 50 percent or less. In other words, suppose that we create a list of numbers, n_1–n_n, each of which corresponds to the likelihood that one of the members of our sample of smokers has reported the truth. We will not be in a position to conclude that the argument of example 6 is strong if we have information that provides reason to think that the result of multiplying n_1–n_n is 50 percent or less since we cannot conclude that the subconclusion of example 6 is more likely than not, given this further information.

3. The final three claims in example 4 do not *quite* compose a statistical syllogism, however, since the percentage cited is 100 percent.

4. If these features were the only features that contribute to the goodness of an explanation, then for an explanation to be good, it would need to display only these features sufficiently well. Displaying these features sufficiently well would be all that is needed for an explanation to be a good explanation. As we have seen, however, there remains controversy about whether these are the only features that contribute to the goodness of explanations—a controversy we will not attempt to settle here.

Part 2 The Virtues of Inquiry

1. The key text for the revival in virtue ethics is Mac-Intyre (1984). Several texts have been important for the development of virtue epistemology. The seminal article is Sosa (1980).

2. This account of virtues as excellent ways of being for goods derives from Adams (2006).

3. The language used here is intentionally vague concerning the debate between reliabilist virtue ethicists and responsibilist virtue ethicists. The present focus on traits of character, however, is plausibly most at home in a responsibilist virtue epistemology.

Chapter 4 Internal Virtues

1. Montmarquet (1993) calls this trait "conscientiousness." Roberts and Wood (2007) call it "love of knowledge."

2. Roberts and Wood (2007), 154–55.

3. The caveat here, that there may be different kinds of support appropriate for different beliefs, is intended to forestall a commitment to evidentialism. Perhaps some beliefs do not require a preponderance of support from evidence, but they must be supported in some other way if they are to be appropriately held.

4. Cf. Zagzebski (2012).

5. This definition is borrowed from Kunda (1999), 112–15.

6. See Baron (2000).

7. See Kahneman (2011).

8. See Pronin (2007).

Chapter 5 Virtues of Intellectual Dependence

1. Cf. Zagzebski (2012).

2. Cf. Fricker (2007).

3. See Titchner (1909).

4. See Linker (2011).

5. Cf. Byerly (2014).

Chapter 6 Virtues of Intellectual Dependability

1. Another option would be for the egoist to retreat to the view that one's goods are more valuable for oneself just because they are one's own. However, this view appears to be a tautology: each person's goods are her goods. What it is for a good to be good (or valuable) for oneself is just for it to be one's own good. But a tautology such as this does not have the force that the egoist wants. It cannot motivate us away from intellectual generosity since no advocate of intellectual generosity denies that my goods are mine and your goods are yours.

2. See, for example, Greco (2010).

3. An expanded version of this argument is given in favor of the value of a more general others-centeredness in Byerly and Byerly (2016).

Glossary of Key Terms

ad hominem **fallacy.** A kind of informal fallacy that directs an argument against a person rather than against an argument. (See section 5.1.)

affirmative statement. A categorical statement that affirms that some or all members of the subject class are members of the predicate class, as in statements of the form "All S are P" or "Some S are P." (See section 2.3.)

affirming a disjunct. An invalid argument form in which one of the disjuncts is affirmed rather than denied in the second premise. (See section 2.2.)

affirming the consequent. An invalid argument form in which the consequent is affirmed rather than denied in the second premise. (See section 2.2.)

ambiguous term. A word or phrase that can reasonably be understood in multiple distinct ways in the context, where the way it is understood makes a difference. (See section 6.2.)

antecedent. The part of a conditional statement that immediately follows the word "if." (See section 2.2.)

appeal to an unqualified authority. An informal fallacy that employs the form of an argument from authority but substitutes someone for X who is not an authority about whether P is the case. (See section 3.3.)

argument. A set of statements where one of those statements (the conclusion) is affirmed on the basis of the others (the premises). (See section 1.1.)

argument from analogy. A kind of argument in which we identify an analogy between two different individuals or groups—a way or range of ways in which the two individuals or groups compared are alike—and then conclude that because one of the two has some further feature, the other does as well. (See section 3.4.)

argument from authority. An argument that concludes that something is true because an authority on the subject has asserted that it is. (See section 3.3.)

assert. To present P as if it is true. (See section 3.3.)

audience sensitivity. A tendency to regulate communications in such a way that one best enables a particular audience—with its particular views, concerns, needs, and abilities—to achieve intellectual goods. (See section 6.3.)

authority. An authority about a statement P is someone who is more likely than not to have a true belief about whether P is true. (See section 3.3.)

available explanation. H is an available explanation for D if the audience of the inference to the best explanation is aware of H as a candidate explanation for D. (See section 3.5.)

begging the question. A rhetorical fallacy in which one employs premises one knows are rejected by one's audience. (See section 6.3.)

best explanation. H is the best explanation for D if there is no other explanation for D that is as good as or better than H. (See section 3.5.)

categorical statements. Statements that assert that a relationship obtains between classes or categories of things. (See section 2.2.)

categorical syllogism. An argument with three categorical statements: two premises and one conclusion. These three statements employ three different terms, and each term is used twice in the argument. (See section 2.3.)

cogent argument. A strong argument with only true premises. (See section 1.2.)

communicative clarity. A tendency to eliminate sources of confusion from one's communications to others. (See section 6.2.)

conclusion indicators. Words or phrases indicating that what comes immediately after them is a conclusion affirmed on the basis of premises supplied elsewhere in the argument. (See section 1.1.)

condescension. A tendency to not treat anyone else's best methods of inquiry the same as your own simply because they are not you. (See section 5.1.)

conditional statement. A statement in which the main logical connective is the "if . . . then" connective. (See section 2.1.)

confirmation bias. A pattern of inquiry in which inquirers disproportionately investigate evidence they have reason to think favors their own view. (See section 4.3.)

conform. An argument conforms to a famous valid argument form if it exactly matches it, or if it matches it except that it uses different letters or puts its premises in a different order. (See section 2.1.)

conjunct. The statement on one side of "and" in a conjunction. (See section 2.4.)

conjunction. A statement in which the main logical connective is the "and" connective. (See section 2.2.)

consequent. The part of a conditional statement that immediately follows the word "then." (See section 2.2.)

constant. A term that refers to the same entity throughout an argument. (See section 2.5.)

constructive dilemma. A famous valid argument form that begins with a disjunctive claim, makes a claim about what is the case if each one of the disjuncts is correct, and ends with a disjunctive conclusion. (See section 2.1.)

contradiction. A claim of the form P · ~P—that is, a conjunction of a statement and its negation. (See section 2.4.)

copula. The form of the verb "to be" that is employed in the categorical statement. (See section 2.2.)

Counterexample Method. A method that provides provisional evidence of the invalidity of an argument by constructing a good counterexample to the form of that argument that makes all of its key logical vocabulary explicit. (See section 2.2.)

credulity. An insensitivity to reasons for treating others' methods of inquiry differently from one's own. (See section 5.1.)

deductive logic. The study of the methods used to evaluate arguments for validity or invalidity. (See section 1.2.)

denying the antecedent. An invalid argument form in which the antecedent is denied rather than affirmed in the second premise (See section 2.2.)

disjunct. One of the statements in an "either . . . or" claim on either side of the "or." (See section 2.2.)

disjunction. A statement in which the main logical connective is the "either . . . or" connective. (See section 2.1.)

disjunctive syllogism. A famous valid argument form that begins with an "either . . . or" statement, denies one of the disjuncts in the second premise, and affirms the other disjunct in the conclusion. (See section 2.1.)

enthymeme. A statement of an argument that leaves some premises or the conclusion unstated. (See section 5.2.)

existential quantifier. A quantifier (represented by the ∃ symbol) that tells us that *there is* something such that an expression following the ∃ symbol is true of it. (See section 2.5.)

Expanded Proof Method. A method used to determine that an argument is valid by constructing a proof of its conclusion using the rules of the Proof Method together with the additional rules of implication, indirect proof, and equivalence unique to the Expanded Proof Method. (See section 2.5.)

explanation. A set of statements where none of the statements is affirmed on the basis of the others and where some of the statements tell the reader why one of the other statements is true. (See section 1.1.)

fallacy of amphiboly. An informal fallacy in which a grammatically ambiguous phrase functions in one way in one claim and in a different way in another claim. (See section 6.2.)

fallacy of equivocation. An informal fallacy in which an argument employs a term with different meanings in different claims. (See section 6.2.)

Famous Forms Method. A method used to determine whether an argument is valid by determining whether the argument's form conforms to a famous valid argument form. (See section 2.1.)

famous strong argument form. An argument form that is such that any argument with this form is strong in the absence of certain additional information. (See section 3.1.)

famous valid argument forms. The five commonly employed argument forms, including *modus ponens*, *modus tollens*, disjunctive syllogism, constructive dilemma, and hypothetical syllogism. Any argument with a form that conforms to one of these argument forms is a valid argument. (See section 2.1.)

good counterexample. A good counterexample to an argument form is an argument that uses this argument form where the premises are well-known truths and the conclusion is a well-known falsehood. (See section 2.2.)

hypothetical syllogism. A famous valid argument form that has conditional statements for its premises and conclusion. (See section 2.1.)

illustration. A set of statements where none of the statements is affirmed on the basis of the others, and where one of the statements is explained or clarified through the use of an example. (See section 1.1.)

induction by enumeration. A strong argument form employing the following pattern of reasoning, where x is any number between 0 and 100 inclusive and A and B are categories:

x% of a sample of A are B.

So x% of A are B. (See section 3.2.)

inductive logic. The study of the methods used to evaluate arguments for strength or weakness. (See section 1.2.)

inference to the best explanation. An argument that uses the following argument form, where D is a datum and H is a hypothesis:

H is the best available explanation for why D. So H. (See section 3.5.)

intellectual caution. A tendency to sensitively regulate one's inquiries in light of known obstacles facing this inquiry. (See section 4.2.)

intellectual courage. A tendency not to be overcome by obstacles to inquiry—a tendency to continue inquiry despite these obstacles. (See section 4.2.)

intellectual egoism. A tendency to think that one's own intellectual goods are more important than others' just because they are one's own. (See section 6.1.)

intellectual empathy. A tendency to imaginatively reconstruct the position occupied by the views and arguments of others within a psychological web in which they make best sense. (See section 5.3.)

intellectual generosity. A disposition to contribute to others' inquiries in a way that displays a deep motivation for promoting others' intellectual goods responsibly. (See section 6.1.)

intellectual injustice. A tendency to treat others' best methods of inquiry differently from one's on the basis of reasons that are irrelevant to whether others' methods or abilities are as good as one's own. (See section 5.1.)

intellectual narcissism. A tendency to direct everyone's attention to one's own self-identified intellectual superiority over others. (See section 6.3.)

intellectual patronization. A tendency to promote another's intellectual goods in such a way that one inhibits the other from acquiring or utilizing intellectual virtues. (See section 6.1.)

intellectual selfishness. A tendency to act as if one is an intellectual egoist. (See section 6.1.)

intellectual snobbery. A tendency to underestimate an audience's intellectual abilities and to forego an effortful presentation of one's ideas in a way that is narrowly tailored to the unique features of the audience, unless that audience is among a select group one regards as worthy of one's best efforts. (See section 6.3.)

interpretive charity. A tendency to interpret others in as positive a light as possible, consistent with a respect for their communicative intentions. (See section 5.2.)

interpretive face blindness. A tendency not to interpret others in a way that is consistent with what one has best reason to think they intended to communicate. (See section 5.2.)

interpretive stinginess. A tendency to resist interpreting what others have said in the most positive light. (See section 5.2.)

introspective vigilance. A tendency to attend carefully to one's own patterns of inquiry, and to root out, correct for, and prevent bad ones to the best of one's ability. (See section 4.3.)

invalid argument. An argument in which the truth of the premises does not absolutely guarantee the truth of the conclusion—an argument in which it is possible for the premises to be true and the conclusion false. (See section 1.2.)

invalid argument form. An argument form—including denying the antecedent, affirming the consequent, and affirming a disjunct—in which some arguments that employ the form are invalid. (See section 2.2.)

irrelevant. If two items are similar in respect R, this similarity is irrelevant to their possession of P if it is not more likely than not that if something possesses R, it possesses P. (See section 3.4.)

key logical vocabulary. The argument's logical connectives, quantifiers, and copulas. (See section 2.2.)

logic. The study of the methods used to evaluate arguments. (See section 1.1.)

logical connectives. Those words or phrases that an argument uses in order to make larger statements out of smaller ones. (See section 2.1.)

love of intellectual excellence. A disposition to conduct inquiries in a way that displays a deep motivation for achieving intellectual goods responsibly. Intellectual goods include true belief, knowledge, understanding, and attitudes that are adequately supported. (See section 4.1.)

main logical connective. The logical connective of a statement that operates on the entire statement, as opposed to simply a subpart of the statement. (See section 2.1.)

mere conditional statement. An "if . . . then" statement that is not used to either affirm or deny either of its component clauses. (See section 1.1.)

middle term. The term of a categorical syllogism that appears in both of its premises. (See section 2.3.)

modus ponens. Latin for "the way of affirming," a famous valid argument form that begins with an "if . . . then" statement, affirms the antecedent in the second premise, and affirms the consequent in the conclusion. (See section 2.1.)

modus tollens. Latin for "the way of denying," a famous valid argument form that begins with an "if . . . then" statement, denies the consequent in the second premise, and denies the antecedent in the conclusion (See section 2.1.)

monotonic. A claim that for any valid argument "P. So Q," the argument "P. R. So Q" is also valid, where P and Q are the same statements in each quotation and R is any statement whatsoever. (See section 3.1.)

necessary conditions. Conditions for the application of a term that are such that, if the term is to be correctly applied, the conditions must be met. (See section 6.2.)

negation. A statement in which the main logical connective is the "not" connective. (See section 2.1.)

negative statement. A categorical statement that denies that some or all members of the subject class are members of the predicate class, as in statements of the form "No S are P" or "Some S are not P." (See section 2.3.)

non-monotonic. A claim that it is not the case that for any strong argument "P. So Q," any argument "P. R. So Q" is strong, where P and Q are the same statements in each quotation and R is any statement whatsoever. (See section 3.1.)

particular statement. A categorical statement that is concerned with only some members of its subject class and that uses the quantifier "Some," as in statements of the form "Some S are P" and "Some S are not P." (See section 2.3.)

post hoc **fallacy.** An informal fallacy in which one too quickly concludes that because one thing occurred after another, it occurred because of the other—it was caused by the other. (See section 4.3.)

predicate. An expression referring to a property or feature of something. (See section 2.5.)

predicate term. The second class or category named in the categorical statement. (See section 2.2.)

premise indicators. Words or phrases indicating that what comes immediately after them is a premise on the basis of which a conclusion is affirmed. (See section 1.1.)

problem of dwindling probabilities. A problem in which in any argument that employs a subconclusion, and in which the premises offer merely probabilistic support for the subconclusion and the main conclusion, the probability of the main conclusion given the premises that are not subconclusions is lower than the probability of the subconclusion given those premises used to defend it. (See section 3.2.)

proof. A proof of an argument is a set of symbolic statements of an argument that begins with symbolized representations of the argument's premise(s) and ends with a symbolized representation of its conclusion, where each other statement in the set is justified by a rule of implication, equivalence, or indirect proof. (See section 2.4.)

Proof Method. A method used to determine that an argument is valid by constructing a proof of the argument's conclusion where each step of the proof is justified by an implication rule, an equivalence rule, or an indirect proof rule. (See section 2.4.)

quantifier. The word in a categorical statement that signals how much of the subject class the statement is concerned with. (See section 2.2.)

rebutting defeater. Any information that challenges the support an argument's premises provide for its conclusion by directly providing support for the denial of that conclusion. (See section 3.3.)

relevant. If two items are similar in respect R, this similarity is relevant to their possession of P if it is more likely than not that if something possesses R, it possesses P. (See section 3.4.)

relevant disanalogy. If X and Y are disanalogous with respect to P, this disanalogy between them is relevant to their possession of Q if there is a difference between the likelihood that something possesses Q given that it possesses P and the likelihood that something possesses Q given that it doesn't possess P. (See section 3.4.)

report. A set of statements where none of the statements is affirmed on the basis of the others and where the statements are offered for the purpose of simply providing the reader with information. (See section 1.1.)

rule of quantifier equivalence. A rule of the Expanded Proof Method that comes in four forms and that allows us to move back and forth from statements that employ the ∀ symbol to equivalent statements that employ the ∃ symbol. (See section 2.5.)

rules of equivalence. The rules of equivalence are rules used in the Proof Method that allow us to move back and forth between equivalent statements in a proof. The ten rules of equivalence are double negations (DN), commutation (Comm), redundancy (Re), contraposition (Cont), association (As), exportation (Ex), material implication (MI), distribution (Dist), De Morgan's (DeM), and material equivalence (ME). (See section 2.4.)

rules of implication. The rules of implication are rules that allow us to make inferences within proofs. The rules of implication of the Proof Method are *modus ponens* (MP), *modus tollens* (MT), disjunctive syllogism (DS), hypothetical syllogism (HS), constructive dilemma (CD), simplification (Simp), conjunction (Conj), and addition (Add). (See section 2.4.) The rules of implications of the Expanded Proof Method are ∀-elimination and ∃-introduction. (See section 2.5.)

rules of indirect proof. The rules of indirect proof are rules that allow us to prove something not directly on the basis of preceding premises but instead on the basis of an assumption that we will temporarily introduce into the proof before then discharging. The rules of indirect proof for the Proof Method are conditional proof (CP) and *reductio ad absurdum* (RAA). (See section 2.4.) The rules of indirect proof of the Expanded Proof Method are indirect ∃-introduction and indirect ∀-introduction. (See section 2.5.)

scope. The scope of a quantifier is the part of an expression to which a quantifier applies. (See section 2.5.)

slippery slope fallacy. An informal fallacy in which one reasons in accordance with a chain of conditional ("if . . . then") statements where the connection between the conditionals' antecedents and their consequents is tenuous. (See section 4.3.)

sound argument. A valid argument with only true premises. (See section 1.2.)

statement. Any sentence that is either true or false. (See section 1.1.)

statistical syllogism. A famous strong argument form with the following form, where x is a number or range of numbers greater than 50 and less

than 100, A and B are categories, and Y is an individual:

x% of A are B.

Y is an A.

So Y is a B. (See section 3.1.)

straw man fallacy. The informal fallacy of representing one's interlocutor as having endorsed a position that the interlocutor did not endorse, attacking this position one has identified, and concluding that the interlocutor's view is false on this basis. (See section 5.2.)

strong argument. An argument in which the truth of the premises makes the conclusion more likely than not without absolutely guaranteeing the conclusion. (See section 1.2.)

subconclusion. A conclusion in an argument that is itself used as a premise in defense of another conclusion. (See section 3.2.)

subject term. The first class or category named in the categorical statement. (See section 2.2.)

sufficient conditions. Conditions for the application of a term that are such that, if they are met, then it is appropriate to apply the term. (See section 6.2.)

theorem. A statement that can be proven without any premises. (See section 2.4.)

trust. A tendency to treat others' best methods of inquiry the same way as one's own in the absence of reason for doing otherwise. (See section 5.1.)

uncogent argument. An argument that is not cogent. (See section 1.2.)

undercutting defeater. Any information that undercuts the support that the premises of an argument provide for its conclusion without providing direct support for the denial of the conclusion. (See section 3.3.)

universal quantifier. A quantifier (represented by the ∀ symbol) that tells us that *for anything* there is, the expression following the ∀ symbol is true of it. (See section 2.5.)

universal statement. A categorical statement that is concerned with all members of its subject class and that uses the quantifier "All" or "No," as in statements of the form "All S are P" and "No S are P." (See section 2.3.)

unsound argument. An argument that is not sound. (See section 1.2.)

valid argument. An argument in which the truth of the premises absolutely guarantees the truth of the conclusion—an argument in which it is impossible for the premises to be true and the conclusion false. (See section 1.2.)

variable. A term the referent of which is left unspecified. (See section 2.5.)

Venn diagram. A diagram of three overlapping circles, one labeled S, one labeled P, and one labeled M,

corresponding to the subject and predicate terms of the conclusion of a categorical syllogism and the middle term of that syllogism. (See section 2.3.)

Venn Diagram Method. A method used to determine an argument's validity that involves representing the premises of a categorical syllogism on a Venn diagram and then concluding that the syllogism is valid if this diagram also unambiguously represents that the conclusion of the syllogism is true. (See section 2.3.)

weak argument. An argument in which the truth of the premises does not make the truth of the conclusion more likely than not. (See section 1.2.)

Bibliography

Adams, Robert Merrihew. 2006. *A Theory of Virtue: Excellence in Being for the Good*. New York: Oxford University Press.

Baron, Jonathan. 2000. *Thinking and Deciding*. 3rd ed. New York: Cambridge University Press.

Byerly, T. Ryan. 2014. "The Values and Varieties of Humility." *Philosophia* 42: 889–910.

Byerly, T. Ryan, and Meghan Byerly. 2016. "The Special Value of Others-Centeredness." *Res Philosophica* 93: 63–78.

Fricker, Miranda. 2007. *Epistemic Injustice: Power and the Ethics of Knowing*. New York: Oxford University Press.

Greco, John. 2010. *Achieving Knowledge: A Virtue-Theoretic Account of Epistemic Normativity*. New York: Cambridge University Press.

Kahneman, Daniel. 2011. *Thinking, Fast and Slow*. New York: Farrar, Straus, and Giroux.

Kunda, Ziva. 1999. *Social Cognition: Making Sense of People*. Cambridge, MA: MIT Press.

Linker, Maureen. 2011. "Do Squirrels Eat Hamburgers? Intellectual Empathy as a Remedy for Residual Prejudice." *Informal Logic* 31: 110–38.

MacIntyre, Alasdair. 1984. *After Virtue: A Study in Moral Theory*, 2nd ed. Notre Dame, IN: University of Notre Dame Press.

Montmarquet, James A. 1993. *Epistemic Virtue and Doxastic Responsibility*. Lanham, MD: Rowman & Littlefield.

Pronin, Emily. 2007. "Perception and Misperception of Bias in Human Judgment." *Trends in Cognitive Science* 11: 37–43.

Roberts, Robert C., and W. Jay Wood. 2007. *Intellectual Virtues: An Essay in Regulative Epistemology*. New York: Oxford University Press, 2007.

Sosa, Ernest. 1980. "The Raft and the Pyramid: Coherence Versus Foundations in the Theory of Knowledge." *Midwest Studies in Epistemology* 5: 3–26.

Titchner, Edward. 1909. *Lectures on the Experimental Psychology of the Thought-Processes*. New York: Macmillan.

Zagzebski, Linda. 1996. *Virtues of the Mind: An Inquiry into the Nature and the Ethical Foundations of Knowledge*. New York: Cambridge University Press.

———. 2012. *Epistemic Authority: A Theory of Trust, Authority, and Autonomy in Epistemology*. New York: Oxford University Press.